WAR IN VAL D'ORCIA

First published in 1947, Iris Origo's *War in Val D'Orcia* forms a valuable eye-witness account of civilian life in Italy during the Second World War. In what has become an acknowledged classic, we see the author providing shelter for deserters, refugee children and escaped prisoners – all were received at her large farm in Southern Tuscany. And despite the strain of life under the shadow of the Gestapo we see, also, the beauty of the Tuscany countryside in which the ordinary values of everyday life still have their place.

Iris Origo, who was made a Dame of the British Empire in 1977, is an Anglo-American who grew up just outside Florence. After her marriage to Marchese Antonio Origo in 1924, she and her husband bought the large farm estate of La Foce, where this diary and other books were written and where she still lives today. Her book of memoirs, *Images and Shadows*, is also available in the *Century Lives and Letters* series.

Denis Mack Smith, who introduces this edition, is an Oxford historian of modern Italy whose first meeting with *War in Val D'Orcia* was an accidental one in a secondhand bookshop. He is the author of *Mussolini, A Biography*.

WAR IN VAL D'ORCIA

A Diary

IRIS ORIGO

CENTURY HUTCHINSON
LONDON

First published in Great Britain in 1947
by Jonathan Cape

This edition published in 1985 by
Century Hutchinson Ltd,
Brookmount House,
62–65 Chandos Place, Covent Garden, London WC2N 4NW

ISBN 0 7126 0804 4

The painting on the cover is 'Oliveto' by G. Colacicchi (Scala)

Reprinted in Great Britain by
Richard Clay (The Chaucer Press) Ltd, Bungay, Suffolk

To
ANTONIO
who shared it all

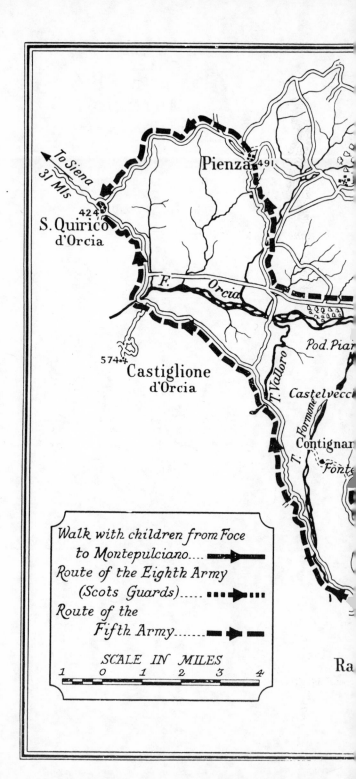

To Siena
31 Mls

S. Quirico
d'Orcia
424

Pienza 491

F. Orcia

574
Castiglione
d'Orcia

Pod. Piar

T. Valloro

T. Formone

Castelvecc

Contignar

Fonte

*Walk with children from Foce
to Montepulciano....* ➤
*Route of the Eighth Army
(Scots Guards)......* ▪▪▪➤▪▪▪
*Route of the
Fifth Army.......* ➤

SCALE IN MILES
1   0   1   2   3   4

Ra

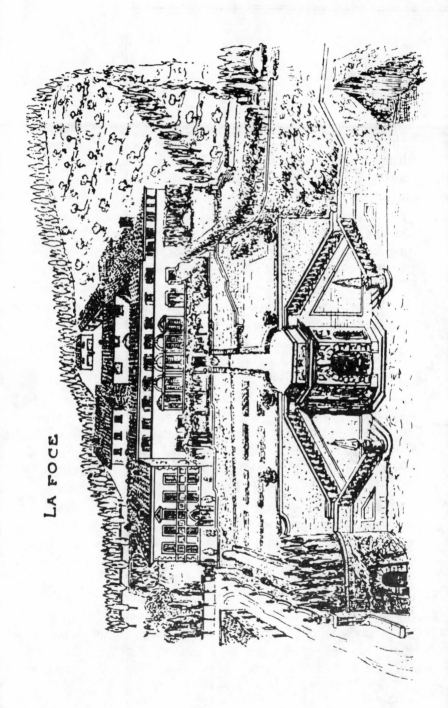

LA FOCE

INTRODUCTION

I first saw this book, a diary covering two years during the Second
World War in Italy, in Italian translation, and remember my immediate impression was of reading a minor masterpiece. The
author is an Anglo-American lady, married to an Italian landowner, who in 1943-4 found herself having to raise a young
family during a time of civil war and foreign invasion in the no
man's land of the remote Tuscan countryside. Assailed by conflicting armies and ideologies, she had to acknowledge a divided
loyalty, since her country of adoption was at war with her country
of origin. But neither this tragic fact nor the politics of fascist
Italy was her principal concern as she noted each day's events,
because for the most part she was preoccupied with the immediate problems of holding her household together and trying to
keep a rural community from dissolution or annihilation.

I came across the diary by accident in a second-hand bookshop
and recollect thinking that its author must be a person of quite
unusual gifts. The subject-matter had a special interest, for it was
a look into the daily life of non-combatant villagers who unex-
pectedly found themselves pitched into the middle of a terrible
and long-drawn-out battle which they could barely understand.
No other book has succeeded so well in portraying this aspect of
the war in Italy. The story is one of confusion and bewilderment
in a peasant society that was suddenly confronted by one of the
greatest conceivable disasters, when in the space of a few months
a whole way of life was changed utterly and beyond any possibility of repair. It is a story of individual tragedy and suffering, but
at the same time of great generosity, courage, and even heroism.
Many soldiers on both sides of the war owed their survival to the
kindness and spirit of disinterested sacrifice shown by the farmers
and farm laborers who lived in the Orcia valley. Their patience
and resignation, but also their humanity and unselfishness, reveal

to us a world that is often unrecorded just because there is no one at hand to record it.

Later when I read her other books I came to know more about the Marchesa Origo. She has written studies of Byron and the Italian poet Leopardi. Another book was about Saint Bernardino of Siena, and she was the first to inform the general reader about that enchanting merchant of the fourteenth century, Francesco Datini. Other personal details of her life and family can be found in a volume of memoirs entitled *Images and Shadows,* published in 1970. We learn from this autobiography that although she has spent most of her life in Italy, her father was an American, a pupil of Santayana at Harvard, who became secretary to the Ambassador of the United States in London and in 1901 married into the Anglo-Irish aristocracy. As a girl, Iris Origo lived part of the time in Long Island. Her father died from tuberculosis when she was only eight, after which she had longer periods in London and Kilkenny at the house of her English grandfather Lord Desart. It was her father's wish that she should be brought up in France or Italy or at all events 'somewhere where she does not belong' in order to become cosmopolitan and free from any narrow patriotism. So the family home was moved by her mother to the Villa Medici just outside Florence. This meant that she grew up in one of the great centers of the Italian renaissance, a palatial dwelling built by Michelozzo for Cosimo de' Medici, the founding father of the most celebrated family in Florentine history.

Here she spent fourteen years in an environment of exceptional privilege, comfort, and wealth. Many friends of the family at Florence were other rich exiles, sophisticated and intellectual if somewhat rootless, and the author of this diary has confessed that she herself felt uncertain about who she was and where she belonged. Marriage to an Italian eventually made it possible to put down roots, and in 1924 the new couple bought a large estate in the heart of Tuscany, where her war-time diary and other books were written.

The estate of La Foce was located a hundred miles north of

Rome, between Siena and Lake Trasimene. This particular area was carefully selected by the Origos because it was a barren region that could be improved by a planned program of intensive cultivation. The Val d'Orcia had been much neglected over the centuries, laid bare by soil erosion and desolated by wars between rival city-states. The new owners set about restoring it to life. Fifteen years of hard work resulted in the establishment of fifty farms, each of about a hundred acres, all grouped round one central *fattoria* where the Origo family lived and where all the general decisions were made about what crops to grow and what agricultural methods to adopt. Each tenant farmer held his individual farm by the usual Tuscan system of *mezzadria*, sharing all produce with the proprietor but depending on him for equipment and capital.

While her husband introduced modern farming techniques and a rational system of cultivation, the Marchesa set up a health center and a school for ninety children. Evening classes were also provided for adults. She found the valley a wild district, with over eighty percent illiteracy, where the peasants were instinctively opposed to any innovation and where witches and witch-doctors helped to regulate the life of the population. But during these fifteen years, there was a gradual growth in prosperity, and the whole society began to change and develop.

Italy at this time was governed by the fascist administration of Benito Mussolini, who had come to power in 1922. Since one of the main principles of Italian fascism was a dislike of the flight from the countryside into the towns, the government had a special interest in assisting the more backward agricultural regions of Italy. Land drainage, reforestation, and road-building all found encouragement and active assistance on the part of Mussolini, and the Origo family was grateful for the results of this at La Foce. Only later did they recognize that during these years, as well as being helped and encouraged to introduce many beneficial social changes, they had been cut off by a 'barrier of privilege' from the kind of person who might have been able to tell them about the cruelties of fascism, its oppression of minorities, its inefficiency, and other less attractive aspects of the regime. In particular it was very difficult for anyone so far away from the main centers of power to have much inkling of Mussolini's growing obsession with making war — or, more specifically, with fighting against what he took to be the decadent democracies of the West and the backward, incompetent Russians. The possibility of losing such a war was inconceivable to him, and after a series of minor campaigns against Ethiopia, Spain, and Albania, he decided to risk the whole future of his country on a bid for world power.

The Second World War began in September 1939 and Italy entered it a few months later as an ally of Nazi Germany. The Marchesa Origo, despite her Anglo-American origins, was allowed to take a job with the Italian Red Cross in Rome, where she dealt with British prisoners of war. Then, in 1942, expecting a baby, she returned to La Foce and began writing her diary. It was not originally intended for publication; nor, she assures us, was it touched up later before publication; these two facts help to explain some of its immediacy and verisimilitude. It was designed as a pastime in the middle of domestic isolation and boredom, as a means of concentrating and clearing the mind by noting down each day any interesting events she heard or witnessed at first hand. She also saw it as a means of preserving a thread of serenity and hope as the months went by, when living conditions became progressively more difficult and the first expectations of a quick end to the war gradually receded. Sometimes she would bury what she had written lest it be found by the authorities and betray her growing doubts, but for the most part events were described without any strong political slant. Any news circulating in the countryside was bound to be more humdrum and less dramatic than in the towns. Often it was at the level of rumor and gossip. There was much more food in agricultural areas, whereas in Rome or Florence everyone resorted to the black market if they could afford to do so. The fascist police and soldiery were also less in evidence in this distant corner of rural Tuscany, and government regulations much harder to enforce. Even newspapers were sometimes hard to find or at least arrived many days late.

But by the time the diary opens, a series of military disasters had brought the reality of war much nearer to everyone, even to those who were remote from the world of government and politics. After initial German successes almost everywhere in 1940, there was a different story to tell by the end of 1942. Many Italians by then had learned to see through the absurd exaggerations of fascist propaganda, and could even envisage the possibility that their country might be invaded. Recent battles at Stalingrad and El Alamein indicated that the tide might well have turned, and gradually it became clear that, short of producing one of the secret weapons that Hitler and Mussolini kept talking about, the fascist powers had no apparent ability to stop the Allied advance in Russia and North Africa.

Mussolini by January 1943 had lost almost all of his large African empire. American troops were in Tunisia, and in Libya the Eighth Army, mostly British, was moving towards Tripoli, coming ever closer to the Italian mainland. Unknown to almost everyone, the Duce himself had by this time become so ill that he virtually ceased to function as a dictator in charge of events, and the Italian war effort was being directed largely from Berlin. Ordinary citizens could not be prevented from observing that many German soldiers were occupying strategic points up and down the peninsula; nor was there any chance of concealing the heavy bombardment of Italian towns by enemy planes using airfields recently captured by the Allies in North Africa. In January 1943, the evacuation of children to escape the bombing of Genoa and Turin suddenly changed the routine of daily life at La Foce.

More than twenty of these refugee children were taken into care by the Origo family. Some of them were orphans; some were sent by their parents to what they must have hoped would be a secure place in the rural seclusion of the Val d'Orcia. One of the new school buildings was converted to house them. A dispensary was furnished, together with an operating room for any casualties in the valley, and housing for a resident nurse. Some teaching had to be improvised for the older children, and various members of the household did what they could to share the work involved. Every locality in Italy had to prepare to be as self-sufficient as possible, since the government was increasingly unable to provide basic services or the efficient distribution of food and clothing. The difficulties of each day are made light of in the diary but can be easily imagined. As well as needing education and health care, the children had to be fed, clothed, and amused, and this provided much of the small-scale drama of the following months.

In June 1943 the Allies made their first landing in Italy when they captured the small Mediterranean island of Pantelleria. This was followed in July by a full-scale invasion of Sicily. Mussolini had promised the Italian public a few days earlier that such an attack had no chance at all of success, and the speedy conquest of Sicily was the final disillusionment that lost him the support of other fascist leaders. When the king, toward the end of July, agreed to his arrest, there was universal rejoicing as two decades of personal dictatorship came to an abrupt end. Iris Origo was probably correct in thinking at the time that the new government of Marshal Badoglio, if sufficiently clever and brave, could have made peace at once with the Western Allies: if only Italy could have either proclaimed itself neutral or turned against Hitler, the damage done by the war could have been minimized. But Badoglio feared retaliation and for several months did not dare come out in open defiance of the Germans. This resulted in a tragic continuation of hostilities, and only in September did Badoglio agree to sign an armistice with the democracies. By that time Hitler had made all the necessary preparations for the Germans to occupy all of central and northern Italy. Not until a year later, in June 1944, did the Allied armies at last reach Tuscany, and this was after huge casualties as they slowly struggled all the way up from the south through Naples and Rome.

The year from June 1943 to June 1944 was one of the most disastrous in the whole of Italian history. Often in previous centuries the peninsula had been fought over by hostile foreign armies as other countries settled their differences on Italian territory and at Italy's expense. But this was the most destructive war of all. And it was in addition a civil war, since Mussolini in September 1943 was restored to power under German supervision to rule an artificial state that ran from the Alps on the north to as far down as Rome. Hitler's army of occupation was thereafter supported by a new extremist militia of Italian fascists.

When Badoglio made his belated peace with the Western powers, he could therefore speak only in the name of the southern provinces. Everywhere else the fascists were more or less in control, except that a partisan movement of anti-fascists, in an attempt to prepare the way for a democratic victory and a restoration of Italian freedom, gradually made itself felt as a challenge to Mussolini's puppet regime. This civil war began on a very small scale but eventually manifested itself in many areas of Tuscany. Deserters from both sides, in need of food and medical help, peopled the woods of the Val d'Orcia. Young men in the civilian population took to the hills to escape conscription into the fascist armed militia. Individual groups of anti-fascist partisans were at large, some of them communist and some anti-communist, occasionally squabbling with each other for political reasons, and other groups were interested less in politics than in loot and intimidation for profit. Always the German occupying force was not far away, and was ready to punish with great savagery anyone suspected of rebellion or of giving help to the enemy.

In various provinces of northern and central Italy there were also more than 50,000 Allied soldiers who had been prisoners of war and who, after escaping from Axis prison camps, were hoping to be able to rejoin their units further south. As well as British and Americans, these included Poles, Yugoslavs, French, Tunisians, South Africans, and some from Central and South America. At La Foce the central *fattoria* was too close to the main roads to be a safe hiding-place except in emergency, but the outlying farms became a temporary home for a stream of refugees, and food was continually being sent to them from stores concealed by the Origo household. Always there was a risk of betrayal and anyone caught could be shot, but a long chain of farmers and peasants showed great bravery and generosity throughout the harsh winter of 1943-4 and passed these escaped prisoners from house to house on their way south. Provisions which had been buried to avoid governmental requisition were dug up for them. Army boots were re-soled or manufactured by the local cobbler. The sick and wounded were secretly cared for in the makeshift field hospital. Information was provided about the safest routes for moving through the enemy lines, and signals were arranged to give warning when German units were in the neighborhood. Or else the refugees stayed to become part of a peasant family, helping in the fields or with the children.

Amid all this turmoil, the Marchesa Origo explains, she was too busy to be afraid, and every day brought new demands on her resourcefulness as every kind of commodity became scarcer. The former barriers between rich and poor for the moment were broken down. Everyone had to confront the same problems and was united by the same tragedies, the same fears and hopes. So great was the uncertainty that no one could plan for even the immediate future, and she commented that 'everything was so clearly dependent on events outside our own control as to be almost restful.' Without any reliable repository of power, without either central government or local government, everyone was compelled to rely on self-help and improvisation. People had to learn how to make their own soap, how to spin and weave the local wool, how to make leather out of skins; a few lucky ones learned how motor vehicles could be converted to run on charcoal. Every day there must have been great suffering to contend with, and a permanent danger of arrest; but it is heartening to read about so many examples of daring, patience, self-sacrifice, and ingenuity. Something not unlike this must have been experienced in countless villages throughout Europe, but rarely can the tale have been told with more persuasiveness or in such simple, controlled language that sets off the seriousness of events by sheer contrast.

Early in June 1944 the German troops were at last forced out of Rome and retreated in the hope of finding another defensive position further north. As the battle raged through Tuscany, the Val d'Orcia found itself for a few days in the front line of the fighting. Nazi units destroyed crops and buildings as they withdrew northward. In one nearby village, every male who could be found was executed as a reprisal and deterrent; in another, all the buildings were burnt to the ground. For those living at La Foce, in addition to the children there were several hundred partisans in the woods to be fed, there were dying men to be nursed, sometimes scores of people sheltering in the main buildings; and every day brought more refugees from the towns who congregated in the farm courtyard hoping for food. Occasionally partisan bands came to take provisions at the same time as German soldiers were billeted in other rooms of the *fattoria*. The children were by now so inured to what was happening that they sometimes continued to play in the garden while the fighting went on around them, not stopping even to look up as the planes swooped. In one last fantastic scene the Marchesa, after being obliged to leave her house in the Germans' possession, marched sixty of her charges eight miles away to Montepulciano. Under a hot June sun along a mined road under shell fire, with corpses all round, this straggling line of children passed through the middle of the battle.

A few days later, fascism disappeared into nothingness, leaving behind it a sense of incredulity that such a regime could have lasted so long with so little apparent support. The same sense of relief and joy had been experienced a year earlier at Mussolini's first fall from power, and would be felt again a year later in April 1945 when the great dictator was executed ignominiously by a partisan unit near Lake Como in the north. Italy once again set herself to repair the damage and pick up the pieces. When Iris

Origo was able to return home, she found La Foce thoroughly ransacked by the retreating soldiers. Most of the farm buildings were damaged or entirely ruined. Everywhere there were bodies to be buried. The fields were still mined, yet the harvest had somehow to be gathered if those who survived these terrible months were not to starve. All these many problems were no doubt confronted with the same patience and ingenuity as before, but at this point the published diary stops.

Things could never be the same again for people living in the valley. Communist administrations took over local government in most Tuscan localities after 1945: this was in reaction to the fascist administration and because after twenty years of dictatorship, people had forgotten what it meant to live under a liberal regime. The whole economy of the area was to change over the next few years, and in most respects for the better. Farmers were impatient with the old *mezzadria* system and with the paternalistic methods of the past. As farm laborers once again began to move into the towns, agriculture was bound to become more mechanized and more subsidized. But one may guess that the work done on this estate in the 1920s and 1930s by the Marchese and his wife will not be forgotten. Nor will the story told in this diary of how a small community managed to survive through the horrors of war.

DENIS MACK SMITH

All Souls College, Oxford, 1983

PREFACE

THE following are the conditions under which this diary has been written:

We live on a large farm in southern Tuscany — twelve miles from the station and five from the nearest village. The country is wild and lonely: the climate harsh. Our house stands on a hill-side, looking down over a wide and beautiful valley, beyond which rises Monte Amiata, wooded with chestnuts and beeches. Nearer by, on this side of the valley, lie slopes of cultivated land: wheat, olives and vines, but among them still stand some ridges of dust-coloured clay hillocks, the *crete senesi* — as bare and colour-less as elephants' backs, as mountains of the moon. The wide river-bed in the valley holds a rushing stream in the rainy season, but during the summer a mere trickle, in a wide desert of stones. And then, when the wheat ripens and the alfalfa has been cut, the last patches of green disappear from the landscape. The whole valley becomes dust-coloured — a land without mercy, without shade. If you sit under an olive-tree you are not shaded; the leaves are like little flickering tongues of fire. At evening and morning the distant hills are misty and blue, but under one's feet the dry earth is hard. The cry of the cicadas shrills in the noon-day. One can only wait — anxiously, thirstily — for the Sep-tember rains, when the whole countryside comes to life again. Then the vintage comes, the ox-carts are piled high with purple and yellow grapes. The farm-houses and the trees around them are hung with the last vestiges of the harvest: the orange cobs of the Indian corn, hanging to dry, gay and fantastic as a Russian ballet décor. Then there is the autumn ploughing, and one last harvest before the winter: that of the olives. The fruits turn from green to red, from red to the ripeness of dark purple; they are gathered and pressed, and pressed again; their oil is stored in great jars, fit for Ali Baba, and their kernels serve us for fuel.

And now we wait for the winter, and with it comes the north wind, the *tramontana*, sweeping across the bare uplands. It drives the farmer indoors; it buffeted and tore the escaping prisoners of war and partisans until they had perforce to take shelter, for months on end, in the stables of the farms.

These farms — fifty-seven of them in number, in seven thousand acres, and housing some six hundred souls — are widely scattered. Each of them, however, is closely in touch with the central farm, the *fattoria* — where stand (beside our villa) the agent's house, the granaries, the cellars, the oil-presses and the dairy, workshops and laundry. The villa is an unpretentious sixteenth-century house, outlined with red brick, with a loggia on the front garden of cypress and ilex, and another formal garden, with a fountain and box-edged flower-beds, facing the valley. When this diary began our house contained my husband, myself and our household; our little girl, Benedetta, was born in 1940, and another, Donata, in 1943, and with Benedetta came her Swiss nurse, Schwester Marie. In the *fattoria* live the *fattore* — whose position somewhat resembles that of the Scotch factor — his wife and two children, and two young assistants of the *fattore* — to whom, in 1943, were added two refugee boys of fifteen. The carpenter, the keeper, two bricklayers and several workmen all live, with their families, nearby. Two hundred yards away are the *ambulatorio* — something between a welfare clinic and a cottage hospital — the school with its two teachers and their families, and the nursery-school — while a little farther off there is the *dopolavoro*, or men's institute, with the local shop. The *Casa dei Bambini*, once a nursery-school for the farm-children, became in January 1943, a home for twenty-three refugee children from Turin and Genoa whose homes had been destroyed by bombs. They are cared for by the nursery-school teacher, Signorina Berettini, and by the district nurse, Signorina Guidetti, who lives above the *ambulatorio*. The Castelluccio — an old castle, about a mile away — houses the parish priest (above the church, which is within the castle walls) and two keepers with their families — and, for six months in 1943, fifty British prisoners of war and their escort.

On the other side of our house, on a southern slope looking down over the valley, stand, between tall cypresses, the little cemetery and chapel which we built in 1933. Our eldest child — Gianni — is buried there, and many of the farmers — and now there is a section given up to those who have been killed here during the war.

The whole does not exactly constitute a village, for there is only one shop; but it forms a complete, self-supporting little world. The land (like practically all the land in Tuscany) is worked according to the *mezzadria* system — a profit-sharing compact which has been in use in Tuscany since the thirteenth century. The compacts — *patti colonici* — between owner and husbandman to-day are almost identical with those drawn up six centuries ago. Now, as then, the landowner builds the farm-house and keeps it in repair; he supplies the money to buy half of what is needed to cultivate and improve the land; he pays for half of the stock of cattle. When harvest comes, owner and farmer share the crops. Like many traditional systems handed down from father to son, the *mezzadria* compact is both very complicated and very elastic. There has always been plenty of healthy grumbling on both sides — and in recent times this grumbling has been fomented and formulated by political agitators. Yet certainly the *mezzadria* has suited the nature of the people and of the soil; it has worked. The interests of the landowner and farmer are fundamentally the same, and in general their relationship has been a satisfactory one. It is not quite that of landlord and tenant, nor certainly that of employer and employee — it is more intimate than the former, more friendly than the latter. It is a partnership.

During the war our little community, always largely self-contained, became almost entirely so, held together by a bond of common interests, anxieties, fears and hopes. Together we planned how to hide the oil, the hams and the cheeses, so that the

Germans would not find them; together we found shelter and clothes for the fugitives who knocked at our door – whether Italians or Allies, soldiers or civilians – together we watched the first bombs fall on the Val d'Orcia bridges, and listened hopefully to the rumours of landings in Tuscany which never came. And together, when the Germans had turned us out, we returned – after the Allies' arrival – to reap the harvest, to start clearing the mines and rebuilding the shattered farms.

Daily life, throughout the war, was much easier than in the towns. For food we were almost wholly self-supporting. We baked our own bread with our own flour – of which one-and-a-half quintals per person was assigned to us; the rest went to the government stores, the *ammassi*. We had our own chickens, turkeys, geese, rabbits, vegetables, fruit, milk and honey. We made our own hams and sausages (being allowed to kill one pig a year for the villa and one for the *fattoria*, while each farm also killed its own). We made cheese out of sheep's milk and occasionally, in secret, we killed a calf and succeeded in getting its hide tanned for leather. For fuel we used, besides a small ration of lignite, our own wood and the kernels of our olives. We made our own soap with a residue of kitchen fats, potato-peel and soda.

As the war went on, everything, naturally, became scarcer. In 1944 first the Germans and then the Goums took away or killed thirty per cent of our cattle, six hundred of our sheep, and all our chickens and turkeys, and the Germans burned out our beehives. Milk and meat became scarce that winter, and eggs, chicken or honey non-existent.

Owing to the lack of sugar, we had to give up making most sorts of jam – except of grapes and of the little Montepulciano plums, sweet enough to keep without sugar. But we still had plenty of flour and maize, and some ham and sausages (buried underground, to save them from the Germans), as well as our own vegetables, and so got through the winter very well – even with the children's extra twenty-three mouths to feed.

The problem of clothing, however, was not so easily solved. In the autumn and winter of 1943, when a constant stream of fugitives — Italian disbanded soldiers and Allied prisoners of war — was passing through our property, all in need of clothes, I was still able to buy (mostly on barrows in the Florence markets) a supply of blankets, trousers, shirts and socks, though never sufficient for the demand. Boots, however, were an almost insoluble problem. We bought some 'black-market' leather and made as many as we could — and also made leather tops to wooden clogs. Our own refugee children also had boots made at home, and jerseys and stockings made of our own sheep's wool, spun on the farm. With the same wool we made babies' jackets for the numerous babies who were born during that winter in the Montepulciano hospital, where many expectant mothers were sent when their homes in Livorno and Grosseto were destroyed by bombing — and we also made babies' clothes and nappies out of old sheets and curtain-linings, and slippers out of strips of felt and carpet. But the increasing scarcity of thread was a fresh difficulty, and in the summer of 1944, before leaving, the Germans took away all that I had left, as well as all the children's winter clothes — so that we had to begin at the beginning again.

The experiences recorded in this diary have been in no way exceptional: thousands of other Italians have had similar ones, and many have had far worse. Indeed, the events here described are, as the reader will see, singularly undramatic and unheroic. Although in the last months of the German occupation the shadow of the Gestapo was never far away, and their spies and punitive expeditions did several times reach this valley, our anxieties were far less intense, far less continuous, than those borne by the people who hid Allied prisoners and partisans in their houses in the very heart of Rome or Milan, who concealed munitions or transmitted information, to whom every telephone call was a peril, every footstep on the stairs a menace. Nor did any active fighting or destruction by enemy property by the partisans of this district compare with that achieved by the partisans of the north, in Piemonte or Lombardy. No, our problems (and those of our neighbours) were of a different nature: they arose from a continual necessity to weigh, not between courage and cowardice or between right and wrong, but between conflicting duties and responsibilities, equally urgent. Every day the need for deciding between them would arise: the request for a lodging of a p.o.w. would have to be weighed against the danger to the farm which sheltered him, the dressing of a partisan's wound against the risk to the nurse and to the other patients in her charge, the pleas of the starving townsfolk who, in the last weeks before the liberation of Rome, came all the way from the city to beg for food, against the needs of the children and partisans whom we must go on feeding here. And when some hot-headed partisans would shoot at a *carabiniere* behind a hedge, or disarm two German soldiers in a village pub, disappearing themselves into the woods and leaving the helpless villagers at the mercy of German reprisals, it was our unpleasing task to attempt to point out the consequences of these methods, or (subsequently) to try to protect the villagers therefrom. Moreover, these were problems which — since the local situation was continually changing, with the arrival of different officials, and with the fluctuations of the military situation — could never be solved: every day each incident had to be met on its own merits. This became, in the long run, distinctly fatiguing, since it was impossible not to conduct a perpetual cross-examination of one's own conscience. At the end of each day prudence inquired, 'Have I done too much?' — and enthusiasm or compassion, 'Might I not, perhaps, have done more?'

What, it may be asked, under such circumstances, was the motive underlying the generous help given to the hunted Allied prisoners of war by the Italian countryfolk, often at the risk of their own lives, from the Garigliano to the Po, from the mountains of Piemonte and the Abruzzi to the fishing-villages of Liguria and Emilia? It would be a mistake, I think, to attribute it to any political — or even patriotic — motive. There was, it is true, a certain amount of anti-German and anti-Fascist feeling, especially among those peasants whose sons had been in the army against their will, or else were still attempting to avoid conscription by the Fascist Republican Army. But the true motive was a far simpler one: it has been described by an Italian partisan as 'the simplest of all ties between one man and another; the tie that arises between the man who asks for what he needs, and the man who comes to his aid as best he can. No unnecessary emotion or pose'.[1] And an English officer, himself an escaped prisoner of war, who owes his life to the help given him in this manner, has expressed his views in almost identical words: 'The peasants' native sympathy with the under-dog and the outcast asserted itself. Simple Christianity impelled them to befriend those complete strangers, feed them, clothe them, and help them on their way ... All over Italy this miracle was to be seen, the simple dignity of humble people who saw in the escaped prisoners not representatives of a power to be withstood or placated, but individuals in need of their help.'[2]

Of the 70,000 Allied p.o.w.s at large in Italy on September 8th, 1943, nearly half escaped, either crossing the frontier to Switzerland or France, or eventually rejoining their own troops in Italy; and each one of these escapes implies the complicity of a long chain of humble, courageous helpers throughout the length of the country. 'I can only say,' wrote General O'Connor to me, 'that the Italian peasants and others behind the line were magnificent. They could not have done more for us. They hid us, escorted us, gave us money, clothes and food — all the time taking tremendous risks ... We English owe a great debt of gratitude to those Italians whose help alone made it possible for us to live, and finally to escape.'[3]

There is a passage in *The Pool of Vishnu* in which L. H. Myers, in attacking certain forms of self-protective egotism, maintains

[1] Roberto Battaglia: *Un uomo, un partigiano*. Edizioni U., 1945.
[2] Major P. Gibson.   [3] General Sir Richard O'Connor, K.C.B., D.S.O., M.C.

that they are not natural to men, but produced by the structure of organized society. 'If one sees,' he says, 'a man struggling at the bottom of a well, one's natural impulse is to pull him out. If a man is starving, one's natural impulse is to share one's food with him. Surely it is only on second thoughts that we *don't* do these things? Society seems to me to be like an organized system of rather mean second-thoughts.' During those crucial months of shared apprehension and danger, when the structure of society did not seem very important, that 'organized system of mean second-thoughts' also, mercifully, disappeared into the background. For a short time all men returned to the most primitive traditions of ungrudging hospitality, uncalculating brotherhood. At most, some old peasant-woman, whose son was a prisoner in a far-away camp in India or Australia, might say — as she prepared a bowl of soup or made the bed for the foreigner in her house — 'Perhaps someone will do the same for my boy'.

The actual keeping of the diary was not always an easy matter. During the first months, when a search of the house did not seem likely (though always possible), it usually lay among the pages of the children's picture-books; since I believed that the nursery bookshelf would probably be one of the last places to be searched. Later on, most of it (together with various propaganda leaflets and my jewellery) was buried in tin boxes in the garden. But the current pages were naturally always in the process of being written — even up to the end, with the Germans in the house, and (since even in times of danger the careless remain careless) were apt to be lying about in undesirable places. During the most eventful periods, too, it was often difficult to find time to write at all. Some passages were hurriedly scribbled at night, others with twenty children in the room — and some in the cellar, during the shelling.

But I felt at the time, and feel now, that any interest this diary might have would come from its being an immediate, first-hand account. I put down each day's events as they occurred, as simply and truthfully as I could, and (though I did report stories and rumours that reached us, since they were part of the queer mental colouring of our daily life) I tried not to make statements of which I had not had first-hand knowledge. And now, on re-reading, I have refrained from 'touching up' the photograph, from changing the colour of events in the light of subsequent knowledge.

I have tried to avoid political bias and national prejudice. But we are all affected, far more deeply than we know — not by the theories, but by the mental climate of the world in which we live. Even our reactions against it show that we are not immune. I have no doubt that to those living in a different climate and seeing the same events from a different peep-hole, many of my judgments will appear mistaken, naive, prejudiced and even wrong. Most certainly I have swallowed propaganda without realizing it; but may I be permitted to ask my readers — are they quite certain that they have never done so, too?

It will, I think, be obvious that I love Italy and its people. But I have become chary of generalizations about countries and nations; I believe in individuals, and in the relationship of individuals to one another. When I look back upon these years of tension and expectation, of destruction and sorrow, it is individual acts of kindness, courage or faith that illuminate them; it is in them that I trust. I remember a British prisoner of war in the Val d'Orcia helping the peasant's wife to draw water from the well, with a ragged, beaming small child at his heels. I remember the peasant's wife mending his socks, knitting him a sweater, and baking her best cake for him, in tears, on the day of his departure.

These — the shared, simple acts of everyday life — are the realities on which international understanding can be built. In these, and in the realization that has come to many thousands, that people of other nations are, after all, just like themselves, we may, perhaps, place our hopes.

IRIS ORIGO

La Foce, 1944

1943

1943

January 30th

The first refugee children have arrived. They were due yesterday evening at seven — after a twelve hours' journey from Genoa — but it was not until nine p.m. that at last the car drew up, and seven very small, sleepy bundles were lifted out. The eldest is six, the others four and five — all girls except one, a solemn little Sardinian called Dante Porcu. We carry them down into the play-room of the nursery-school (where the stove is burning, and supper waiting) and they stand blinking in the bright light, like small bewildered owls. White, pasty faces — several with boils and sores — and thin little sticks of arms and legs.[1]

The Genoese district nurse who has brought them tells me that they have been chosen from families whose houses have been totally destroyed, and who, for the last two months, have been living in an underground tunnel beneath the city, without light or sufficient water, and in bitter cold. Their fathers are mostly dock-labourers; two of them have been killed.

The children eat their warm soup, still too bewildered fully to realize where they are — and then, as they gradually thaw and wake up, the first wail goes up — 'Mamma, Mamma, I want my Mamma!' We hastily produce the toys which we have prepared for just that moment; the little girls clutch their dolls, Dante winds up his motor, and for a few minutes tears are averted. Then we take them upstairs and tuck them up in their warm beds. Homesickness sets in again — and two of them, poor babies, cry themselves to sleep.

[1] In theory, the evacuation of these children was planned by the Fascist organizations in each province. In practice, we waited for three months for the Genoa Fascio to send us the children for whom we had applied — and then, as none came, I asked the Principessa di Piemonte to request her Red Cross inspectresses in Turin and Genoa to select twelve especially needy cases — whereupon the children arrived in a fortnight.

It is only comparatively seldom that the so-called 'turning-points' in a country's history — so convenient to the historian — are actually observable by those present at the time. But the dropping of high explosives commands attention; and in the days after the first raids on Turin and Genoa, in November, everyone in Italy said: 'Now it's come; now it's our turn.'

The intention, presumably, of the raids was to produce panic: the immediate result was rather resentment. Partly of the kind that the Allies wished to produce, resentment against Fascism: 'This is where They (the Fascists) have landed us.' But there was also the effect produced on every other bombed civilian population; a healthy, elementary reaction of resentment against those who were dropping the bombs.

And already in these first days of confused bewilderment, compassion and pain — when one began to meet the first refugees and to hear the (now all-too-familiar) stories of crowds crushed in the doorways of shelters, of homeless children, of anger and fear and pain and mismanagement, it became clear that the country was going to be divided between those whose resentment took one or the other form: either against their own government or against the Allies.

Among the first were, naturally, all those whom one may call the professional anti-Fascists, the Opposition, and to these must be added the ever-increasing numbers of the disillusioned, of all kinds, sincere ex-Fascists, gradually disgusted by graft, mismanagement, and bluff; members of all three Services, suffering from a similar disillusionment; members of the upper classes, whose allegiance to Fascism was really chiefly to the god Success, and whose first anti-Fascist and anti-German wobblings began with the first glimpse of failure, only kept in check by an even greater fear of 'bolshevism'; and finally a number of simply bewildered, frightened, common citizens, afraid that the next bombed city would be their own. Among these last the Opposition deliberately circulated alarmist rumours and catastrophic prophecies. 'Tripolitania will fall in a fortnight — Tunisia in three weeks — Then there will only be half an hour's flight between the Allied bombers and every town in Italy — Sicily will be invaded — no, Corsica, and Sardinia, and from there the Tuscan coast. Every beautiful building in Italy — Rome, Venice, Florence — will be destroyed. It's the end of Italy, for ever.' These prognostications naturally led to the question: what can we do to avoid this tragedy? Even now, said the Opposition, it is not too late. Turn out the Fascists, demand the King's abdication, and form a temporary military dictatorship, to sign a separate peace.

This proposal, however, was far from universally acceptable. 'Let us show the English that we can take it as well as they have!' was the cry of many people throughout the country — not necessarily Fascist or pro-German, but roused to anger and national pride. 'Must we turn traitor and be despised by the whole of Europe?' No, they maintained, the only decent course was to swallow for the present all political differences, and stick it out until the end. Some even hoped in a renewal of the Italian spirit, a revival of national unity and valour, such as was seen after Caporetto; but they were few. Most of them admitted that defeat was now inevitable, but maintained that the only course, nevertheless, was to go on fighting. To the moral argument was added a profound conviction that the Opposition's faith in the Allies' terms was excessive. 'Contempt is all that we shall reap.'

In November, nevertheless, the King's abdication and a separate peace were openly spoken of everywhere, even in the Senate. The programme of the Opposition, according to its supporters, was sanctioned (though of course not publicly) by the Vatican, was supported alike by Monarchists, Republicans, Communists and Liberals, and was to be carried out by the Army, led by the Principe di Piemonte. The programme was the following: the King's abdication, seizure of the Fascist leaders, and assumption of the government by a military dictatorship, headed by the Prince of Piemonte. Then an immediate request to the Allies for an armistice, and, in due course, after a 'period of transition', a Liberal coalition government, headed by Bonomi. According to the more optimistic members of the Opposition, the temper of the country is now already ripe for these events, a sufficient majority of the Army is ready to move, and the Prince would be prepared to take the responsibility, provided his father had abdicated of his own free will.

How many responsible people would really now be prepared to follow such a course, and how many would condemn it — whether on grounds of principle or of expediency — I have no idea. Each party, of course, claims that the other is only a despicable minority. Feeling runs high, and my chief dread is of a situation like that in France: inner conflict (combined with the activities of the Gestapo) followed by chaos.

February 10th

The second batch of children has now arrived: six little girls from Turin. They are older than the Genoa children — eight-to ten-year-olds — and much more self-possessed; but they show more clearly the effects of what they have been through. One of them, Nella, is suffering from a mild form of 'St. Vitus' dance'; another, Liberata, has sudden fainting-fits. All are very nervy and easily become hysterical. But all — the 'big girls' from Turin and the 'little ones' from Genoa — are quite astonishingly well-behaved. We have had, of course, to struggle with their hair (some of them have had their heads shaved), but otherwise their 'habits' contrast most favourably with what I have heard of the little evacuees in English villages — and their manners are charming. All of them have had their homes destroyed by air-raids — and most of them have parents working in the Turin factories, and fully realize that they will be bombed again. At post time they hurry up to the *fattoria* — and if for three days one of them has no letter, they go about with white, pitiful faces. Each child has at once had a medical examination and is now under the district nurse's daily care — the older ones go to the school next door, the little ones do some nursery-school lessons with their own teacher. I have written long letters to each of their mothers, and we have taken a photograph of them to send home. Perhaps later on, their mothers will be able to come to see them.[1]

Already the children's characters are beginning to define themselves. Of the older girls Liberata is the leader: by far the most intelligent and sensitive, and already 'mothering' the little ones, she is a born school teacher — and no doubt will become one some day. Of the others the most engaging is fat Anna Gotta — as round and pink as an apple — who insists on tying a minute bow of blue ribbon in her single inch of hair (she, too, has had her head shaved) to show that she is not a boy.

Children such as these, all over Europe, have had to leave their own homes and families, and are arriving — bewildered but hopeful — among strangers. There is something terribly moving in this exodus — something, too, so deeply wrong in a world where such a thing is not only possible but necessary, that it is difficult not to feel personally responsible. For the present we can try to salve our consciences by giving them food, shelter and love. But this is not enough. Nothing can ever really be enough.

April 1st

Three months of this year of waiting have already passed. Military events have been less rapid than was expected here in January. Tripolitania has fallen, but the acute phase of the struggle in Tunisia has only now begun. However, it is fully realized that that cannot last more than another few weeks; the eleventh hour has come. What then?

Since January a marked change has come over public opinion. The active resentment and dismay which followed upon the

[1] In the course of the first summer, all the mothers in turn managed to come — and after seeing how well and happy their children were, begged me to take yet one other brother or sister — so that the children's numbers gradually rose to twenty-three. In June 1944, when the front passed on beyond us, all these children became completely cut off from their parents — and for eight months remained without any news of them.

Allies' landing in North Africa and the bombing of Italian cities has given place to a despairing apathy. The whole country is sunk under its leaden weight. There is now no hope of victory, and the number of those who say, 'We must hold out with Germany until the end' is becoming smaller. But as the time left for any other measure becomes shorter, as the menace (indeed, the certainty) of bombing, invasion and total defeat draws nearer, no one comes forward to take a decisive step. It is hardly fear of the police (many of whom, indeed, are heartily anti-Fascist) or even of Germany. The general discontent finds open expression in every class, from the senator to the taxi-driver. Every night the streets of Rome are placarded with posters or strewn with pamphlets saying 'Fascism must go'. Everyone cries 'How long, oh Lord, how long?'; everyone says quite openly: 'It is Fascism that has brought us to this.' But still it is all talk; no one will take a risk, or a responsibility.

The King himself remarked a few days ago: 'It is like the time after Caporetto. Only now the events are greater – and the men smaller.' Every day a fresh rumour, a fresh shadowy plan arises – never to take a definite shape. Part of the Senate, it is rumoured, would support a provisional government formed by members of the King's Council, the *Collari dell'Annunziata*, for the purpose of deposing Mussolini, turning out the Fascists, and entering upon negotiations for a separate peace. Last week colour was given to this rumour by the unexpected bestowal of the *Collare dell'Annunziata* on Grandi. The diplomatic negotiations, it was said, would be entrusted to him, with Cini representing the *industriali* and the financial interests of the North, while a temporary military dictatorship would be headed by Marshal Caviglia or General Ambrosio (the chief of staff). Many, however, maintain that it is already too late to save the King's position, and such a step would be possible only after his abdication, under the leadership of the Principe di Piemonte. The true anti-Fascist Opposition, however, is violently opposed to these plans, or any others that would imply collaboration with the moderate

24

Fascists — and attempts to influence both the Prince of Piemonte and the Vatican to take up the same attitude.

Thus we have in this country, besides the ever-diminishing nubmer of Germanophile Fascists (headed by Farinacci):

(1) The various branches of 'moderate Fascists', each with their own axe to grind and their skin to save.

(2) The 'Opposition', consisting mostly of the old Liberals, but who have succeeded in enlisting a promise of co-operation from the Monarchists, the Republicans, and some of the Communists, and who are in touch with the Vatican, and with the house of Savoy through the Principessa di Piemonte. Some of the chief *industriali* of the north would probably co-operate with them; some with the moderate Fascists.

(3) The Army, almost entirely anti-Fascist, but with no really outstanding figure to take on the military dictatorship which would probably succeed any attack upon Fascism.

(4) The Vatican, working for peace at any price, with distinct pro-Ally and anti-Fascist sympathies. Here the outstanding figure is Monsignor Montini. The Pope is a Saint — but a saint, it is said, lacking in determination.

(5) The House of Savoy: the King a dark horse, and the Prince almost equally so. The Princess intensely anti-German, and consequently anti-Fascist.

(6) The increasingly discontented, resentful, murmuring masses of the people — hungry, bombed, apprehensive. In the towns, in the country, the key-note is apathy. And everywhere, talk, talk, talk, and no action. Resentment without a sense of responsibility. The fruits of twenty years of Fascism. And on the part of those elder citizens who remember a different Italy, a profound sadness and sense of shame.

April 12th

   Meanwhile the time is short. Two days ago, the English 8th Army and the American 1st Army joined forces; Sfax has fallen; Rommel is in full retreat. The American air-raids on Cagliari — totally undefended after the first two attacks — have been entirely different in quality from any executed by the R.A.F. The long queues of women and children waiting in the main street to enter the few shelters were repeatedly machine-gunned; the dead are over six thousand; and the few survivors have now taken refuge permanently in the caves round the town. A further horror is added by the fact that, during the first air-raid, the terrified lepers escaped from their hospital and have now mingled with the rest of the population.

When the first raids began, the following gentle prayer was said by the Sardinians:

> Ave Maria, gratia plena,
> Fa' che non suoni la sirena,
> Fa' che non vengano gli aeroplani,
> Fa' che si dorma fino a domani.
> Se qualche bomba cade giū
> Madre pietosa, pensaci tu.
> Gesù, Giuseppe, Maria,
> Fate che gli inglesi perdano la via.
> Dolce cuore del mio Gesù
> Fa' che gli inglesi non vengano più.

A less bitter war prayer can hardly be imagined. But now, after the machine-gunning and wholesale destruction, the tone has much changed and much bitterness is felt. In Naples, too, recent air-raids have not confined themselves to 'military objectives'. A few days ago the first great daylight raid by American flying-fortresses took place, and presumably heralds others. Worse than any raid, however, was the damage caused by the explosion, in the harbour, of a ship laden with munitions — a masterpiece of folly, since the ship was known to be on fire for three hours before the explosion, and was to be seen gently smouldering in the harbour, while officials argued with each other as to whether or no it would be advisable to take it out to sea. In the subsequent inquiry the officials (German and Italian, military, naval and civilian) all attempted to lay the blame upon each other.

Six days ago Mussolini departed in an armoured train for Bavaria — presumably to meet his colleague and to decide whether the Axis is to continue. It is certain that Italy cannot defend herself without German help, both in men and war material. Germany is therefore forced to choose whether it will, on the whole, be cheaper for her to let her weaker ally make a separate peace, or to provide the means of defending her.[1]

April 14th

Mussolini has now returned and the official bulletin announces that the Axis still holds, but without specifying what help, if any, Germany will give to Italy. Sousse and Kairouan have fallen, and the Navy have refused to convey back to Italy the convoys of retreating troops, declaring that in view of their numerical inferiority and of the complete incapacity of the Air Force to defend them, any such attempt would be suicidal.

April 16th

C.A. arrives from Rome with the news that Germany will send no military help for Italy's defence, that the order in Tunisia is to resist until the end, without attempting to bring any of the troops home, that a landing in Sardinia is expected before the middle of May. In Rome the Chief of Police, Senise, has been dismissed and the most varied rumours, all catastrophic, are spreading.

---

[1] According to Monelli (*Roma 1943*) it was Mussolini's intention, on this occasion, to issue a solemn statement of the rights of the smaller nations of Europe — a sort of Axis Atlantic Charter. This idea had been suggested by Bastianini, the Foreign Minister, but Ribbentrop would have none of it. As for Hitler — at the end of one of the two leaders' interviews, lasting two and a half hours, Mussolini said: 'To-day Hitler has had a mono-logue — to-morrow I will speak.' But that to-morrow never came.

April 23rd

Still the resistance in Tunisia continues. The English radio emphasizes the sacrifices which the Axis is prepared to make in order to gain time to prepare the defence of the Continent. Seventy-four Junkers carrying reinforcements were shot down in one single convoy, and, according to the B.B.C., the losses in men crossing the Mediterranean to Tunis, before even reaching the field of battle, amount to fifty per cent.

E., arriving from Rome, brings the various current rumours: as soon as Tunisia has fallen, the invasion of Sardinia is expected, but after that one school of thought expects the invasion of Southern France, the other that of the Tuscan coast. If the latter, it is said that the Italian line of defence is to be the Tuscan Apennines: i.e. a line from Spezia to Pesaro. Others say the Apennine foothills round Monte Amiata, in which case this valley will be one of the battlefields.

Talk about separate peace proposals has almost completely died down, but it is said that General Messe, whose report on the battle of Mareth contained very clear accusations against the good faith of his German allies, might, later on, be chosen by the King to head a military dictatorship.

May 2nd

Within the last month a new factor has been introduced into Italian warfare: the day-bombing by the 'Liberators'. Already after Cagliari, Naples and Trapani, the Italians had begun to realize that new daylight air-raids were different, not in degree, but in kind, from any experienced before. And now, Grosseto. On Easter Bank Holiday, at two p.m., a squadron of twenty-six Liberators flew over Grosseto. Having dropped some bombs on the airport, they then proceeded to fly very low over the main street of the little town, leading from the central square to the 'amusement park'; this was already crowded, with the merry-go-rounds in full swing. Owing to the suddenness of the attack, the alarm did not sound until the planes were already overhead, so that the street was full of people in their Sunday best, and all the way down the street the crowd was machine-gunned. The planes then went on to the amusement park, and machine-gunned the tents containing the merry-go-rounds, where children were riding,[1] and even pursued some people who tried to escape into the surrounding wheat-fields, two cars racing down the road, and four children in a field, herding some geese. Then, wheeling back over the town, they again swooped over the square. There a small crowd had gathered round the parish priest, who was giving absolution to the dying under the church porch — and this crowd was machine-gunned once again. One of the bombs fell upon the surgery of the hospital, destroying most of the first-aid kit, so that as the wounded began to pour into the hospital, the surgeons and nurses found themselves without bandages, swabs or ligaments. Subsequently the wounded were moved to the hospital at Montepulciano; and their photographs (especially those of the wounded or mutilated children) have been published in the papers.

These tales have done great harm. Yet I do not think that, when all is over, the dispassionate historian will be able to maintain either the Fascist thesis — that these air-raids have at last aroused the Italian people to hatred of the enemy — nor certainly the Allied one, that they have only awakened resentment against Fascism. I have met, of course, individuals who have bitterly felt one or the other of these emotions. But in the great mass of the nation, the keynote still appears to be a dumb, fatalistic apathy — an acceptance of the doom falling upon them from the skies, as men living in the shadow of Vesuvius and Fujiyama accept the torrents of boiling lava. All this, they seem to feel, is merely part of war — of the war which they did not, do not want. But they are not ready to do anything about it — not yet.

---

[1] These tents may, of course, have been mistaken for military ones.

May 3rd

The prisoners of war have arrived — fifty of them, all British, from the camp at Laterina, near Arezzo. As far as public feeling is concerned, they could hardly have come at a worse moment. The memory of Grosseto is still fresh, and the keepers'

CASTELLUCCIO

wives who live in the same building (an old castle half a mile from us) are prepared to barricade themselves in.

Very quickly, however, these fears were dispelled. Antonio met the men at Chianciano station, helped them to get their kit loaded into our ox-carts, and started them on their twenty-mile tramp to the castle. He soon discovered that the Italian officer who is in charge of them is himself married to an Englishwoman, and is a bank-clerk who used to work in Threadneedle Street — and one of the prisoners, a Guardsman, has a Maltese wife. By the time they reached the castle the most cordial relations were established, and on arrival the men were delighted with their quarters: two large rooms on the ground floor of the castle, giving on the court, another big room (once the stables), a dining-room, a kitchen and a wash-room, with twelve basins and two showers – all freshly whitewashed and perfectly clean, if primitive. The thick walls of the castle, with high, barred windows, are a sufficient safeguard against any attempts to escape – and indeed, one of the prisoners, as he saw Antonio testing one of the bars with the carpenter, remarked humorously, 'If you're doing that for me, sir, don't bother!' Beds for the prisoners (double-tiered bunks, with straw-filled sacks for mattresses) are provided by the Italian Army – also the cooking utensils, and the prisoners' food. An Italian lieutenant is in charge, with a guard of ten men (mostly very small Sicilians), and the prisoners are represented by their corporal – a stolid Yorkshireman named Trott, gardener, we soon discovered, to the Earl of Durham! At the end of the evening he came to Antonio to express the men's appreciation of their quarters – and then, as Antonio asked whether they had any request to make, 'Well, sir, if we could have a bit of a field in which to knock a ball about ...' This can be managed, and also a bit of a kitchen-garden, for them to grow their own vegetables. Their rations as a working-party are better than those they had in camp – four hundred grs. of bread a day, as opposed to two hundred, meat twice a week, etc. And they supplement their rations with magnificent Red Cross parcels (a five-kg. parcel a week for each prisoner) containing in each parcel a tin of butter, one of marmalade or treacle, cocoa, potted meat, dried beans or peas, bacon, fifty cigarettes and a cake of excellent soap – bounty at which we all gape. The *fattore* and keepers are much impressed by the men's discipline and the order in which they are keeping their quarters: the experiment has started well.

May 7th
        I have now been up to the castle, having tactfully kept away for the first three days. The men had just finished their

evening meal, after their day's work. I looked at their quarters and was shown the contents of one of their parcels, but only talked to the corporal and the cook. I found the first sight of them extremely moving, but do not think I showed it, said very little, and stayed only a few minutes. My best chance of being able to be of use to them is to be as inconspicuous as possible. The officer has already accepted, on their behalf, a parcel of books and some packs of cards (strictly speaking, forbidden, unless they have passed through the censor's office) and seems to be well-disposed. But any local gossip might make trouble. Most of the men were captured at Mersa Matruh, about a year ago, and have been for nine months in the camp at Laterina, of which their chief complaint is intense boredom. All seem thankful to be here instead.

May 13th

The last Italian troops on Cape Bon — with enemy troops in front of them, the British fleet behind, and bombed from the sky — have surrendered to the Eighth Army.

The prisoners have settled down now. It is very odd to hear broad Yorkshire spoken in the fields and to see them marching down the road.

May 14th

Arrived in Rome, for the birth of my baby. No one expects Rome to be bombed, but presumably there will be bombing of the coast towns and air-ports.

May 15th

Yesterday afternoon the sirens sounded, and the alarm lasted about an hour. This morning we learn that Civitavecchia was bombed, just as three troopships, packed with troops bound for Corsica, were leaving the harbour — no doubt following upon 'information received'. All three ships were hit and sunk; the soldiers, packed in the hold, were almost all drowned.

May 16th

I have now heard, in one afternoon, the view of three members of the Opposition. Each of them holds a different view of what course should be pursued by Italy, when, and how. It is hardly encouraging.

The extremists advocate immediate action by the King: deposition of the Fascist Government, followed by a military dictatorship and an immediate appeal to the Allies for an armistice. A petition sent to the King by the Young Monarchists of Piemonte reflects these views, and implores the King to act before it is too late. 'Many Italians have still faith in the Monarchy, but every day their number is decreasing . . . From the Alps to Sicily (where your subjects are dying under fire from a people they have never felt to be their enemy) a single cry of acclamation would welcome the step for which we are all waiting . . . The war of imperialist Fascism is irremediably lost — and now the Fascists, in the hour of failure, are trying to turn what was only a party war into a national defeat . . . Sire, separate the fate of this Nation from that of a single brutal, megalomaniac faction. Destroy every link between your dynasty, which gave unity and a constitution to our country, and those who have deprived her of liberty and of a right to citizenship among civilized peoples . . . We affirm, Sire, that against Germany the Army would fight again as it fought at Vittorio Veneto.'[1]

Thus the extremists of the Opposition (Monarchists, Liberals, and even some Republicans). The more lukewarm advocate a half-way measure: a proclamation by the King that he is no longer in agreement with the policy of the Fascist Government — thus throwing the whole odium for the continuation of the war upon the Fascists — even if this should lead to the King's becoming

[1] This petition, of course, was conveyed to the King in the greatest secrecy. For some days a copy of it was hidden behind a picture in the house where I was staying.

practically a prisoner in his own country. It is difficult, however, to see how this would benefit the Italian nation at large.

Finally there are those, even among the Opposition, who are whole-heartedly against any attempt to make a separate peace. 'Let us not conclude,' they say, 'a grotesque war with a still more grotesque attempt at peace, one that can only end in ignominious failure. By any attempt to break the Axis we shall merely precipitate the occupation of Italy by German troops — reserves which Germany will draw from the Russian front, thus strengthening the Russian position, and retarding the progress of the English and Americans here. Is that really what we wish? Moreover, we shall then learn, as Poland and Czecho-Slovacchia have learned, what it is to be occupied by a hostile and vindictive Germany; we shall become a battlefield, despised on both sides as traitors, destroyed by both combatants. No, there is nothing left for us now but passive endurance, until the final defeat of Germany.'

The only point on which all are agreed is that in any case no move is possible until after the beginning of the next Russian offensive. As to the defence of Italy, it appears that there are only seven Italian divisions in the whole country, while there are thirty in Jugoslavia and Croatia. And so we go on waiting.

May 17th

Last night another air-raid alarm, at eleven-thirty p.m. As there was a good deal of firing, apparently just above our heads, we went down to the shelter — the old dungeons of Palazzo Taverna, where Lucrezia Borgia was imprisoned — very deep and very damp. There we found an odd assortment of people: old Princess P., half blind, in a black woollen dressing-gown and shawl, with her daughter wearing three rows of pearls and carrying the family jewels, together with a large crowd of women and children from the surrounding slums; the sleepy babies wailing and the women reciting litanies. After half an hour we went upstairs again and waited until the all clear at one-fifteen.

The planes appear to have been in the direction of Ostia. I trust that my baby will not select one of these nights for its arrival.

May 18*th*

To-day we learn that the planes dropped some bombs on the airport at Ostia, but not on the town, and flew over Rome (of which every stone must have been distinguishable in the clear moonlight) on their way there and back, dropping numerous leaflets. These are adorned on one side with a large skull and cross-bones, on the other by a map of Italy, showing how easily all the principal Italian cities can be reached by the Allies by air − with an appeal to the Italian people to throw off the Fascist and German yoke before it is too late.

A good deal of family discussion takes place as to whether I had not better return to the country for the baby's birth, but I prefer to remain here, within reach of a doctor and nurse. The bombing of Rome is problematical: the baby's arrival certain.

Meanwhile each day and night continue to be of an unequalled, indescribable beauty. Never have I seen a more lovely Roman May. The flower-stalls are piled high with irises and roses and madonna lilies, the fountains play, the cafés on the side-walk are thronged with pretty young women in summer hats ogling the tight-waisted young men who still, in astonishing numbers, walk up and down the pavements. In the *Giardino del Lago* the children sail their boats and watch the Punch and Judy shows and feed the swans, while an occasional plane swoops overhead. And yet the sense of menace is there. At night the streets, lit only by moonlight or starlight, are of an uncanny beauty − silent and deserted, with no eye to see.

May 20*th*

The papers continue to publish accounts of objects containing explosives which are supposed to have been dropped by Allied planes, with the object of mutilating women and children: fountain-pens, pencils, watches, lip-sticks, and even dolls and cough-drops! — and they publish photographs of children wounded by picking up these objects. Some are supposed to have fallen at Civitavecchia and Ostia, but I have never met anyone who has actually seen or touched one. Every child in Rome has been solemnly warned never, never to pick up anything in the street or it will go off with a bang — but on the whole the stories are received with scepticism. 'It's the Germans who have dropped them,' is a frequent comment.

May 24th

There is a lull in the air-raids and it is rumoured that negotiations are in progress, and that, if successful, they will lead to a coup d'état.

May 26th

According to the same rumours, the date of the coup d'état is to be between June 20th and 30th. The bombing of Sicily and Sardinia continues with unabated vigour.

May 27th

A. reports that a German tank corps is now installed at Chiusi. The children of the Principe di Piemonte, who were to have come to Chianciano for safety, are to remain in Rome. (The trunks, which had already arrived at Chiusi, have now gone away again.) Apparently one of the current rumours is that the Allies' invasion will take place on the coast of southern Tuscany near Follonica — in which case the Val d'Orcia will be on their way, and our British prisoners will see their friends arriving.

May 30th

The members of the clandestine opposition in Rome, passing from one secret meeting to another, attempting to find common ground in the points of view of parties as widely at variance as the Communist and the Liberal, the Republican and the Monarchist, are undoubtedly showing great courage. Belonging to the most varied categories — parish priests and Communist workers, ladies of the Princess's entourage and university professors, Army officers and students — they are united by a common enthusiasm, which leaps (in a manner sometimes alarming to the dispassionate observer) beyond all intervening obstacles to the ultimate goal: the destruction of the Fascist regime. Meeting secretly in each other's houses or in obscure little cafés, hiding their papers behind picture-frames, in books, in the soles of their shoes, there is in their doings a certain flavour of Mazzinian conspiracy. But the risks they are taking are real, and already arrests are beginning — mostly as yet among university students and intellectuals, and in Milan and Bologna among the Communists.

The Principesse di Piemonte, for some months now, has been in touch with most of these groups, and is said to convey their aspirations to her husband and, sometimes, to her father-in-law. In this difficult task she has shown great tact and unfailing courage.

Food in Rome is becoming scarcer: fruit and vegetables are practically unprocurable. A chicken costs three hundred lire. The milk ration is two hundred grs. per day (less than a cupful). Flour, ham, etc., can still be bought in the black market, but at a price far beyond the reach of the average purse. Yesterday a friend, who has six small children, sold twelve silver spoons and bought a ham. At the same time, small restaurants continually spring up, provide excellent meals (mostly consumed by high Fascist officials) at exorbitant prices — and then, after a few weeks, are closed by the police, only to open again elsewhere. It is generally expected that the harvest-fields will be destroyed by the Allies with incendiary bombs.

May 31*st*

In the course of this last week, Churchill and Eden have both clearly expressed the Government's determination to pursue the bombing of European cities 'until the total destruction of the Axis powers'. Yesterday Mr. Attlee repeats this statement, in reply to a question in the House by Mr. Stokes as to whether 'an increasing body of public opinion' in England has not come to regard 'the indiscriminate bombing of civilian populations' as 'morally wrong and strategically lunatic'.[1] Mr. Attlee replied: (*a*) That there had *not* been any such 'indiscriminate bombing'; bombing has taken place only where, for military reason, it was considered to be the most efficacious, and (*b*) that the bombing would continue 'in spite of any representations by the members of neutral nations' (from which we conclude that some such protest must have taken place). Finally the B.B.C. reports that yesterday's German raiders over England bombed a country church in which a Sunday school service was taking place, killing twenty children, and machine-gunned children playing on a beach. An article in the *New Statesman* is quoted, stating that those of its readers who previously demanded the invasion of France or Italy, but now deplore these air-raids, are 'severely confused'.

June 3*rd*

News of fresh arrests — for anti-German propaganda — in Perugia and Bologna.

[1] April 1945. Having now received a copy of Harold Nicolson's *Friday Mornings*, I find that on June 4th, 1943, he devoted an article to the examination of Mr. Stokes's remarks. 'I admit,' he wrote, 'that Bomber Command are better judges than is Mr. Stokes of what is, or is not, strategic lunacy. But it is an important fact that the only two places in the world where such points of conscience can be raised with fearless indiscretion are the British Houses of Parliament and the American Congress. It is in fact the truth that there are many people in this country who are distressed by this fierce bombing of crowded cities and who have every right, under a free constitution, to make their opinions heard. And even those who, like myself, have come to a compromise with the paradox, "In order to conquer evil, one must commit evil," find it difficult in this matter to steer a steady course between hypocrisy on the one hand and sentimentality on the other.' Harold Nicolson, *Friday Mornings*, p. 168.

June 4th

The most recent rumours are even more contradictory than usual. On the one hand, it is said that the King is at last about to move: the coup d'état will take place, followed by negotiations for a separate peace. On the other hand, equally definite news is given that it is now too late for any such action, for already the German occupation (in all but name) has taken place. According to these accounts, there are already a quarter of a million Germans in Italy (spread all over the country, so that their numbers are not as yet generally realized). In Sicily and Sardinia large reinforcements have already arrived. Near Rome, Capannelle and Ciampino are being turned into large German airports; and in the province of Siena there is a German tank corps at Chiusi. Moreover, within the last five days the personnel of the German Embassy has been increased by one hundred and fifty members, and it is expected that the Gestapo will soon get seriously to work.

June 9th

At four a.m., in the Clinica Quisisana, my second daughter, Donata, is born. During the long night before her birth I heard from the next room, through my own pain, the groans for morphia of a young airman whose leg had been amputated.

June 10th

The third anniversary of Italy's entry into the war. No celebrations. A rumour had spread that there were to be air-raids all over Italy, and all day many mothers have kept their children at home. Nothing, however, occurred until six p.m., when a few enemy planes flew over the town — and a few more during the night. The air-raid warnings in the hospital (even though nothing happens) are rather uncomfortable, owing to one's enforced immobility and the jumpiness of some of the patients.

June 14th

Antonio returns from Siena, with an account of the methods used by the Fascist militia to obtain 'volunteers'. Five of our peasants, none of whom were Fascists, having been called to the colours with their class, went to Siena. There they were shown, singly, into a room where a captain of the militia (by flattery and promises of safety, of frequent leave, and remaining in his own province) 'invited' each of them to join the militia instead of the Army. All, except one, refused – and were stormed at as 'Bolsheviks, anti-Italian, etc.' The fifth, simpler than the others, signed his name on an enrolment form – but, on coming out, met his friends, compared notes, and assembling all his courage, hurried back to the captain to annul his signature. After a good deal of abuse, he believes that he succeeded, but in the evening he came to us, sweating with anxiety. 'What will happen to me? Have I done right or wrong?'

The present condition of the militia is also indicated by a letter received by Antonio a few days later, requesting him to 'make a gift' to the militia of a motor-car, 'for use in Sicily'. He has not replied.

June 18th

More political arrests are in progress all over the country – university professors, students, workmen. It is said that General Raffaele Cadorna,[1] the son of the Cadorna of the last war, has had his division taken away from him, 'for anti-Fascist sentiments'.

June 19th

The Principessa di Piemonte has gone to Sicily to accompany some Red Cross workers and to investigate conditions in some of the hospitals, of which a deplorable account has reached

[1] He subsequently commanded the Partisan forces in northern Italy.

her (lack of equipment, lack of medicines, dirt, etc.) through
Edda Ciano. According to the latter's own account, she said to
the Princess: 'You are just like my father. You go everywhere
and see nothing!' But this may be apocryphal.

June 21st
    News that a large Allied convoy has left Oran — bound
for where?

June 23rd
    We return to La Foce. A comfortable, ordinary journey,
by train.

July 6th
    The German offensive in Russia has begun. The air-raids
in Sicily are intensified. A 'state of emergency' has been proclaimed in Crete. Everything seems to point to the approach of
a fresh move on the part of the Allies. Meanwhile Mussolini has
made a long and violent speech, stating that resistance is for Italy
a matter of 'life or death' and that the invaders, if indeed they
come, are not to be allowed to pass the highwater-mark (*il
bagnasciuga*) on the Italian shore. The Duce then passed on to
the measures to be enforced by the Fascist Party, and stated that
he is prepared to bear the full weight of his responsibility: 'One
day I shall demonstrate that this war neither could nor should
have been avoided.'
It is perhaps significant that this speech (which is only published a fortnight after it has been made) should have been
addressed neither to the Senate nor to the assembled people in
Piazza Venezia, but only to the Directorate of the Fascist Party.
Querulous and violent, it is generally considered deplorable.

July 8th

News from Rome that the Army's coup d'état is to take place before the end of the month. I do not believe in it: there has been too much talk for too long.

July 10th

The long-expected news has come at last: Allied troops landed last night in Sicily. The Italian bulletin at one p.m. tells but the bare fact, adding that fierce fighting is in progress. The B.B.C. adds that the troops are those of the Eighth Army, commanded by General Eisenhower, and that there are also some Canadian divisions, but gives no details as yet about the landing, beyond stating that there are supposed to be four hundred thousand Axis troops in Sicily, of whom one hundred thousand are Germans.

All day German planes fly over the valley, bound southwards.

At ten p.m. the broadcast from America in Italian follows the news of the landing with an appeal to Sicilians to throw off the Fascist yoke, and a vague statement of the peace conditions that would be offered to Italy by the Allies. 'For the Fascists and for the Army which is supporting them, unconditional surrender. For the Italian people, an opportunity to fill once again an honourable place among the free peoples of Europe.' The Algiers radio states: 'The battle of Africa is over; the battle of Europe has begun.'

July 11th

Donata's christening — a day of strange contrasts. We wake at five a.m. to a dull booming sound — a naval bombardment, we presume, from enemy ships on the Tuscan coast, or perhaps the bombing of Grosseto or Livorno, perhaps a preface to invasion. All day we listen in eagerly for an explanation of this sound, which is never forthcoming. The bulletins, both from

Rome and London, tell of further landings in Sicily. Meanwhile Donata's little festa takes place. Baskets of flowers and small presents are brought to her by the children on the place. The guests are gathered, and at eleven Mons. B. celebrates Mass[1] in Gianni's chapel. The introit is appropriate: 'The Lord is my light and my salvation: whom shall I fear? The Lord is the protector of my life: of whom shall I be afraid? . . . If arms in camp should stand together against me my heart shall not fear.' At five-thirty we all go to the Castelluccio church for the christening: at the church door are gathered a large crowd of the peasants and of children, who afterwards come back to the garden with us.

When all is over, and the children are gone, we turn on the radio: the landings in Sicily continue.

July 12th
    Last night British troops entered Syracuse.

July 13th
    We spend most of the day speculating as to what the next move of the Allies will be: France? the Balkans? Sardinia and the Tuscan coast? Meanwhile Turin is bombed once again — the most severe raid, according to the B.B.C., yet made on any Italian town. We try to prevent the news from reaching the refugee children, whose families are still there.

The news of the landing in Sicily somehow reached the British prisoners yesterday, and they celebrate it at night, singing and dancing. To-day the Maresciallo dei Carabinieri has come from Pienza to inquire who had told them: one of the workmen is suspected, and has been arrested.

[1] This same Monsignore, during the German domination in the winter 1943-44, played a heroic part in helping to hide and protect fugitives from the Germans and Fascists — hiding partisans, Jews and Army officers (regardless of all the rules of the cloister) in his convalescent home for nuns in the Sabine hills, and providing yet others with false papers with the Vatican stamp. Even the catacombs of Priscilla served once again as a hiding-place — from the German soldier now, as centuries ago from the Roman.

43

July 16th

Bombing all over Italy: Genoa, Bologna, Naples, Parma, Foggia. Simultaneously a broadcast of Churchill and Roosevelt to the Italian people urges them to overthrow the Fascist regime, and offers them 'an honourable capitulation' and 'a respected place among the free peoples of Europe'. Germany, says the message, has betrayed the Italian people: Mussolini and Fascism have betrayed them. If they do not capitulate, Italy will be destroyed. It is for the Italians to decide whether they will die for Mussolini and Hitler or live for peace and liberty.

Fierce fighting in the plain of Catania. But the Axis air defence is negligible, and apparently no reinforcements from Germany have arrived.

July 17th

Leaflets are scattered by Allied planes over Rome and other cities, containing Churchill's and Roosevelt's joint message to the Italian people.

Letters arrive from the children's families in Turin: Liberata's mother writes that her house has been hit for the second time; Nella's parents, that they are only alive 'by a miracle'. They add, 'pray for us'. The other children have no news as yet. Lentini is occupied: fierce fighting still continues on the Catanian plain. American troops are marching on Girgenti. Allied bombings now centre on the toe of Italy, rather than on Sicily.

The Italian papers publish Churchill's and Roosevelt's message, calling it 'an invitation to shame and dishonour'.[1]

July 19th

This morning, for the first time, bombs are dropped on Rome. The one o'clock Italian bulletin gives the news laconically (while the raid is still in progress) adding 'the damage is being

[1] They do not, however, print the statement in the second half of the message, that 'the Germans have betrayed and abandoned their Italian ally both in Russia and on every battlefield in Africa' — and it is said that this omission has been ordered by Mussolini.

ascertained'. At two-thirty the B.B.C. broadcast in Italian states that bombs have been dropped on the railway station and 'military objectives' and that leaflets have been scattered all over the town, to inform the citizens of Rome that the Allies intend to confine themselves to military objectives and to avoid 'monuments of religious or cultural interest'. For this reason the raid has been in broad daylight.

Nucci's father arrives from Turin, with details of the last raid there. It has been by far the most serious that has yet taken place. The Fiat works have been hit, and the electric cable factories, as well as the older parts of the town, several churches, and Don Bosco's *Casa della Divina Provvidenza* — in spite of the vision granted in 1940 to the Mother Superior, by which Pope Pius X himself assured her that the institution would remain untouched.

July 20th

Caltanisetta is taken. More details of the raid on Rome: five hundred Liberators bombed the city for three hours — according to the B.B.C. hitting only the station, marshalling-yards, airports, and government buildings; according to the Italian radio, destroying the Basilica of San Lorenzo, and hitting the hospitals of the Policlinico, the Verano cemetery, and many workmen's houses. Directly after the air-raid the Pope left the Vatican and visited San Lorenzo. Kneeling on the steps of the ruined church, and surrounded by an enormous crowd which had gathered as soon as his presence was known, he recited the *De Profundis* and imparted his blessing to the crowd.

July 21st

Succeed in telephoning to E. in Rome. The town is still without water and no trains are running. The Pope's visit to San Lorenzo aroused great popular enthusiasm — so great, indeed, that his car was injured by the faithful who surrounded it, and he had to go home in another one. All night the porticoes of St. Peter's are thronged with a great crowd, in the belief that there, at least, no bombs will fall. Once again, the faithful take refuge in the shadow of St. Peter's.

July 22nd

A panic-stricken letter from Turin, from Liberata's mother, implores me to take in her other children, too. 'Let them sleep in a cellar, but save them from certain death ... I can't think any more; I have seen too many horrible deaths. It is worse than a massacre, so many corpses under our house ... Help me, help me, I must save my children somehow. . . .' We have wired to them to come. Still no news of Marisa's father, who lived in the quarter which has been most completely destroyed.

July 23rd

Late in the evening, Liberata's mother, sister and brother arrive from Turin, exhausted and terrified. They were buried under their house, have slept for the last ten days in a stable, and have nothing left in the world but the rags they have on. They have uttered no single word of resentment or complaint.

July 24th

Marsala is occupied by the Allies. Bologna is bombed. According to E. who has just arrived from Rome, the city is full of rumours: the coup d'état is at last about to take place. It is said that at Mussolini's recent interview with Hitler, the latter demanded, as the condition of his sending reinforcements, that the conduct of the war in Italy should be handed over entirely to the German Command, and the whole of Southern Italy (including Rome) abandoned: the first line of defence to be on the Apennines, and the second on the Po.[1]

July 26th

The long-expected news has come at last: Mussolini has fallen. The news was given by radio last night, but we did not hear it until this morning. Mussolini has resigned, the King has appointed Marshal Badoglio in his place and has himself taken over the command of the Army. A proclamation of Badoglio's announces: 'Italy will keep her pledge; the war continues.'

As the broadcast closes E. burst into my room: 'Have you heard? After twenty years — after twenty years ...' We all have a lump in our throat. Hope — perplexity — anxiety — doubt — then hope again — infinite relief. A weight has been lifted, a door opened; but where does it lead? We spend the day in speculations, fed by driblets of news. First a proclamation of martial law, with the institution of a curfew at sunset and a prohibition of any public meetings: moreover, it is forbidden to carry fire-arms or to circulate in any private vehicle; a few hours later we hear with delight of the disbanding of the Fascist militia: its members are to be incorporated in the regular Army. In the evening comes the list of the new Cabinet; mostly permanent officials or under-secretaries. It is clearly to be a moderate, traditional government of administrators, not of 'great men'. Italy has had enough of heroes. But still innumerable questions are unanswered. What has happened to Mussolini and his satellites? And above all — increasingly with every hour — what about Germany?

[1] Subsequent accounts of this interview give a different version. According to Badoglio, Mussolini (accompanied by his Chief of Staff, General Ambrosio, by the Foreign Minister Bastianini, and the Ambassador to Germany, Alfieri) had gone to meet Hitler with the intention of informing him of the true condition of affairs in Italy and of convincing him that Italy must now get out of the war. Whether or not this was Mussolini's intention, it is certain that Ambrosio had plainly informed the Duce of the military situation, and that both he and Bastianini expected Mussolini at last to attempt to extricate his country from this impasse. But when the meeting took place, only one person spoke — Hitler — and when the Italian delegates returned home, a flat little communiqué merely announced that 'questions of military character have been discussed'. Nothing more. (Monelli, *Roma 1943*.)

July 27th

Slowly, some of these questions are answered — though not the most important. To-day's papers publish, without comment, the motion of the *Gran Consiglio* (assembled on Sunday, July 25th, for the first time since December 1939) — the motion that brought about the end of Fascism. Presented by Grandi and signed by nineteen out of the twenty-six members of the *Gran Consiglio* (including Mussolini's own son-in-law, Ciano, and De Bono, Bottai, Federzoni, Bastianini and Rossoni) it is a more complete and ignominious recantation of the Fascist doctrine than any that could have been composed by its enemies. In it the Fascist leaders recognize that in order to obtain 'the moral and political unity of all Italians in this grave and decisive hour' it is necessary to proceed to an immediate restoration of all the functions of the State, 'restoring to the Crown, the Grand Council, the Government, the Parliament and the Corporations all the duties and responsibilities by our constitutional laws'.

In consequence the Council moved that the Prime Minister, Mussolini, should hand over the military command to the King. With this motion — affirming, as it does, the necessity, in a time of crisis, of returning to a constitutional government — the Fascist doctrine stands condemned by its own adherents. Mussolini, like all other dictators, is betrayed by his own men.[1]

July 28th

To-day fuller details reach us. It appears that when Grandi (of whom Mussolini had been jealous and suspicious for a long time) presented his motion to the assembled Grand Council, Mussolini drew forth a voluminous *dossier* of the errors and misdeeds of his lieutenants during the past twenty years. These, he stated, he had suppressed until now, but would now

[1] Of all the Duce's followers, only one man — Senator Morgagni, the head of the 'Agenzia Stefani' — was faithful to him at the end. Five minutes after the broadcast giving the news of Mussolini's resignation, he shot himself, leaving on his desk a note saying: 'The Duce has resigned. My life is over. Long live Mussolini.' (Monelli, *Roma 1943*.)

48

make public. A 'discussion' took place which lasted ten hours and ended with a vote of nineteen to seven, in favour of Grandi's motión. Meanwhile, all over the city the news had spread that something was afoot. At three a.m. on Sunday morning the long black police cars which had brought the Fascists to Palazzo Venezia drove away again, and the anxious satellites (industrial magnates, financiers, politicians, diplomats, and smart young women) who had been waiting anxiously all night in the hall of the Excelsior, were called to the telephone or to the houses of their friends. By dawn, the news began to spread all over the city; in the afternoon, Mussolini went to Villa Savoia, and before evening he and his friends were under arrest, while the broadcast at ten-forty-five announced his fall and the King's proclamation. The next morning a great crowd of working people from all the outlying quarters surged into the centre of the city and made its way to the Quirinal, singing Mameli's hymn: *Fratelli d'Italia, l'Italia s'è desta!* They broke into all the offices and club-rooms of the Fascio; destroyed every bust and statue of Mussolini, set fire to the offices of the *Messagero* and the *Tevere* and carried in triumph on their shoulders any officers of the regular Army that they encountered. The only bloodshed was at the Viminale, where some of the militia fired into the crowd — whereupon the Carabiniere fired back, killing several Blackshirts. Similar demonstrations took place in Milan, Turin, Bologna, Florence — with the result that by eleven o'clock on Monday morning a special broadcast issued a firm order of Badoglio's, that all public meetings and processions would be dispersed by the police. 'This is no moment to give way to impulsive demon-strations. The gravity of the hour requires from each one of us discipline and patriotism, dedicated to the supreme interests of the nation.'

Meanwhile we listen-in eagerly to the foreign broadcasts, for comments from abroad. The first statement of the news from Germany affirms that Mussolini has resigned 'on account of his health'; and subsequent statements refrain from any comment whatever, merely emphasizing Badoglio's affirmation: 'The war goes on.' What lies beneath this restraint?

From England, too, official comment in the first two days is very cautious. Then yesterday evening came Churchill's statement to the House: 'The keystone of the Fascist arch has fallen ... we may reasonably expect very great changes.' After describing the welcome given to Allied troops at Palermo, he comments: 'I cannot doubt that the main wish of the Italian people is to be rid of the Germans and to restore their democratic institutions. The choice lies with the Italian people.' If, however, the Italians have not the will or the courage to free themselves from Germany, 'we shall continue to make war upon Italy from every quarter, by land, air and sea ... Italy will be covered with scars and bruises from end to end'. The P.M. warned the House against the mistake made by the Germans in occupied territory, that of 'destroying all forms of local authority'. 'We certainly do not desire to reduce Italy to anarchy and to have no authority left with which we can deal.' But, he emphasized, the real enemy is Germany, the real point at issue, Hitler's destruction — and for this unconditional surrender is a necessity. 'The affairs of Italy must be handled with this supreme end constantly in view.' Subsequently, the B.B.C. commentator is not sparing in his picture of the methods ('by fire and steel') to be used to 'encourage Italy's decision'.

The main points of this speech were subsequently reprinted on leaflets dropped over the Italian towns, entitled 'Out with the Germans — or fire and steel'.

July 30th

Yesterday, at the first meeting of the new Cabinet, the *Camera dei Fasci e delle Corporazioni* was officially dissolved. No political parties may be formed and no political activities are to be permitted, until four months after the end of the war, when a constitutional parliament will again be elected. For the present, Italy remains under martial law.

Simultaneously comes the news that the liberation of political prisoners has begun. The 'Special Tribunal for the Defence of the State', instituted in 1926 by the Fascist regime, is suppressed, and its duties will be taken over, during the war, by military tribunals.

V., arriving from Ferrara, brings tales of rioting in some of the northern cities. In Milan, he says, many Fascists have been killed or beaten up by their old enemies; there is still shooting in the streets. In Ferrara a leading Fascist, who had shot a boy of twelve for singing *Bandiera rossa*, was attacked by the boy's relations, and only saved his life by jumping into the canal. There have been similar incidents in Turin, Bologna, Genoa and Florence — and numerous strikes in factories, where the workmen refuse to go on working under Fascist foremen. The Fascist Party secretaries throughout Italy have been arrested — partly for their own protection — and the prefects are under temporary arrest in their own houses.

A broadcast this morning warns the Italian people to mistrust 'false and unfounded rumours of sensational events, which are evidently being spread by irresponsible and unpatriotic individuals, who wish to create a disturbance of the peace'. These rumours — as they have reached us here — include the suicide of Hitler and the desertion to the Russians of the thirty Italian divisions in the Balkans.

Gayda is removed from the *Giornale d'Italia*, his place being taken by its founder, the Liberal Bergamini.[1] The *Lavoro Fascista* changes its title to *Lavoro Italiano*. All the papers, of whatever political complexion (including the republican and socialist *Lavoro* of Genoa, the *Stampa*, etc.) publish appeals to Italians to celebrate their new-found liberty by discipline and unity — and not to forget, in their delight at internal changes, that the enemy is still at their gates.

[1] In October, Bergamini and other Liberal editors were arrested by the new Fascist Party.

July 31st

The papers announce that all railway and post-office employees are to be 'militarized'. All Fascist provincial secretaries, vice-secretaries and *squadristi* are to be called to the colours — this last a most popular measure.

Demonstrations in the various towns continue, and to-day the B.B.C. (quoting the Swiss papers as its authority) affirms that they are not only against Fascism, but for peace. 'Marshal Badoglio's Government, however,' it adds, 'has given no sign of implementing the Italian people's wish for peace.'

Undoubtedly the majority of the Italian people *do* want peace, but how many, in order to obtain it, are prepared to break with Germany and to submit passively to Allied occupation I have no idea.

August 1st

To-day the B.B.C. announces that the lull which has lasted since July 25th is over: the bombing of Italy will begin again. Throughout the night Radio Algiers has broadcast this news to the Italian people, warning them to keep away from factories producing war material, and from airports, railways, etc. So now we are once again expectant.

Meanwhile the Italian radio broadcasts a denial of the news given by the B.B.C. of serious riots and demonstrations in Italian cities, of the occupation of Trieste and Udine by German troops, and of sabotage by the railway workmen of northern Italy. Here, in the depths of the country, we have no means of knowing what the facts are.

August 3rd

Yesterday I went to see the B.s (ardent Liberals) who have recently arrived from Rome. To the tale of Mussolini's downfall they add the following details: On leaving Palazzo

Venezia at three a.m. on Sunday morning, after the meeting of the Grand Council, the Duce went home, still firmly convinced that under no circumstances would the King dispense with his services, and later in the morning asked for an audience. In the afternoon he went to Villa Savoia, and offered his services to the country once again. This time, however, they were refused. What took place at the meeting between the two men, who were alone, is not known. What is certain is, that when Mussolini came out and looked around for his car, the officer on guard at the gate requested him instead to enter a Red Cross closed ambulance, in which he found his doctor waiting. And so he drove quietly away — from Villa Savoia and from power.

The B.s believe that Badoglio's Government has had every intention from the first moment of making a separate peace, and is now playing for time. So convinced are they, that they have already made arrangements for their young nephews and nieces to leave the Veneto, which (since they presume that a German invasion would ensue) would become a battlefield. They are certain that, as soon as war is declared *against* Germany, innumerable volunteers will flock to the colours. Another friend, on the contrary, expressed his conviction that the spirit of resistance in the country *against the Allies* is increasing daily. The truth is that we none of us have the faintest idea of what is going on behind the scenes — everyone interprets such events as he has heard of, in the light of his own desires.

August 4th

Letters from friends, commenting on recent events. M.G.V., the wife of a young diplomat, writes from Rome: 'I would not have missed the last few days for anything in the world. Every day life becomes more interesting. We are all waiting ... for what, no one knows ... The curfew is very strict and not agreeable in this weather — but it may last a year! We all go to bed in the deepest darkness and silence, with an occasional gunshot in the night. Daily life is normal, and every face smiling. It is as if we had at last succeeded in holding up our heads again. Fancy! by Monday morning there was not a single Fascist left in the town! And then everyone is kinder, more humane, more polite!' On the other hand, another young woman, who works in our office, writes that she feels hopelessly confused and bewildered. 'Not for nothing have I been brought up for twenty years under the Fascist regime. I can't yet realize how it is possible to live under a Liberal Government.' Finally yet another (once an ardent Fascist) writes: 'I can't tell you what I have been feeling. Surprise, hope, fear, disgust at some of the revolting performances of the mob, then hope again, doubts, fears . . . I have only one desire, the same that I have had through all these last months: to save Italy's honour. The task of the King and of the Government is terrible and I pity them. Forgive me if I can't say more.'

The daily press, for years practically unreadable, has suddenly become interesting again. Most of the papers are again edited by old Liberals who are also experienced journalists, and many different shades of opinion find expression in their columns. Most of the articles are very moderate in tone, and even those that most rejoice at the return of liberty are prodigal of warnings as to how that blessed state must be defined and safeguarded. 'Our liberty will only be safe when we shall no longer need to talk about it. As soon as possible let us leave this vague expression and pass on to practical problems: for then only will freedom have life,' writes U. Morra in the *Popolo di Roma*.

A number of German tanks drive down our road to the Val d'Orcia (only for manœuvres — as yet) and in the evening, going into the kitchen, I find two German soldiers and an interpreter sitting there; they have come to ask if they can buy a sheep. The interpreter is a quiet, civilized man, the head of a small business in Milan, where he has lived for many years. He comes from Hamburg, where his father and mother were buried beneath the ruins of their house in 1941; and he now has had no news of his three sisters there. Later on six other German officers come tramping up the garden path. All are very young, but all have been through the Russian campaign; they are now quartered at Citta della Pieve. At ten o'clock we all go indoors, to listen to the news. One of them looks round the library: 'What a lot of English books you've got!' 'Yes,' says Antonio, 'my wife is an Englishwoman.' There is a moment's silence; then we all laugh. But as we go on talking, I wonder how many more such German officers have come into this country in the last ten days – and whether, by their coming, Italy's fate is not already decided.

The tone of British propaganda since the fall of Fascism has caused much resentment, with its insistence on 'unconditional surrender' and its bland assumption that peace at any price will be welcomed by the Italian people. The Italians feel that they have succeeded, at a considerable risk, in ridding themselves of Fascism, thus kindling a spark which may start similar conflagrations all over Europe – and that the Allies, who for years have been urging them to this course, have now shown that they are utterly indifferent to the liberty of Italy, except as a stepping-stone to Germany's destruction. An article in the *Corriere della Sera* of August 5th reflects this feeling: 'Our enemies went on repeating that they were fighting against Fascism and not against Italian people. Fascism has been overthrown. What have they to offer to Italy? Nothing but a vague promise of generosity, a threadbare velvet glove over the iron hand of "unconditional surrender" . . . Many of us, in those unforgettable days, hoped for clearer statements, which would forecast a consciousness of a new, united Europe, more certain of equity and justice. . . .'

Fully to understand the Italian attitude in this matter it is perhaps necessary to look back and realize how widespread is the conviction among Italians that the war was a calamity imposed upon them by German force – in no sense the will of the Italian people, and therefore something for which they cannot be held responsible. Recently I came across my diary for June 1940, in which, when Italy's entry into the war appeared inevitable, I tried to explain to myself the reasons which, psychologically, had rendered possible the fundamentally false position of the Italian people.

'Is it possible,' I wrote, 'to move a country to war against its historical traditions, against the natural instincts and characters of the majority of its inhabitants, and very possibly against its own instincts? Apparently it is possible. In a people as profoundly individualistic and sceptical as the Italian, eighteen years of Fascism have not destroyed the critical spirit, and this is allied to an inborn fluidity and adaptability which causes them (now as in the past) to interpret all general statements and theories in the light of the particular occasion, and thus to attach no undue importance, in the field of politics, to abstract formulas or absolute doctrines. Thus most Catholic Italians (though not all) in these last twenty years have not allowed themselves to be unduly dismayed by the abstract claims of the Fascist doctrine that the rights of the State should prevail over those of the Church, but have been content to accept the fact that, in actual practice, it has been easier in the last twenty years than in the fifty years of intense anti-clericalism after 1870, to bring up their children in a Catholic atmosphere at home. They are prepared to yield in principle, where they can gain in practice. And it is this same fluid adaptability (which can be interpreted by those temperamentally opposed to it as a cynical opportunism) that has rendered possible the German alliance. The Axis, regarded purely as a temporary policy of self-interest, forced upon them by the "intransigent" attitude of the democracies, has been accepted by a people which, in accepting it, yet has not modified its instinctive antipathy for Germany, and for the barbaric and brutal aspects of the German *Weltanschaung*.'

So I wrote in 1940 – and now Italy, with Fascism overthrown, is reaping the consequences of the disastrous alliance.

Meanwhile we hear that four more armoured German divisions

have crossed the Brenner — among them, Hitler's own *élite* division. It begins to dawn upon us that the choice — if indeed there ever was one — is already made. This autumn will not bring peace to Italy.

August 12th

More German gunners arrive here for manœuvres in the Val d'Orcia, and camp beneath Radicofani. Their officers inform us that they are there in order to be able to move rapidly towards whatever landing-point in Tuscany may be chosen by the Allies: Grosseto, Piombino or Livorno.

August 13th

Rome is bombed again; the same quarter as before, near the station. Also, last night, Milan and Turin.

August 14th

C.A., arriving from Rome, brings depressing news. According to his account, Badoglio's Government *did* start out with a definite intention of making a separate peace, but (though this is difficult to believe) had no clear plan of action with regard to Germany. In the first four or five days after the coup d'état, the Germans were completely taken aback and bewildered — von Mackensen hurried off to Germany — and the German General Staff (at Frascati) had received no instructions. Decisive action on the part of the new Italian Government (seizing the German General Staff at Frascati, and closing the Brenner) might possibly have been effective; but instead it shilly-shallied for three days, awaiting Guariglia's arrival from Ankara, and then embarked on diplomatic negotiations to persuade the Germans to retire from Italy of their own accord — a proposal which Germany did not

57

even consider. Italy no longer has any choice: she will go on with the war, not because she has decided to, but because she must.

August 15th

My birthday, which we celebrate together with Benedetta's by having a children's party. In the middle of Blind Man's Buff a military lorry drives up and two German officers come clanking down the garden path. They belong to the division, encamped beneath Radicofani, which crossed the Brenner on July 28th. Their own company, however, is to go in a few days to Salerno — where, they tell us, the Allied landing is now expected. They deny that the first line of defence is to be along the Apennines; it is to be, they say, from Salerno to Brindisi, to prevent the Allies from cutting across Italy to the Adriatic. Several divisions, however, will still remain in Tuscany. As they sit, very correct and polite — drinking their glasses of wine and proposing a formal toast — I feel that they are the most highly specialized human beings that I ever encountered: the 'fighting man'. Both of them (one from Mecklenburg, one from the Saar) are under twenty-five; both have taken part in the campaigns of Poland, France, Russia — and now Italy. One of them, risen from the ranks, commanded for six months a company of Russian deserters, who are now fighting against Russia (he says that there are now two hundred thousand of them) under German and Russian officers; the other was at Stalingrad. To one of them I say: 'You must have gone into the Army straight from school.' 'No,' he replies. '*Schon in der Schule war ich Soldat.* I belonged to the Hitler Jugend.' We ask about the Russian front. 'We'll hold them back all right; we *must*.' It is impossible to convey the depth of the conviction in his voice, both then and later, while he expounded to us the familiar doctrines which had been taught him: the needs of *Gross Deutschland*, Nordic racial superiority, the inevitability of Germany's entry into war (in spite of all Hitler's efforts to make peace with England), his pride in his country and his men, and above all his unshakable certainty, even now, of victory. He was not being a propagandist, but simply stating a creed, a creed to which he brought an absolutely single-minded, self-denying devotion, with no half-shades of humour, self-criticism or doubt. Add to this, admirable health, iron discipline, and the vigour and courage of youth, and arm and clothe such an army well — and the results are formidable: the results that Hitler intended to produce, and that fifty Mussolinis could not produce here.

August 17th

Last night the first bombs fell in the Val d'Orcia. As we were sitting in the garden after dinner, we heard planes approaching and then saw their lights, between us and Monte Amiata. There were three distinct booms, and then we saw a fire on the mountain, above Campiglia, which smouldered for about half an hour before it died out. This morning we learn that the bombs (presumably dropped by some plane on its way home) fell near an isolated farmhouse, wounding three people.

A neighbour comes to tell us that on July 28th (three days after Mussolini's fall) as he was travelling to Florence, the news spread down the train that an armistice had been signed. At Pontassieve flags and carpets were hanging from the windows; at Florence the great bell of the Bargello had been rung; people were weeping for joy and embracing each other. But after half an hour the rumour was contradicted and the excited and disappointed crowd had to be dispersed by the police.

At Bologna, too, on one day of that week, a similar rumour had spread, and armoured cars were stationed in the squares, to prevent rioting. But now, day by day, such hopes are fading — and with them the short-lived popularity of Badoglio's Government. Moreover, the King is now sharing some of the unpopularity which previously was directed against the Fascists.

In the Romagna people are already clamouring for a Republic; at Terni, after the air-raids, the King was hissed by the crowd.

In the evening we hear that Messina has fallen; the Axis troops have been evacuated to the mainland. The Sicilian campaign is over.

August 21st

Once more, with the Sicilian campaign ended, we are embarking upon a period of suspense. At Quebec, the Allied leaders are, presumably, making their plans; in southern Italy and in France air-raids are increasing. The common citizen sits and waits — but with an ever-increasing dread of invasion and diminishing hopes of peace.

August 30th

Quebec is now over — and certainly no statement has come to raise our spirits. The bombing of southern Italy (as well as the more severe attacks on Germany) continue, and the only speculation left to us is what point of landing the Allies will choose: Naples, Civitavecchia, or Tuscany. What we do not know here, in the depths of the country, is what is happening in the towns. Certainly in the north there seems to have been more trouble than in Tuscany. From Turin the mother of one of our children, who works in a war factory, writes of continual rioting in the streets and frequent strikes, of troops and machine-guns in the streets. V., too, coming from Ferrara, says that the workmen there are completely out of hand; they refuse to work under their previous foremen or to observe working hours, and many of them have struck work altogether. 'What's the use?' is the universal cry. We are only waiting.

From Rome comes the rumour of a Fascist plot to seize the government once again, in which Cavallero, Starace and Muti are said to have been the leaders — but with German backing.

All are now arrested, and Muti, in attempting to get away, was shot. Badoglio is said to have made a strong protest to the German Embassy.

A cryptic letter from Rome says that 'Victoria (England) has had the permission to stay near Civitavecchia very soon'. From this I conclude that the Allies' landing near Rome is to take place with the Italian Government's consent and that the consequent seizure of the city will be followed by capitulation. There are still, however, the German troops in southern Italy to be reckoned with — not to mention those in the north.

Most people have now got to the point of exasperation where almost any news would be welcome; anything is better than this prolonged expectation.

September 1st

The radio announces that General Cavallero has committed suicide, 'unable to survive the dishonour of betrayal'.[1] So also has Frontoni (the head of the Infant Welfare organization, who was one of the administrators of Ciano's enormous, ill-gotten fortune). The arrest of ex-Fascist leaders is now in progress, pending an inquiry into the methods by which their large fortunes have been acquired. Ciano, however, and Grandi have been allowed to escape, though Ciano's fortune has been seized.

It is difficult to overstate the depth of the depression that has overtaken the members of this unhappy country. While the majority of the people want nothing but peace, and the Army is clearly demonstrating its reluctance to fight, the intransigence of the Allies' terms is only equalled by the firmness of Germany's refusal to remove her troops. Whatever happens, Italians now realize that their country must become a battlefield; and their only choice (if indeed it still is one) is merely whether they shall remain half-hearted participants or passive spectators. There is

[1] There now appears to be little doubt that he was shot, by Kesselring's orders.

a bitter irony for listeners here in the exhortations of the B.B.C. to the Italian people to rid themselves of the Germans: so might one urge a sheep to rid itself of a wolf.

September 2nd

To-day the Pope's appeal for peace falls here upon ears only too thoroughly converted. But I fear it will cut little ice elsewhere.

September 3rd

The long-drawn-out suspense is over: British and Canadian troops of the Eighth Army landed this morning at Reggio, Calabria. The invasion of the mainland has begun. We hear the news from the B.B.C. at eight a.m. and it is confirmed by the Italian bulletin at one p.m.

September 4th

A friend writes: 'There is a patrimony common to all humanity, made up of decency, sensibility and civilized behaviour, which is every day diminishing and will soon be bankrupt. I envy the only people whose hands are still clean, the Swiss, with ideologies which are reflected in the simple acts of everyday life.'

September 6th

A letter sent by hand from Rome informs me that a second landing is expected within the next ten days, 'in your part of the country'. (Civitavecchia? Grosseto? Piombino?)

I spend the afternoon blackberrying with the children, and reflect (without really believing it) that within a fortnight this peaceful scene may look very different.

September 7th

Drive to Montepulciano. At the Siena cross-roads we are stopped by a barricade across the road; sentries from the Montepulciano garrison ask for our permits. Cannons, thinly concealed by branches and leaves, have been placed on points commanding the hillside and there are trenches around the hill beneath the road. For whom, we wonder, is all this intended? The little town is as crowded as on a market day, but now only with soldiers (the 'Ravenna' Division, recently back from Russia). A rumour has reached the B.s that the armistice has already been signed, and will probably be made public to-morrow or the next day. But what steps have been taken about the Germans is not mentioned. We sit on the terrace overlooking the peaceful valley, drink our tea, and speculate as to what will happen, if indeed this news is true. The doctor comes to call, and tells us that twenty-three of the Calabrian soldiers of the garrison have deserted in the last few days, on the pretext of returning home 'to defend Calabria'.

September 8th

Drive for the day to Siena with Antonio, Schwester and the baby, whom I am still nursing. An exquisitely lovely, still morning; no sign of trouble anywhere, except an occasional plane overhead. But on the way we say to each other: 'I expect this is the last of these jaunts.' We drive through the familiar villages through which we used to pass on our way back from the Palio, greeted by cries of *Chi ha vinto?* Now all of them are full of troops, and the road is barricaded at S. Quirico and Buonconvento by soldiers, who ask for our permits. At Siena, a very odd day. Antonio goes to see the new Prefetto, Schwester and I go off shopping. At intervals I return to a friend's house to nurse the baby, and we lunch with the A.s at the *Cannond'Oro*. But all these familiar occupations are interspersed with startling news: the bombing yesterday of Naples, which has destroyed the whole centre of the town, the bombing of Frascati (C.A. tries to telephone all day, but cannot find out whether or no his house is still standing), and then, finally, the news that a great Allied convoy is already in sight of the Bay of Naples, and a landing imminent.

We drive back, saying: 'Here it is at last!' Naples to-day, and presumably Grosseto to-morrow. Then, as we stop at the Buonconvento barrier, we see that the soldiers are grinning from ear to ear. 'Soon you won't need these permits any more!' 'What do you mean?' — 'Haven't you heard? The Chaplain has just told us. Badoglio has spoken on the radio. There's been an armistice. *E' la pace, la pace incondizionata!*' (The speaker, a small private, clearly thought this superior to any other kind of peace.) 'Thank you,' says Antonio grimly, and we drive on.

As we get nearer home and the dusk falls, we see bonfires blazing in front of the farms: the news has got here, too. And at eight-thirty p.m. we hear the official broadcast, and Badoglio's proclamation: 'The Italian Government, having recognized the impossibility of continuing an unequal struggle against over-whelming opposing forces, with the intention of saving the nation from further and graver misfortunes, has requested General Eisenhower, Commander-in-Chief of the Anglo-American Allied Forces, for an armistice. The request has been granted. Consequently any act of hostility against the Anglo-American Forces must cease on the part of the Italian Forces everywhere. They will, however, resist any attacks that may be made upon them from any other quarter.'

Immediately afterwards we hear the same news from the B.B.C., followed by Admiral Cunningham's proclamation to the Italian Navy, telling them to sail their ships at once into Allied ports.

Outside the peasants are rejoicing, the bonfires continue, we hear sounds of laughter and merry-making. The household look at us with excited faces, in which delight is marred by a dawning uneasiness. 'What do you think will happen next? What about the Germans?' What, indeed, about the Germans? Presumably they will at once occupy the chief Italian towns. Presumably, too, they will continue fighting at Naples, and later on form another line of defence along the Apennines. But what is to be the Italian part in all this?

We spend the evening in grim silence. The German radio tells us nothing. Antonio can only think of the betrayal, the dishonour. Moreover, it is incomprehensible to us both why the Government—having clearly intended to take this step from the first—should have waited to do so until now, and like this. By declaring on July 25th that 'Italy will be true to her word. The war goes on', Badoglio deliberately and gratuitously took upon the shoulders of the new Government the heritage of the Fascist policy, which it could have disavowed; and by failing to close the Brenner immediately, he allowed the entry into the country of the large numbers of German reinforcements with which we — and the Allies — will now have to deal.[1]

September 9th

Wake in the morning to fresh news: the Allies have landed south of Naples. While we are still breakfasting, the A.s arrive. They have heard that the greatest part of their beautiful villa at Frascati (together with most of the little town) has been destroyed, and they are now on their way to Rome. During the morning the telephone (which strangely enough has not been cut) rings unceasingly, each time bringing further bad news. Rome, we hear, is already cut off, and a bombardment is audible along the coast (presumably preceding a landing). There is also firing between Rome and Frascati, where the German General Staff is quartered. There are four Italian divisions round the capital (these eventually prove to be six), but will they succeed in holding it? The A.s, who are determined to get home, are told that it is not possible; the Roman railway-line is cut at Monte

[1] Between July 25th and August 6th — when General Ambrosio complained to Von Keitel of the number of German troops entering the country — six German divisions crossed the Brenner. 'You told me at Feltre', said Ambrosio, 'that you could not spare me a single division — and yet now ...'

Rotondo and the roads are blocked by the Germans, who are requisitioning all cars. I try to telephone to E., near Bologna (who was to have left for Rome to-night), but am told that the telephone lines with Emilia have been cut since early this morning; and at lunch time we hear that Bologna, Padova and Verona are already occupied by the Germans. There is a rumour of another Allied landing near Rome, but this is contradicted in the evening. The Roman radio continues to repeat Badoglio's proclamation, but gives no other news; any other information reaches us by telephone, or from the B.B.C. and the Swiss radio. In the evening we hear (by telephone) that the King and Badoglio have already left Rome, but hesitate to believe it.

I walk up to the castle and tell the British p.o.w.s about the armistice, and of their consequent liberation. Orders have come from the main p.o.w. camp at Laterina to 'protect' them from any German attempt to seize them; the protectors, in our case, being the seven small soldiers of the escort with their seven rifles, and the completely useless lieutenant, all of whom are on the point of leaving. Antonio explains the situation to the prisoners, pointing out that, although they are now free, they would be unwise to set off along the roads, where they would run straight into the Germans. As soon as the Allies land farther north, he says, we will at once let the men know, and they can then make their way across country to join their own forces.[1] The men agree that it is best to wait, and I promise them a map, so that they can become familiar with the lie of the land. Meanwhile we close the main door of the castle and show them a tower staircase at the back, by which they can escape in the night if the sentry gives the alarm. 'We aren't going to Germany if we can help it!' they say. 'But if only you'd arm us, sir!' — 'What with?' Antonio replies. As we are leaving, four of them return from the *fattoria*, carrying a demijohn of wine. 'Hullo, Ginger! Just in time to celebrate!' And we leave them to it.

[1] This proved to have been bad advice, alas! — since the difficulty of avoiding the Germans became increasingly great later on.

I look in at the *Casa dei bambini* where the children greet me shouting 'Peace has come!' I try to explain to them, without being alarming, that they can't go home at once, and may not receive any letters for some time.

In the evening we hear of more fighting round Rome, but no details. Badoglio issues a second, explanatory proclamation.

September 10th

Hear by telephone that Chiusi is now occupied by German troops, who are in control of the railway and are requisitioning cars on the roads. The telephone with Rome and with the north is cut. No post; no buses to Chiusi; no papers. Our only source of news is now the radio. The distant rumble which we heard during the night turns out (according to the B.B.C.) to have been the bombing of Grosseto by the Allies. We wonder whether it heralds an Allied landing. Meanwhile, in preparation for the passage of troops, we spend the morning in preparing a hidden store of wheat, potatoes, cheese, wine, etc., which we wall up or bury in various hiding-places. We also bury a store of petrol and take the wheels off the cars.

Later in the morning we walk up to the Castelluccio. The prisoners are spending the day in a creek nearby to escape the attention of any German troops that may be passing by, and we arrange with the lieutenant that they had better be moved to-morrow, in small parties, to scattered farms off the road. I give Corporal Trott a map of the district and also some Italian phrases for the men to learn by heart before they start off across country. 'Where are the Germans? I am a freed British prisoner. I do not want to meet the Germans. Where are the British? How many kilometres?' and so on.

On our way back we meet one of our peasants, in uniform, on his way back to his regiment from leave. 'What am I to do now?' he asks. He has just met some other soldiers in plain clothes, who have escaped from Bologna and Verona and who have told him that all officers and men who can do so are running away, while the rest are being put by the Germans into concentration camps and taken to the north. Later in the day yet other fugitive soldiers turn up.

At one o'clock we learn that Badoglio 'is absent from the capital on a tour of inspection' and that Caviglia has temporarily taken his place. This is the last Italian broadcast from Rome. At tea-time the B.B.C. tells us that they are fighting around the city but we still do not know who is winning. In the evening the German bulletin informs us that the Italians have capitulated. German troops will occupy a thirty miles' radius round the capital, and 'will defend the City of the Vatican'. Some of the Italian troops in southern France have crossed into Switzerland, where they will presumably be interned, after which German troops have closed the frontier between France and Switzerland. Part of the other troops in Southern France are fighting against the Germans; others have already capitulated. German troops under General Rommel have seized all the important towns of Emilia, the Veneto and Lombardy — and are now marching upon Milan.

Walked up to the castle with Benedetta to say good-bye to the prisoners. They practise their Italian sentences (which, as taught by a Sicilian soldier to a Yorkshireman, acquire a very peculiar flavour) and examine the places on the map where I tell them there are German troops, and those where there might perhaps be an Allied landing. 'We've got a fifty-fifty chance of escape, don't you think?' says one of the men. Then, lifting Benedetta on the table, they all sing to us: 'Roll out the barrel', 'Tipperary', 'Land of hope and glory' — and finally, when Benedetta has blown them a good-bye kiss, 'Auld lang syne'. As we come out of the castle we see, slowly winding up the valley road, a lorry full of Germans. Are they coming to fetch the prisoners? For a few minutes we all stand waiting, rather breathless — then the lorry takes the other turn, towards Chianciano. Less than an hour later, the captain of the Carabinieri at

Montepulciano telephones to Antonio. Is it true, he asks, that we have got twenty German 'Tigre' tanks stationed here? Rumours move fast: in an hour, a single lorry has turned into twenty tanks!

September 11th

The morning news confirmed that Rome is now held by the Germans and that they have control of the telephone and the radio — but we hear that an agreement has been signed between General Kesselring and Count Calvi di Bergolo (the King's son-in-law), who is now in command of the city, by which the German troops are to remain outside the capital. The same bulletin informs us that the King and Badoglio have now joined the Allies, thus leaving the country without any government. In the morning I drive down to Chianciano with the children and hear fresh rumours of an Allied landing near Ostia — which, however, proved to be unfounded.

September 12th

A bad day. We wake to Marshal Kesselring's proclamation, by which all the territory occupied by the Germans (which, except for a few pockets of resistance, is now the whole of Italy north of Rome) is placed under German martial law. Strikes or any other attempts at resistance will be tried by court-martial. Trains, telephones, and posts will be under German control; no private letters are allowed, and all telephone conversations will be severely controlled.

At eight-fifteen the B.B.C. gives some of the terms of the armistice. The territory of Italy and Corsica are to be occupied by the Allies as bases. Airports and ports are to be defended by Italian troops, if necessary, until the arrival of the Allies. Italian troops in the Balkans and in France are to be recalled. Italian planes and ships are to proceed to Allied ports, and the Merchant

Marine is to be put at the disposal of the Allies. British prisoners are to be freed and, if necessary, defended by Italian troops against any German attempt to recapture them. The Italian Government is to use its troops, if necessary, to enforce these measures.

Under present circumstances, these terms have an ironic ring — all of them (except that regarding the Navy, which has been scrupulously observed) being nullified by the debacle of the Italian Army. At Rome six divisions, fully armed and on their own ground, have been unable even to hold the capital against the Germans. In France, Italian troops have fled across the frontier, and those which have remained have now capitulated. In the cities of northern Italy there seems to have been some sporadic fighting, but here, too, considerable numbers of officers, as well as of men, have simply torn off their uniforms and fled. The first train to Rome yesterday passed through Chiusi packed with men even upon the roof, and to-day our woods are full of many others who have escaped on foot.

At Montepulciano this morning the disarming of the 'Ravenna' Division by the Germans took place: the men's guns and tunics were removed, and those who wished to were allowed to take their mules away with them. At S. Quirico the garrison appears to have made an attempt at resistance, and we hear sporadic firing all through the morning. The whole thing is a grim comment on the illusions of those members of the Opposition who proclaimed (and sincerely believed) that 'against the Germans the Army will fight again, as it fought upon the Piave'. But how can one expect an army to fight, when its leaders have fled? The King and Badoglio are safe in Sicily: and to Italians of a different stamp, nothing is left but bitter humiliation and shame.[1]

[1] At the time of writing these comments, many facts were unknown to me — as to most other bewildered people in this country. We did not know, for instance, of the long-drawn-out negotiations which preceded the signing of the armistice — of General Castellano's two journeys to Lisbon in August, followed by that of General Zanussi (accompanied, as a pledge of good faith, by General Carton de Wiart) and of his subsequent two journeys to Sicily — journeys executed in the greatest secrecy, under the constant menace of discovery by German spies. We did not know of the Allied refusal

Bewildered and confused, we sit listening to the radio – from which at one o'clock Radio Roma, for the first time, gives the news in German, and an hour later the B.B.C. relays the bells of St. Paul's ringing out in honour of the 'victory' over Italy.

Meanwhile we have our local problems to solve, that of the British prisoners. With the arrival of German troops in Montepulciano their danger has become considerable. The lieutenant and the soldiers of the guard are already in plain clothes, preparing to go home, and the prisoners themselves are scattered in various farmhouses. But there can be no question of concealing them for long. Too many people know of their presence here, including the shopkeepers of Montepulciano, where we drew their rations. While we are discussing what to do, one of our men comes running up the road with a false alarm: the Germans are already on the place! They've got as far as one of our farms, Pian Porcino: there's been some shooting! (All this turns out later to have been purely imaginary.) Antonio hurries down to the farms where the Englishmen are living, and offers them a choice: those who

---

(whether owing to fear of the information leaking out or to a more fundamental distrust) to inform the Italians of either the precise date or place of their intended landing – nor of the Italian Government's assumption (on insufficient grounds) that the landing – and simultaneous announcement of the armistice – would not be until September 15th, so that Eisenhower's announcement on the 8th came to them as a thunderbolt. We did not know that – owing to erroneous information from Italian G.H.Q. – the organized plan of a descent of Allied paratroops in the neighbourhood of Rome, to protect the city, was given up at the last moment. Nor did we know to what an extent the Germans – naturally suspicious of betrayal from the first day of the coup d'état – were continually pressing the Italians as to their intentions – ('Can you give me your word of honour,' said Ribbentrop to Guariglia already on August 6th, 'that you are not negotiating for an armistice?') – so that all orders had to be given, all preparations executed, with a degree of secrecy which completely paralysed them. (This was carried so far that Badoglio preferred to risk losing all the Italian troops in the Balkans – half a million men – rather than to send instructions which might leak out.)

Nevertheless, when all this has been said, a deplorable impression remains – of panic among those who left (so suddenly, that secret compromising papers were forgotten), of utter confusion among those who remained behind. Thus the divisions round Rome, at the critical moment, were found to be short of both petrol and ammunition – and many O.C.s in other parts of the country, in France, Albania, the Aegean, etc., never received any orders at all – other than those implied in Badoglio's declaration – and were left (often in the midst of overwhelming German forces, whom they had considered their allies until the preceding hour) to deal with the situation as best they might. There were single, sporadic episodes of firmness and valour – but the whole story remains one of tragic mismanagement and irresponsibility.

wish to take their chance of getting away must leave at once; the others he will try to keep on as farm labourers, pointing out to the Germans that we are short-handed. And if the Germans threaten to take them off to Germany, we will try to warn them in time. The sergeant says that he will tell the men, and those who wish to go will be gone to-morrow. I spend the morning in the front garden with the children, expecting to see the Germans arrive at any moment, and thinking of ingenious ways of detaining them — but no one comes, and directly after lunch Antonio goes down the valley again, to take the men some maps, a compass and some money. Two of them, he finds, have already started: six more have decided to start at dusk. We have told them plainly that their chances of getting through are poor — but, says the sergeant, there is no holding them.

Before going to bed, a final piece of news brings a climax to the day: German paratroops have succeeded in freeing Mussolini.

September 13th
　　More fugitive soldiers pass by, all through the day, and many of the men from our own farms have now come home. One who has returned from the South of France (acquiring an Army mule on his way) tells us of some severe local fighting there; another, from Genoa, says that a portion of the garrison in the harbour attempted to resist and two hundred men were killed, but that the barracks were promptly surrounded by the Germans, and the men there disarmed, marched to the station, and sent home. In the course of the morning, we hear a few gun-shots across the valley, but never discover their origin. Antonio goes down to see off the prisoners, and discovers that thirty-two of them have now set off, so that only eighteen are left — the least adventurous, but possibly the wisest. In the evening the captain of the Carabinieri calls Antonio up to inquire about the prisoners, and Antonio explains the situation, pointing out that he needs

their labour. 'Go on feeding them, and keep quiet about it,' is the captain's advice.

The German radio (which now alone gives the Italian news) does a good deal of crowing over Mussolini's release, but gives no details. It also describes large crowds gathering in Piazza Venezia and calling for the Duce — a statement which it is difficult to believe. The B.B.C. tells us of severe fighting, without much progress, on the Salerno beaches; the Eighth Army has occupied Cotrone — a long way away.

So now, once again, we are under German rule; once again we must begin to wait. Looking back on the last few days, I realize that we have all been stunned by the suddenness and swiftness of the news, and also stimulated by the numerous small local jobs to be attended to. It is only now that the full grimness of Italy's situation is sinking in.

September 14th

The German-controlled Radio Roma gives an account of the diplomatic conversations which took place immediately before the armistice. According to this account, Guariglia, Badoglio and the King himself (on September 1st, 4th, and 8th respectively) gave clear and personal assurances to the German envoys that Italy's new Government would not break faith with her ally but would go on fighting.

Drive with Antonio, Schwester, and the baby to Montepulciano — with the grey mare, since we are warned that the Germans are still requisitioning all cars. The only German, however, whom we encounter is a lorry-driver fast asleep in the shade under his car. The roads are empty and the aspect of the countryside unbelievably peaceful. The B.s — although, as Liberals, they have desired the armistice — join with us in deploring the methods by which it has been accomplished, and especially the King's and Badoglio's flight.

Antonio goes down to Chianciano for news (we are still without letters, papers or telephone) and finds four German hospitals in the Chianciano hotels. The wounded are beginning to arrive. At the post-office we receive a bunch of delayed letters, a week old, but are told that none will now be accepted or delivered.

Meanwhile, although we are cut off from all our friends, life at La Foce is not lacking in variety. In the course of the afternoon, Antonio was first called upon for help by a German lorry-driver, who had got stuck at the bottom of our hill. (Once a Communist, he told us, he changed his views at Stalingrad.) Next we walked down the hill to give the day's news to the British prisoners — many of whom, according to the sergeant, are now very jumpy and undecided. Half an hour later we were talking to another Allied p.o.w. — a French-Canadian who, with a friend, had found shelter this morning in one of our farms. He had escaped, with two hundred others, from a train in Florence that was taking prisoners up to Germany. He told us, too, that the Allied p.o.w.s at Laterina have broken down the barbed wire round the camp and escaped — three of them being shot in the process: so some of them, no doubt, will soon turn up here too. Finally, walking home, we stopped at a farm where a soldier had just returned from Jugoslavia. At the Jugoslav stations, he told us, German troops were waiting with machine-guns, but the engine-drivers slowed down the trains before each town, thus enabling the Italian soldiers to jump out, make a wide circuit round the towns on foot, and then jump again on to the next train that passed. At the next farm, one son had just returned from France; another from Russia.

Germany, England, Canada, Jugoslavia, France, Russia — the farms of the Val d'Orcia are now linked with them all. Perhaps it is a forecast of the future.

We wake to bad news. The tightening-up process has begun. This morning Radio Roma announces the names of the new 'technicians' appointed by the Germans as *commissari*, in place of the Badoglio Cabinet. All Italian officers and soldiers are to report at once to the nearest German Command — and corps of volunteers, organized by the Germans, are to continue the war against the Allies. The rest, we presume, will be sent to Russia or to labour camps. There will be many tears all over the country at this order, shed by all those whose sons and husbands have only just got home. Finally, all freed British prisoners of war are ordered to give themselves up immediately to the nearest German Command, where they will be treated according to the Convention of Geneva. Anyone sheltering them or feeding them is required to notify the nearest German Command of their whereabouts within twenty-four hours. Those failing to obey these instructions, or continuing to give shelter or food to p.o.w.s after that date, will be dealt with by German martial law.

Our thoughts go at once, not only to the Englishmen on this estate, but to all the other p.o.w.s who are roaming about the countryside. Antonio goes off to Montepulciano to speak to the captain of the Carabiniere and returns with the news that the British prisoners' presence at La Foce has already been notified by him to the German O.C. of Chiusi, who merely replied: 'All right; I'll see to it.' This leaves us much where we were before. We discuss what advice to give to the men and come to the conclusion that their chances of being left in peace by the Germans are now exceedingly slight: those who wish to, had better make a bolt for it, while they still can. On the other hand, their chances of getting through to Naples are presumably even more slender than before. Antonio is about to hurry down to them, when the butler, Angelo, puts his moonstruck face in at the door. saying: 'Please, sir, the Germans have come!' But it is a false alarm: they have merely come to requisition our motor-bicycle, and after an hour they leave, taking it with them.

An absurd incident brings a comic relief to their visit. While Antonio is firmly declaring, 'No, we have no spare tyres — all of them have been requisitioned — no, no tyres whatever are concealed upon the place', Angelo, with a beaming smile, inexplicably appears in the *fattoria* yard, wearing a tyre upon each shoulder. Antonio, dreading serious trouble and a search of the whole farm, turns his back on him — but still Angelo stands in the yard, wearing his tyres like a garland. Finally the German can stand it no longer. 'For God's sake tell that silly ass to go away!' he says. 'I haven't seen anything, but tell him to go away.'

As soon as the Germans have left, Antonio hurries down to warn the prisoners — but scarcely has he gone than there is a knock at the door. 'The Germans are back again.' I go downstairs, thinking: 'Now we're in for it,' and the officers' first words, 'About those prisoners', are hardly reassuring. But in a moment I realize that they are not talking about *our* men, but about two others — 'Americans', they say, in plain clothes, whom they believe to be in the district. No, I say, we have not seen them, and my husband is out — and the Germans go away again.

Late in the afternoon I go into the wood behind the house, wondering whether the two American prisoners are in hiding there. And indeed, before I have gone two hundred yards, I meet one of them: a queer, unprepossessing little man in ragged clothes, certainly not an American, and who can speak no European language but a few words of French, in which he goes on repeating, 'Tunis, Tunis'. There is something distinctly fishy about him — and though I point out the road to Monte Cetona, offer him some food (which he refuses) and say, 'Germans are after you: get out as quick as you can', Antonio meets him an hour or so later in the opposite direction. An odd detail is that he and his companion have a piece of paper on which is scrawled, 'Ask for La Foce'.

To-day the news from Salerno is better. *Purchè facciano presto!*[1] says everyone, especially those whose sons and husbands have just come home. Very few, if any, of these Italian soldiers will obey the order to report to the Germans. They propose instead to hide in the woods and (since the actual numbers of the Germans here are very small, and the Carabinieri will certainly not be over-zealous in carrying out their orders) I think they will probably get away with it. Of our British prisoners, several who had left have now come back, having discovered the ubiquitousness of the Germans and the scarcity of water. It is now settled that they are to stay on for the present, as if belonging to a regular working-camp. But when they are at work in the fields, they will always have their kit with them and keep one man on the look-out, so as to be able to bolt in time if the Germans approach. There is a cave at the top of the hill where they can camp out, and we will meet them at the edge of the woods, after dark, with food.

While Antonio is arranging this with the prisoners, the same Germans as yesterday came back again, this time to fetch a battery and an air-filter. They behave like old acquaintances. 'Very jumpy your household seem to be, when they see us!' says the sergeant who pretended not to observe our tyres yesterday, a stout butcher from Berlin — and before they leave they produce photographs and anecdotes of their children. Both refuse to talk war or politics: 'No, we're not political blokes,' they say — and they leave with a promise to bring us a sack of boots (stolen from the Italian military stores in Siena) for our workmen. It is all very odd — and very unlike any preconceived notions of war.

Antonio is sent for by the German lieutenant who has been left in command at Chiusi. When Antonio mentions his address, 'Ah, you're the man who has got the British prisoners!'

---

[1] 'If only they hurry up!'

says the lieutenant. 'I can't spare any men now to take charge of them, but I could perhaps send up a Carabinieri.' — 'Sorry, I can't spare any men either,' says the captain of the Carabinieri. 'Well, then' — says the German to Antonio — 'I'll give *you* a couple of rifles, and you can see to the guard'. Antonio begins to laugh. 'No, I really can't do that.' — 'Well, then — you really think these men won't make any trouble now?' — 'Certainly not.' — 'You'd better be responsible for them. And we'll leave it at that.' Surely a very odd conversation.

In the afternoon we walk down to the prisoners' farm and tell them of this arrangement, but warn them to continue to keep a sharp look-out, in case the situation should suddenly change. We also tell them the war news, which to-day is better, advance parties of the Eighth Army having joined up with the Fifth near Eboli.

In the evening we turn on the radio and suddenly hear Mussolini's voice — 'once', as he remarks, 'well known to you'. After relating the dramatic circumstances of his capture and of his release he proceeds to a violent attack upon the King — and ends with an appeal to Italians to unite once again under his leadership to form the new Republican Fascist Party. But nothing will come of all this. Too profound a disillusion, too violent a revulsion, is associated for all Italians with Mussolini's name — and now no emotion is left but a weary passivity. That spring is broken.

September 19*th*

Talk to one of our contadini, Fosco Nisi, who has been a prisoner in Russia. He has a remarkable story to tell. Left behind (in February of this year) by the Italian troops in retreat, he and one companion — both with frostbitten feet — slowly made their way across the snowbound Ukrainian plain. Every night they slept in a Russian peasant-house and everywhere were fed, lodged and treated with the utmost kindness. The houses, he said, were poor, but clean and well kept: 'They are as civilized as we are!' At last their feet got so bad that they could drag themselves no farther, and the peasants took them to a small civilian hospital in a village about a hundred and twenty-five miles from Kiev, where they developed typhus and were cared for by the local doctor with the utmost kindness, and with exactly the same food and treatment as he gave to his own patients. Soon after their arrival, Russian troops occupied the village, but, on discovering the two Italianski, merely ordered that they should continue to remain in the hospital, under the doctor's care. Later on, when they were convalescent, the Russians retreated, and the village fell into German hands, but they treated the two Italians less well than the Russians had done, and left them behind in the hospital.

Finally the two men set off on foot to cover the hundred and twenty-five miles to Kiev, were transferred from there to a German military hospital at Warsaw, and only after many months and much red tape, at last rejoined their regiment at Naples — two days before the armistice! Then came the night of the last great air-raid on Naples (worse, he says, than anything he met with in Russia) and finally the last and most bitter of his experiences. On the day after the armistice, the barracks were surrounded by German troops and tanks. The colonel — a professional soldier — reviewed his men on the barrack square. They stood — anxious, bewildered, waiting for orders — and he bade them look at the German tanks around them. 'On my own personal responsibility,' he said, 'and to avoid useless bloodshed, I order you to lay down your arms.' As Fosco told me this, tears of humiliation sprang to his eyes. 'Three years a soldier,' he said, with a helpless gesture, 'and then that.' Now, like the rest of the men who have come home, he will spend his days hiding in the woods, rather than obey the German command to join the colours again.

Indeed, our woods seem likely to be thickly populated this autumn, sheltering not only Italian soldiers, but an ever-increasing number of Allied escaped prisoners (there were fifteen thousand in the camp of Laterina alone) who are waiting for an Allied landing in Tuscany.[1] Every day now some of them appear at the *fattoria* or at the various farms, travelling mostly in small parties of two or three — to ask their way south, get some food and then go on. Most of the farmers, though aware of the risk to themselves, are eager to shelter and help them. They are a very mixed lot: not only British, Americans, Canadians, and South Africans, but also Tunisians with more than a touch of Arab, who can only speak a few words of French, South Americans who can only speak Spanish, and Boers who can speak no European language at all. Many of them have succeeded in getting hold of civilian clothes, although we have warned them that this renders them liable to be shot as spies. This evening, as we were walking down a lane, we suddenly met one of them — a tall, fair young man, who looked at us with some anxiety, clearly wondering whether he had better turn tail and bolt. 'Good evening,' we said — and he almost fell over with surprise. He was a South African who had escaped on the day of the armistice from Laterina, and had been wandering about ever since. 'It's very lonely,' he said naively, 'with no one to speak to.' This is already his second escape, since he had already tried to get away from a camp near Foggia and had been recaptured — and he was very nervous, obviously wondering, as we walked along, how far he could trust us. Then, as we reached one of the farms where our p.o.w.s are living, and Sergeant Knight came running downstairs to thank us for the tomatoes and the *Illustrated London News*, the South African's face cleared and, coming upstairs, he found a room full of Englishmen, a map, news, and some food. Never have I seen a man more astonished and more relieved. He told the other men later that I am the first Englishwoman he has ever spoken to — and he did not expect to find her in the Val d'Orcia.

[1] These expectations were not entirely unfounded — since General Castellano's first suggestion to the Allies was that the Allied landing should be near Grosseto.

September 21st

Better news to-day. The Fifth Army now holds the road on the Sorrentine peninsula, the Eighth Army has reached the plain of Foggia. The Germans have evacuated Sardinia and are now fighting against Italian and French troops in Corsica.

An unpleasant bit of local news is that a reward of L.1800 has been offered by the Germans for the capture of any British prisoners of war, or information as to their whereabouts. In the province of Livorno (i.e. along the coast, where a large number of prisoners must have made their way in hope of a landing, and where there is already a food shortage) the reward is higher: L.5000 and an increase in rations. The radio also repeats the penalty for sheltering p.o.w.s — trial by court-martial.

Walk down to the Englishmen and tell them to warn any compatriots of this reward, and of the danger incurred by the farmers who shelter them. We also warn them that at the road-men's cottage in the valley there is a family of ardent Fascists who are reported to be on excellent terms with passing German troops, and who might make trouble.[1] 'It's the sort of thing one reads about in books,' says one of the prisoners with gusto, 'us hiding here and all that.' We all enjoy this idea very much. But privately I hope that the more dramatic episodes of that sort of book (arrival of brutal German troops, hair-breadth escapes by British prisoners, court-martial of those responsible for sheltering them, etc.) may not come our way.

September 22nd

Two other German officers appear during Antonio's absence in Siena, and ask for the keys of the garage: they require, they somewhat unnecessarily explain, a car. I show them ours, but say that it has no tyres — hoping, as I speak, that Angelo will not again stage one of their reappearances. They will see to the

---

[1] They do, later on, and hand over to the Germans a prisoner whom they succeed in capturing in his sleep, in one of our farms.

tyres, they reply, and will come back to-morrow to fetch the car. I ask for a receipt, remarking with sickly humour that I will frame it with the receipt for the motor-bicycle that has already been taken away from us — whereupon they suddenly click their heels, formally introduce themselves, apologize, and remark: *C'est la guerre.* Yes, indeed, say I.

September 24th

Yesterday we were told the names of the Ministers of the new German-appointed Fascist government, of whom the only familiar names are General Graziani at the Ministry of War and Buffarini-Guidi (one of the most odious figures of the regime) as Minister of Interior — all the others being obscure 'squadristi'. Mussolini is the self-appointed Foreign Minister.

The nominal existence of this government, to which no one pays any attention, does not prevent the German Command from issuing its own orders — which to-day include fresh instructions for the mobilization of Italian recruits for labour camps in Germany, and a description of the penalties inflicted on some young men in northern Italy for sabotage: trial by court-martial and reprisals against their families.

Two of our farmers, whose sons were with their regiment in Pistoia, have now received notes hastily thrown out on to the railway line, saying: 'We're being taken off, we don't know where.'

September 25th

A Viennese officer from Chiusi (who has come to take away our car) tells us that General Rommel is now coming south, to take command of the German Army at Naples. A second line of resistance is being prepared by the Germans south of Littoria. Part of the British Fleet has been seen off Livorno, about thirty miles out to sea. (Alas, only by the eye of the imagination.)

Every day it becomes more obvious that the next stage of the war, in which every region of Italy in turn will become a battle-field, is going to take a very long time.

September 26th

To-day, for the first time, Florence has been bombed — also Pisa, Livorno, Verona and Bologna. In Florence the intention was clearly only to hit the military factories and the marshalling yards, but although the factories at Rifredi were hit, the station at the Campo di Marte was missed completely, while bombs fell on the adjoining streets and squares. There has been much loss of life, as the alarm did not sound until after the first bomb had fallen, and the children's hospital is among the buildings hit.

V. arrives to beg us to give shelter to his son, who has left his regiment and is in hiding in Rome. Some of his companions are trying to get through to join the Allied forces with papers provided by the Vatican, bearing a forged stamp of the German Command. V.'s account of Rome is grim. Conte Calvi has been arrested and sent to a concentration camp and the 'Piave' Division which he commands has been disbanded. The S.S. rule over the city. Seven German soldiers have been killed by the population and now six thousand hostages have been demanded by the Germans. Sealed trucks leave daily for Germany by rail, carrying Italian soldiers to labour camps. There are frequent rumours, as yet without foundation, of Allied landings. The universal cry is: 'May they come soon!' But now the weather has broken and the autumn winds may make landings difficult — and, moreover, the Germans have now had time to bring down reinforcements.

New orders issued by General Kesselring award the death penalty for the possession of firearms, for sabotage, or for sheltering or in any way assisting members of enemy forces. The Fascist Government also issues a proclamation awarding the death penalty to those who give help to prisoners of war.

V. and his fugitive son arrive, with long, cadaverous and unshaven faces. At Chiusi they have met a train from the south packed with terrified boys of sixteen and seventeen, whom the Germans have taken from their homes at Castellamare and are taking up to labour camps in Germany.

Last night the Viennese lieutenant returned, bringing with him his 'Herr Major'. The latter — a quiet, elderly landowner from Brandenburg — says that it is absolutely necessary for Antonio to report the presence of our p.o.w.s to the German O.C. at Siena. He himself, he says, will go with Antonio, 'to avoid unpleasantness'. So now no choice is left us. The major says firmly that he does not for a moment believe that the O.C. will allow us to keep the prisoners here without a guard. They will either take them away to Germany at once, or else send some men to guard them here — with a view to removing them as soon as the Allies get nearer. 'After all,' he says, 'you're living in an invaded country. You can hardly expect us to leave enemy troops at freedom in it.'

When at last he has gone to bed, we sit up discussing what to do next. Somehow we *must* save them, but how?

Early in the morning (with the Germans still in the house) we hurry out to meet Sergeant Knight in the wood and explain the situation to him. We tell him that there is just a chance that Antonio may be able to persuade the Germans to leave the p.o.w.s here, but that it is a very slight one. He had better tell the men how matters stand, so that they may always keep a sharp look-out (lulled by a false sense of security, they had got slack) and always take their kit down to the fields with them, so as to be able to get away at short notice. Sergeant Knight hesitates, then shakes his head. If he tells the men ahead, he says, some of them will bolt at once, to-day — and we shall undoubtedly be held responsible. He will keep the news to himself, at any rate, until Antonio gets back from Siena to-night, and then we can decide together what is to be done. Antonio accordingly goes off to Siena in the

German car — and returns with bad news: the O.C. has received orders to recapture all Allied prisoners in the district and take them up to Germany — and he will send a lorry to fetch the men to-morrow morning.

After dark, in pouring rain, we again meet the sergeant and tell him of the orders. But still he firmly refuses, for our sake, to warn his men until the last moment — for fear that they should bolt to-night — 'forgetting', he says, 'all the gratitude that we owe you'. We then make plans for to-morrow. We have already sent down extra rations and, rain or shine, the sergeant must see to it that *all* the men, taking their kit with them, go down to work in the morning — to a field half a mile away from the road and sheltered from it by a hillock, on which the sergeant will be on the look-out. As soon as he sees the German lorry he will signal to the men and they will then have about a quarter of an hour in which to scatter and escape towards the hills. The lie of the land is almost ideal — hillocks and scrub, in which the men can conceal themselves — and unless the Germans are very many or very nippy, it seems unlikely that they will ever get near enough to shoot. When everything is settled, I give the sergeant some small parting gifts — a pocket-torch, our last slab of chocolate, and a map, on which I have marked a suggested route southwards through the mountains, avoiding the coast, which is now full of Germans. We shake hands, ask him to write to us when he gets home — we neither of us say 'if' — and as he disappears into the wood I have a lump in my throat. 'That's a good chap,' says Antonio. 'Good luck to him — to them all.'

September 29th

It's all over — and all has gone well. The Germans were due at ten, and as the time drew nearer, I sat with Antonio on the terrace, waiting to see their lorry appear on the valley road. They were late — a not very pleasant hour of suspense. If some of the men do not get away, I thought, we shall feel that we have betrayed them: if they do, will Antonio not pay the penalty? At last the Germans arrived — in a large lorry, escorted by a motor-bicycle. The men were armed with tommy-guns, but there were only five of them, with an Italian maresciallo. Antonio went out to meet them and warned them that the prisoners always kept a sharp look-out, but they were very confident. And the lorry, with Domenico to show them the way, set off down the hill. Antonio, the *fattore* and I hurried off to a view-point above the pine wood, and anxiously watched the scene. Sergeant Knight had been as good as his word: the men were all at work, and he was on the look-out. We saw the lorry draw up at the bridge, and then, a minute later, the first little group of men (dark shadows on the pale clay hillocks) running for cover. Then a pause — and then the Germans arrived, in single file — to find only some spades and hoes in an empty field: for Tette, the Italian foreman, had had the fright of his life and had run away too. (As he described it later: '*Camò disse il sergente . . . e non c'era più nessuno!*'[1] The Germans hunted about half-heartedly, went to one or two of the farms — and then, not without some slight dismay, we saw the lorry turn back towards La Foce. But as the Germans came into the house, I saw that they were grinning, '*Das war Pech!*' they said. 'If we had known the lie of the land we'd have brought more troops — or saved our petrol.' And in due course they went back to Siena.[2]

Only after their departure did we discover that four of the prisoners, who had omitted to take their kit down to the field, actually went back to their farm to fetch it, and started packing in a leisurely manner. Meanwhile the Germans went to the door of that very house and (while the Englishmen were still lingering upstairs) asked the old farmer's wife in the yard whether she had seen any *Americani*. '*Americani?* No, certainly not!' she replied, in so convincingly blank a tone, that the Germans, without bothering to search the house, went away again. When Antonio

[1] ' "Come on", said the sergeant—and then no one was left!'
[2] We learned, however, later, that this was the first incident that caused us to be regarded with suspicion.

asked her about it afterwards, he saw that she did not even realize that her lie had been dangerous. 'They might have put me in prison? Nonsense — what would they do with an old woman like me? Anyway, they asked for *Americani*, and we've only got *Inglesi* here!'

So all the prisoners have got away. In every farm there is a deep regret at their going. Everywhere they have become a part of the family. They played with the children, helped the housewife with the chores, shared their rations — and *bon citti* (good boys) is the general affectionate verdict. On their side, too, there was an equal liking. Perhaps when they get home, to Yorkshire farms and Midland towns, they at least will speak well of the Italians.[1]

September 30th

Better news at last. Yesterday the Fifth Army broke through the German lines on the Salerno mountains and entered the plain of Naples; to-day they are within ten miles of the city. The good news came, alas, just too late to hearten the prisoners before they left.

C.A., arriving from Rome, confirms V.'s grim account of the city. Complete paralysis and confusion reign. In each ministry there are two heads: a *commissario* appointed by the Germans and a minister appointed by the new Fascist Government — not to mention the recent Ministers of the Badoglio Government who are either in hiding or in prison. But in reality the country is ruled only by German martial law. The Germans, paying no attention whatever to the Fascist Government, issue their own orders — and everyone trembles before them. There has been a certain amount of looting — mostly of empty houses, or of those belonging to prominent ex-officials — and official 'requisitions' of all cars, motor-bicycles, etc. Every Jew, rich or poor, has been required to pay a tribute of fifty golden lire — under threat of

[1] I have received letters from some of them and I learned that eighteen of them got home safely. But nothing, alas, from Sergeant Knight.

imprisonment for two hundred of the Jewish community. The Italian police are completely ineffective. A few nights ago a party of armed Fascists broke into one of the Carabiniere barracks, where a Fascist from Milan was imprisoned, demanded his instant liberation, and took him away with them. The only police force that still has some authority is that of the *Africa Italiana*. The streets are empty. The categories of people who have good reason to be afraid include all ex-officials (Fascist or anti-Fascist), all officers (who have been ordered to report to the German Command), all private soldiers of the classes 1910-25 (who may be sent off to labour-camps), and to these must be added all those merely stricken by blind panic. Thus C.A., who has a large dairy farm at Ostia, says that they are obliged to throw away a large quantity of milk every day, because the Roman lorry-drivers refuse to come and fetch it, while at the same time babies in the town are starving. Of the boys of the Naval Academy in Venice, which had moved to Brioni, half were able to make their way to join the British Fleet, but the other half were caught and are now prisoners in Germany.

Travel by train has now become practically impossible. V. took thirty-eight hours to get from Chiusi to Ferrara— twelve hours of the time being spent waiting in Chiusi, where the only train was packed to overflowing with terrified women and children escaping from Naples to the north — they themselves did not know where. At Livorno the German O.C. has taken fifty hostages, in reprisal for attacks upon German soldiers, and has issued a proclamation announcing that if there is any further trouble, five of them will immediately be shot and the whole population of the suburbs of Livorno will be evacuated without notice.

October 1st

Naples is taken at last and the road is open to Rome. It seems probable, however, that the Germans will fight rearguard actions all the way, and it is said that they have prepared a second line of resistance at Terracina, and another at Nettuno. God knows how long it will be before the Allies get here.

Yet another Italian government, meanwhile, has been constituted by the Allies – consisting of the King, Badoglio, Roatta, Admiral De Curten and Acquarone. An official comment of the B.B.C. speaks of this government as 'provisional' and as merely having been set up 'to co-ordinate the Italian Forces to fight against the common enemy'.

Graziani, after a meeting of all the Italian officers of the district in the Theatre Adriano in Rome, has succeeded in enrolling four thousand officers in the service of the Fascist Republic. (Subsequently we hear that these enlistments were obtained under threat of deportation to Germany.) So now we have the prospect of civil war.

October 2nd

C.A., who has come here to fetch his baby, hesitates whether or not to take her back with him to Rome, where it is expected that the Germans, before leaving, will destroy both the aqueducts and the electric power stations. On the other hand, he is afraid of being separated from the child, without news, during the German retreat, if he leaves her here – and in the end they all set off.

We spend the morning in looking for our old oil-lamps, in case all electricity is cut off later on, and Antonio decides to go to Florence to fetch my furs, which are stored there – as in Rome the furriers have been looted and in Florence both Settepassi and Parenti have suffered the confiscation of all their jewellery and silver.

M.R. arrives, by a cross-country train, from her place in the Val di Chiana. Being near the camp at Laterina, they see a constant stream of prisoners passing by. The farmers give them help and shelter, but one of the neighbouring landowners, a violent

Fascist, has performed one of the meanest acts that I have yet heard of. He engaged six men to look for fugitive prisoners in the woods, with orders to offer them food and help, and persuade them to come to the *fattoria* — where they were promptly handed over to the Germans. Let me add that this is the *only* case of this kind that I have heard of. Everywhere else the farmers here have been eager to help the prisoners — even at considerable risk to themselves.

October 3rd

Benevento is occupied by the Allies — but their progress is slow. Apparently the Germans intend to use delaying tactics all the way up Italy, until they reach their main defence line on the Po. The B.B.C. exhorts its listeners in England to be patient — but this is less easy for those living here, who are still enduring Allied bombings, as well as increasingly severe German and Fascist repressive measures. To-day the Podestà of Chianciano came up to see Antonio and told him that the Germans, with the assistance of the 'Fascistoni', are now threatening to arrest one member of each family that has a soldier in hiding, and keep them as hostages until the soldier gives himself up. The only hope is that — in this district at least — they will not have enough men to carry out this threat.

October 4th

The Allies land at Termoli. They are now in control of the whole Gargano peninsula, but their progress on the western coast is still very slow.

More details of the destruction committed by the Germans before leaving Naples — gas and electricity plants destroyed, water cut off, motor-buses and trams carried away. No doubt the same will happen in Rome later on. No single drop of oil is available for lamps. We succeed triumphantly in buying some acetylene lamps in Montepulciano — but have not as yet achieved any acetylene cylinders. Spend the day in packing linen, blankets, silver, etc., to be concealed in an attic which we will wall up in preparation for the German retreat.

October 7th
Allied progress imperceptible. Bologna severely bombed again.

Antonio returns from Florence triumphantly bringing with him some acetylene cylinders. The town is occupied by the Germans, whose behaviour has on the whole been 'correct', but who are so much hated that all the misdeeds that they have not as yet committed are attributed to them, as well as those which they have. A certain number of houses and villas, including Villa Palmieri and Villa Papiniano, both belonging to English people, have been requisitioned by the German Command, who are also settled in the Excelsior and the other principal hotels. The shops have been emptied, but the soldiers pay (at an exchange rate of ten lire for one mark) for what they have taken. More serious is the requisitioning from all the chief factories — the Galileo, Pignone, etc. — of metals, machinery and precision instruments, and the directors have been warned that, before the arrival of the Allies, all machines will either be destroyed or taken to Germany. A similar warning has been given to the owners of the principal industries in Milan and Turin.

Much as the Germans are disliked and dreaded, however, these sentiments are as nothing compared with those awakened by the members of the new Fascist Party — and with reason. Here is a true story. A few days ago, at the bar of the Excelsior, the radio played *Giovinezza*. One of the men present (a business man called Piaggio) remained seated. 'Get up,' ordered one of the Fascists. The other shrugged contemptuously. Whereupon the Fascist drew a revolver and shot him. Most of the other people in the room ran away, but some Germans picked up the wounded man and took him to the hospital, where he lay for some days at the point of death, having been hit in the kidneys. No one attempted to arrest the Fascist, who is still at large.

October 8th

Antonio makes a second trip to Florence, to fetch some more acetylene, and brings back surprising news: Contessa A.G., one of the Queen's ladies-in-waiting, and several other people with Court connections, have suddenly been arrested by the Fascists. Contessa G., most correct of old ladies, and over sixty-five, together with the others, has been taken to the women's prison at S. Verdiana. No charge is specified.

October 9th

The telephone rings, to say that Bruno S., the son of our keeper, who was a carabiniere in Rome (a boy of nineteen, to whom we are all much attached) is now on his way to . . . somewhere in Germany. He passed through Chiusi station early this morning, a prisoner, in a train full of other carabinieri in the same plight, and succeeded in giving this message for his family to a porter on the platform. Poor child – his state of mind can easily be imagined – and now, that of his family. We send for his father and give him the news, and there is little that we can add in the way of comfort. There appears to be no way of finding out what will happen to these 'interned soldiers', as the Germans call them – and it is still uncertain whether they will be allowed to write home. Later in the day we hear that *all* the carabinieri have been taken prisoner in their own barracks, which were surrounded in the early morning, while they were still in bed, and that the capital is now policed only by the Germans and by the Fascist militia.

The Mayor of Chianciano, who has come up to tea, tells us that so far there is only one single member of the Fascist Party in Chianciano – the local Segretario del Fascio, a hotel-keeper called N. On September 1st he appeared in the Mayor's office and declared: 'Here, in your presence, I solemnly reconstitute the Fascio of Chianciano!' but since that day no other member has joined him, and he says quite openly that, when the Germans leave, he will have to go with them. He cannot, however, be dismissed as harmless, since he acts as a spy for the Germans and has already enabled them to make several arrests.

October 10th

To-day N. has performed a further good office for the Germans who are looking for billets, by bringing them here. They found the Castelluccio suitable for their purpose, and inform us that they will arrive here on the day after to-morrow with fifty lorries, about a hundred and fifty men and an officer. They will be quartered at the Castle, but have taken our garage as a work-shop and repair-shop.

We spend the afternoon in hurriedly packing up all that we wish to store away, and in preparing to move some of our refugee children into the villa, so that none of its rooms may be empty. We also warn V., whose son is in hiding here, and the B.s, who are planning to send us theirs, that this is no longer a safe hiding-place.

The broadcasts of the Fascist Republican Party (from Munich) now begin, after the strains of *Giovinezza*, with the following remarkable statement: 'I believe in God, Lord of Heaven and earth. I believe in justice and truth. I believe in the resurrection of Fascist Italy. I believe in Mussolini and the final Italian victory.'

October 11th

Our 'thirty-two boxes, carefully packed, with the name printed clearly on each,' are now ready, stored, and walled up. As the last brick was set in position, we began to remember the things we had omitted to put away, as well as to regret those which we have packed, but will probably need. It is, however, quite impossible to attach importance to any material possessions now. All that one still clings to is a few vital affections.

Lately a few letters have begun to trickle through again, bringing news of friends in other parts of Italy. From near Bologna E. writes of the occupation of their village, Pianoro, by German troops. Her father, old General D. (now aged ninety) remembers the day, in 1859, when as a child of five, he saw the Germans turned out of Bologna. 'Remember this always, my child,' said his father then, 'the Germans are gone for good.' And now they are back again.

From Florence N. writes that they have decided to stay on there with the children, bombs or no bombs. P. is convinced that the safest place is the very heart of the town – 'so we may move to my in-law's house, in the shade of Arnolfo's tower. I have no real grounds for taking any one decision rather than another, but perhaps by staying put in one's own centre one can be of some use ... When we go out we always expect (and frequently have) air-raid warnings, but one ends by leading much the same life as usual. For food we are still managing, but the expense is frightful. One feels escaping from one's control everything on which one was accustomed to rely, and everything is so suspended that one is very conscious of one's own littleness'.

October 12th

Here the German troops have come – and gone. Yesterday morning we saw the first motor-bicycle drive up, and a sergeant dismounted and said that he had been sent to meet the column, which had left Nemi at ten a.m. the day before. Then, as Antonio began to talk about arrangements, he grinned: 'Yes, I know – but I've got fresh orders in my pocket. About turn!' And indeed, as soon as the first lorries arrived, a few hours later, they were sent back to Nemi again. It seems an unnecessary expenditure of petrol, tyres and energy. We feel great relief, but do not expect to remain undisturbed for long.

October 13th

Drive to Montepulciano, and find the whole little town much agitated. Late yesterday evening a lorry full of Germans arrived there, arrested all the men in the club and all those that they encountered in the street (including my hairdresser, who was going home from his work) and kept them in the police-station all night. This morning they released those that they did not want and took three away with them; four others are still under arrest at Montepulciano. It appears that all those arrested belong to a list of anti-Fascists, furnished by local Fascist spies. Entering the little town, one has a strong impression of bewildered anxiety and fear. Half the population is shut indoors, while the rest stand about in little groups, whispering fresh tales (mostly totally unfounded) of German cruelties or Fascist regulations. Everyone has something to fear, or thinks he has — which, after all, comes to the same thing. In the B.s' drawing-room, where we sit huddled round the radio, each member of the party has some private source of anxiety. M.B. herself is tormented by anxiety for her two grown-up sons (officers in the Army and Navy) whom she hourly expects to be arrested and implores not to leave the house — for her younger boy of nineteen, who might be taken away for *Arbeitsdienst* — for her brother, a leading anti-Fascist in the Veneto, whose house near Padua has been requisitioned — and for her husband, who, as Podestà of this town, is likely soon to get into trouble. Signora T., her guest, is equally anxious about her anti-Fascist husband, who, when she last heard of him, was in hiding in Rome, staying in a different house every night — while her eldest son is in the same position as the B. boys. The grown-up sons are fuming to leave at once and take their chances of getting through the German lines, to join the Allies: the younger

95

ones are fretting at the restriction of their life indoors. A neigh-bour comes in: her husband, the captain of the Carabinieri, is in an even less enviable position, since the Carabinieri in the pro-vince are daily expected to share the fate of their comrades in Rome, and in many small towns have already run away. Here, however, the captain is still sticking to his post. As each new person comes in, the others ask eagerly: 'Have you any news?' One caller has heard that at Foligno bands of escaped British prisoners, with Italian soldiers and officers, are conducting a regular guerrilla against the Germans. (Two British prisoners who came through La Foce yesterday, too, told me that they had been accosted by an Italian officer who invited them to join a similar band.) Another repeats an anecdote which has been told her by her maid, who has just returned from Arezzo. Some Ger-man soldiers went into a bar and asked for a drink. 'Wish it may poison you!' muttered the barmaid, as she handed it to them. 'No, no!' replied the soldiers good-humouredly in excellent Italian. 'Don't give the poison to me; keep it for your chief and mine!' — So we sit and whisper, and presently a British broadcast in Italian announces sensational news: Badoglio's proclamation that Italy has declared war against Germany.

October 15th

It is now five weeks since the armistice. Italy has nominally four governments (the Germans in the north, the Allies in the south, the Fascist, set up by the Germans, and the Badoglio Government, supported by the Allies) and two armies: that of Graziani and that of Badoglio. In actual fact the only effective governments are two: that of the Allies in the south and that of the Germans here — wherever there are enough troops to enforce it. Elsewhere each little town or community rules itself — fairly successfully, since there is (at least in this district) a temporary truce to party politics and a general feeling of unity in con-fronting the general misfortune. The great majority of the Army is in hiding; the police are under arrest, or are expecting to be arrested. Mussolini and Badoglio alike are merely distant voices off stage.

What are the Italians feeling about it all? Those whom I have seen fall into four categories. First there are those who (even if not pro-Fascist or pro-German originally) are profoundly shocked and humiliated by what they consider to be the King's and Badoglio's betrayal, and by the manner of its execution. They feel that neither the Fascist misrule nor the Germans' behaviour can justify this betrayal nor retrieve the national honour – and some of them have disregarded the orders of their superior officers and have joined the German forces.

More numerous, however, are those who feel like the writer of the following letter: 'What I feel is this: ours has been (without wasting time over various excuses which won't affect the judgment of the world at large) an unforgivable betrayal. On the other hand they (the Germans) with their unlimited meannesses, dirty tricks and double-crossing, have forfeited any right or chance of getting allies. So I won't fight on their side – nor, since we *have* been guilty of betrayal, against them, although I think them disgusting.' Practically all the other officers in the writer's regiment (one of the best in the country) share these sentiments.

At the other end of the scale are the anti-Fascists who (even if uncomfortable about the King's and Badoglio's personal conduct) desired and approve the armistice, welcome the declaration of war – and await the arrival of the Allies as friends, liberators and benefactors. Some of these have already attempted to join the Allied forces: others are organizing (together with some of the fugitive British prisoners) guerrilla bands and local sabotage in the parts of the country still occupied by the Germans. In this part of Italy, so far as I can discover, the numbers of these partisans is as yet comparatively small: in Piemonte, I am told, they are numerous and armed, and are in hiding in the mountains until the time comes, with the approach of the Allies, to launch an attack.

Finally there is the great mass of the Italian people, who hold none of these extreme opinions — but *'tira a campare'*.[1] Profoundly disillusioned, cynical, tired, fully conscious that more suffering and privations still lie ahead, they are a defeated nation — and the only universal incentive still left is that of self-preservation. Those who have some sons of military age are engaged in hiding them: those who took part in any of the activities of the Badoglio Government are in hiding themselves; those who have any valuable possessions are concealing them too. Everyone, on a larger or smaller scale, is struggling to obtain the minimum of necessities to support life this winter: food, fuel, light, clothes, boots, medicines. Since it is evident that the Germans are taking away many of these objects, the hatred of them is increasing, and the arrival of the Allies is awaited with impatience and high hopes — hopes so high that it is difficult to believe that disappointment will not ensue. Everyone, however (whatever their political attitude) realizes clearly that every additional week of German occupation increases the country's impoverishment and prolongs the period of suspended action. Whatever prospects the Allies may have in store for us it will be better than the present state of affairs — since then it will be possible to begin again. So we sit and listen to the B.B.C., which reports five miles' progress, eight miles' progress ('a tedious business' says the announcer, and we agree) and go on waiting.

October 16th

Antonio goes down to Chianciano and returns with the news that at Magione a German captain, as he was driving through a wood, was shot at and killed: he was buried yesterday at Chianciano.

In the evening a Moroccan soldier turns up here, an escaped prisoner from Laterina. He can speak only a few words of English and Italian and is very completely lost — travelling north, although he says he wants to get to Rome. We give him food and shelter

[1] 'Just rubs along.'

for the night and point out the road to the south. 'Me ship,' he says. 'Me not swim.' Very slight are his chances of getting home again.

An ominous short paragraph in the *Corriere della Sera* refers to the treatment given to the Italian soldiers who are imprisoned in Germany. They are not considered prisoners of war, but *internati* (i.e. directly under the control of Himmler), but the Fascist Government will 'attempt to obtain a mitigation of fate of those who are willing to fight on the side of the German Army'. Poor Bruno!

October 17th

An eventful morning. As we are walking back from church, we hear four or five shots nearby, in the direction of the *Dopolavoro*, and a minute later are told that a German lorry has just gone by. Antonio walks down the road in the direction of the shots, while I send the goggling children indoors and the nurse gets the bed in the clinic ready. After a few minutes Antonio returns saying, 'It's nothing' — but adds to me in English, 'It's some Allied p.o.w.s firing, presumably at some Germans, as there's a German lorry on the road. When I reached the turn an Allied soldier shouted to me: "Get out! Germans here: we'll shoot!" ' Half an hour later Antonio walks down the road again, and this time finds two very shaken Germans standing by their lorry, which is lying in the ditch. What has happened is this: the Germans (a sergeant and a driver) were coming slowly down the road, when they met four American soldiers. They stopped the car and the Americans fired six or seven shots (those we had heard), shooting the windscreen to pieces, hitting the radiator, and only narrowly missing the two Germans, whom they then forced to get out of the car and stand in the ditch with their hands up while they searched and disarmed them. This was going on at the very moment that Antonio appeared at the turn of the road, but the lorry was between him and the Germans, so that he did not see them, though they saw him — and thought, they afterwards said, that he was the leader of the partisans. The Americans then emptied the petrol tank, pushed the lorry into the ditch, removed the crank — and disappeared into the woods.

While this was going on and Antonio had gone down the road a second time, V. (who with his son was hurrying up to hide in a remote farm) told me that the Moroccan prisoner who arrived last night was still hiding in the wood-shed, so I hurried there to warn him to get away before the Germans came back to search the place. No one was in the shed. I called in English and French, 'Come out.' No answer. But I had the feeling that someone *was* there, in the pig-sty beyond the shed. I went into the yard, in front of the sties, and called again. Then, very cautiously, a black head appeared behind the gate-bars of one of the sties. 'Jerries, tedeschi,' I said. 'Bang! Run!' The ragged figure stood up. 'Tedeschi? Me English!' — 'Yes, I know. Go! Allez!' — 'Me English. Sank you!' And he was off into the woods.

Five minutes later the German sergeant came up to the farm and telephoned to the O.C. at the Chianciano hospital. He was a red-haired, simple young man, much shaken, with the loquacity that sometimes follows a narrow escape. 'Whew!' he said — sinking into a chair and mopping his face, 'that was a narrow shave! I've been through France and Russia, but this — whew!' An hour or so later three German officers came up from Chianciano, asked some questions, and looked at the scene, where there was nothing to be seen but some broken glass. One of them, however, did not seem entirely satisfied. 'Somebody must have lent a hand,' muttered one of the soldiers to another, and the officer pointedly asked Antonio about our prisoners, and whether they really had left: *ganz bestimmt?* But in the end they went away again.[1]

In the evening we heard that all four Americans had been seen at the top of the property, heading south.

[1] This episode became the second black mark against us.

October 19th

We hear from the Carabinieri at Pienza that the Americans of Sunday's incident are not escaped prisoners, but parachutists. This morning a German plane flew low over the district, on the look-out — but nothing more has occurred. We also learn that on Saturday night the Americans slept in one of our farms — and offered to arm the farmer with a tommy-gun if he would join them.

Yesterday evening a strange young man, driving a buggy, drove up to our door. He introduced himself as an officer of Genova Cavalleria, who had driven himself successfully through the German lines, all the way from Piemonte to Tuscany. When his regiment was disbanded on September 12th, near the French frontier, he decided to try at least to save some of his horses and set off with five men and seven horses, travelling across country and hiding whenever they met the Germans. But as they got towards Piacenza the Germans became too numerous and he reluctantly sold all the horses except his own, which he harnessed to a small buggy — and so, dressed as a *fattore*, drove quietly across Italy. Two days more and he will be at his home, Spoleto.

He told us that, of the four thousand officers in Rome who, according to the Fascist radio, had 'spontaneously adhered to the cause of the Axis', and who had started off in German trains for the north, only eight hundred got as far as Florence: all the others had succeeded in escaping on the way!

October 20th

The battle of Volturno is over, but the Allies' progress is still very slow; and as the Germans slowly retreat, they have ample leisure to leave utter destruction behind them. If the 'liberation' of Italy goes on at this rate, there will be little enough left to free: district by district, the Germans are leaving a waste land. Gone are our hopes of a decisive action before Christmas! A grim, long winter lies before us, at the end of which none of us can tell whether our homes will still be standing, or our children safe; and we must meet it with what we can muster of patience, courage and hope.

October 21st

Yesterday Arezzo was bombed, to-day Orvieto. We heard the noise of Arezzo's bombing as we stood watching the sowing and the oxen slowly plodding across the fields. And this morning, as we were playing in the garden with the children, thirty shining Liberators, on their way to Orvieto, passed over-head — the first that I have actually seen.

Hear of the arrest in Florence of M.C.C. and her family — for having sheltered a British prisoner for several days in her house in town (she had been unwise enough to speak of it freely, saying how nice he was). There is now a regular chain of people in Florence who give help to Allied prisoners, many of whom are hidden in the woods and the surrounding hills. Courageous friends walk up into the hills and meet them, provide them with money, clothes and blankets, and guide those who need it towards the south — while the farmers provide them with food and shelter.

News of Bruno has arrived on a Red Cross postcard from Udine — where nurses meet the trains taking prisoners up to Germany and write down the addresses of as many as possible, so as to be able to send back news to their families. At some stations, where the nurses have received permission to take baskets of grapes to the prisoners, they have concealed small saws in the bottoms of the baskets — thus enabling the men to saw through the bars of the train's windows, and escape.

October 28th

A boy of fifteen from the Montepulciano G.I.L.E. (a school for Italian children evacuated in 1940 by the Fascists from Tunis, Cairo, Malta, etc.) turns up. He says that he has run away from his school for fear of being taken by the Germans for *Arbeits-dienst*, and states that a lorry has already arrived at their school to fetch some of the boys. 'Those who have relatives in Italy to plead for them,' he says, 'may be let off – but I've got no one. My father and mother are in Alexandria.' He has been walking about for six days, and now asks whether we will take him in at one of our farms. I telephone to the Mayor of Montepulciano, and find out that no boys have been taken away from the school, only some young men of military age who previously belonged there and had recently returned, after running away from their regiments. We persuade the boy to go back, and Antonio gives him a letter for the head of the school, asking for him not to be punished – but two hours later he is found in another of our farms, in precisely the opposite direction. Germans or no Germans, he is not going back to school! So we settle him at one of our farms.

Occasional p.o.w.s pass through, asking the way south. All know the name of this place, and we get the impression that someone farther north is passing them on to us. Not far from here, in the wild wooded country beyond Castiglioncello, there is said to be a large band of p.o.w.s, as well as Italian soldiers and officers, who are in hiding there. God knows how they will get through the long, cold winter!

October 31st

Grosseto and Genoa bombed yesterday, and Genoa and Perugia to-day. From here we see the lights in the sky and hear the bombs from Grosseto and Perugia.

The new Fascist Republican Government has announced the formation of 'special tribunals' for the trial of ex-Fascists who have 'betrayed their faith' and for other Italians who 'in speech or action have attacked the Fascist regime' – an indictment sufficiently wide to embrace all those against whom any Fascist may have a personal grievance. For those who were once members of the Fascist Party, the only penalty is death; for the others, from five to thirty years of imprisonment.

November 3rd

To Montepulciano for the day. Hear from a friend of B.'s who has just arrived from Rome (on a German lorry — there is now no other way) that whole Jewish families have been deported from Rome by the Germans. The old Ghetto was surrounded by troops, and men, women and children driven out of the houses, packed into closed lorries and driven off — no one knows where. At Arezzo this week, when the young recruits of the 1925 class failed to report, the police arrested instead their wives or mothers, who were kept at the police station until the men turned up.

B. also tells of terrible poverty among the numerous refugees from Grosseto and Livorno in Montepulciano. Their subsidy is eight lire a day for an adult and three for a child: a starvation allowance. And even this has now been taken away from all the men of the 1920-25 classes, so as to force them, by starvation, to rejoin the Army. B. is attempting to organize a communal kitchen, so that they may have at least one nourishing daily meal, but the supplies from Siena are delayed.

Our nurse, visiting a patient at a farm, finds a carabiniere in hiding. According to his account about a thousand men are now concealed in the Spineta woods — Italian officers, Allied prisoners of war, parachutists and Italian soldiers — and are being fed and supplied with ammunition (difficult as this is to believe) by Allied planes.[1] This man returns to his farm occasionally at night and goes back the following night, taking such provisions with him as his family can supply. I arrange that if, later on, medicines, blankets or other comforts should be needed for any of his

[1] This was, at that time, pure invention. Indeed, to my knowledge, none of the partisans in our district ever received food supplies by parachute, though, in the last weeks of the German occupation, some arms and dynamite were thus supplied to them.

companions, he will come by night to our clinic and collect what is required.

November 4th

Spend the day in the beech wood, picnicking with the children. As we are lunching on the fringe of the woods a shining white plane appears from the clouds and dips very suddenly, just above our heads, then circles over the Spineta district. Is it, we wonder, one of the planes bringing supplies to the hidden 'bands'? At the Pietraporciana farm, according to the farmer, small parties of prisoners are constantly turning up, and are fed and lodged at the farm for the night — then sent on south. I cannot, however, be certain whether or no my informant knows about the Spineta band — part of which is said to be hiding here in the woods above Castiglioncello — and naturally refrain from pressing the point. He shows me a note left behind three days ago by a British major, addressed to 'the O.C. Allied Army of Occupation, Sarteano District' (a foreshadowing of the future which gives me quite a turn) acknowledging the kindness and hospitality received at the farm and asking that compensation should be given to its inhabitants. For several hours I walk in the wood hoping to find some trace of the Spineta band, but in vain.

A letter from friends in Florence tells of an 'epidemic' of arrests, and advises me to go on nursing my baby, as a form of self-protection from being arrested! Another friend, living near Grottaferrata, fifteen miles from Rome, writes of 'this nerve-wracking waiting, waiting ... Every day I do some planting and sowing (from force of habit) while asking myself "What for? Perhaps you will not see any of it, and you and your plants will be destroyed!"' Her daughter, whose husband is in the Foreign Office, is in daily fear of her husband's arrest; her four sons, of military age, are all in hiding in various parts of the country. 'In Rome,' she writes, 'one can't find any workmen, as none of them will go out for fear of the man-hunts. Even here the peasants won't go outside their own gates.'

November 5th

A friend returning from Florence brings accounts of fresh arrests in the provinces of Florence and Pisa: mostly innocuous old Senators, whose only crime is that they are known to be loyal Monarchists. It is said that the cause of the arrests is the severe treatment of Fascist officials by the Allies in southern Italy — these Monarchists being taken as hostages to protect the arrested Fascists. But if so, it is difficult to understand why most of the people arrested have been let out, after only a week or ten days in prison. In Rome there have been similar arrests among Ciano's entourage. In Florence the Prefect is a fanatic, and has issued most inconvenient orders. One of the most unpopular is that ordering all employers to give a gift of a thousand lire to each of their employees, to celebrate the *28 ottobre*! This at a moment when all work is at a standstill, and when it is impossible to get hold of any ready money. The banks only allow their clients to draw five per cent a month of their deposit and will cash no cheques.

November 7th

An unidentified plane has dropped some bombs on the Vatican, injuring several buildings, though fortunately not St. Peter's. The German radio, of course, claims that it is an Allied plane; the B.B.C. denies it.

November 8th

The first snowfall. Bitter cold. How will the prisoners and other fugitives in the woods survive the long winter? The boy from the G.I.L.E., who is now settled at one of our farms, comes up to ask for clothes — having nothing on but a linen jacket and a thin vest. There is also a constant stream of fugitive soldiers and evacuated women and children, all begging for clothes. We are giving what we can of our own, and are making jerseys and baby-jackets with every scrap of wool, using the fringes off old counter-panes; slippers with old strips of carpets and curtains; and babies' nappies with old sheets — but soon it will all be exhausted.

November 10th

Bombing of Turin and Genoa has begun again — as well as of the railway farther south. Daily the B.B.C. tells of 'four miles' progress; two miles' progress' — it seems infinitesimal. The B.B.C. reports, too, with satisfaction, the results of the Moscow Conference; but here it seems very remote indeed. As the circle in which our life moves grows smaller and smaller, and the immediate menace more threatening, our mental horizon shrinks to that of the peasants; and with this narrowness creeps in something of their scepticism towards all vague schemes for the future, all remote Utopias. We speculate, instead, at most, on the news from the surrounding provinces — for each province, now, has (in practice, if not in theory) its own laws, depending on the temper and attitude of the local Fascist Prefect, or of the German O.C. And soon even this local news will not reach us, for everywhere the screw is being tightened.

November 11th

By order of the Fascist Government, all men who were still in the Army on September 8th (and who are now in hiding throughout the country) are to report before November 25th, to receive temporary leave. This means, presumably, that the authorities have at last realized that there is no possibility of getting these men to fight again, and that the whole work of the country is being held up while they are still in hiding. But many will be very wary of reporting themselves — fearing a trap. And the order does not, of course, apply to the younger classes (1923, '24 and '25) which are about to be called up — to form, we are told, the nucleus of the new Republican Army — and whose members are at least as reluctant to join the colours as their elders.

November 12th

Antonio returns from two days in Rome, having gone there by car with the Mayor of Chianciano and a German permit. The only disadvantage of this form of travel is that, since the only cars on the road are presumably German, they are occasionally machine-gunned by Allied planes, but the journey passed without any incident. As they got nearer to Rome (supposedly an 'open' city) the numbers of Germans increased, and when they reached the town, they found it full of troops, with German sentries even at the doors of the Excelsior. Two floors of the hotel are taken by the Germans, the rest are empty, since the advent of Germans in a house in Rome to-day has the same effect as that of a negro family in a New York apartment house: the other tenants move out. Moreover many families, who have reasons for wanting to keep out of the limelight, have moved away from their own houses to those of friends, so that completely empty houses are to be found beside others absurdly overcrowded. The whole process, indeed, of covering one's tracks has now been brought to a fine art, and many people are now still living, although hidden, in the heart of Rome, while special offices furnish them with false identity cards and ration cards. Some of those who have most cause for fear — Jews, officers, or members of the recent Government — are known as the *sepolti vivi* (buried alive — from the name of the perpetually-cloistered nuns) and live in walled-in rooms, their food being handed down to them by their families through a trapdoor in the roof. Others are hidden in convents, in the catacombs, in attics, even in the domes of churches; they meet, in secret, in churches, cellars and caves and there mature the plans of the ever-increasing 'Resistance' movement. Other members of the same movement — many of them women — circulate freely in the city, changing their sleeping-place as often as possible. It is they who carry messages from one group of the movement to another — who find hiding-places for Allied p.o.w.s — who furnish arms to the patriots and information to the Allies. Some day the full story of their adventures will be told.[1]

Recent arrests have been directed not so much against anti-Fascists as against members of the Ciano group and Monarchists. They include, beside numerous ex-Fascists, ladies of the Court, and smart women of Ciano's set. Of the seven thousand Jews of the city, about one thousand have been taken off by the Germans — all the rest are in hiding. A friend in the Red Cross writes to me (in a letter sent by hand) 'The Ghetto is deserted. It was surrounded by troops armed with machine-guns, and all those who were still there were dragged away — men, women and children. In one house a woman and a child of eight had hidden in the attic, leaving a baby of one month in the room below, for fear that its cries would give them away. When they returned, the baby was gone. In short, all that we had heard about the treatment of the Jews in Poland, we have now seen here.'

Many members of the Foreign Office have disappeared — including our friend M.R. and her husband, who, with another couple, have set off on foot for Naples. It seems, however, very doubtful whether they will get through, as we hear that south of Frosinone the German patrols have orders to shoot at any civilians going southwards. The complete German control of the country is all the more remarkable in view of Kesselring's admission to a German woman married to an Italian, that, on the day of the armistice, he was taken completely unawares, and found himself isolated at Frascati, cut off from all other German troops, and with *no* orders from Germany or from his Embassy. At that moment, he said, nothing would have been easier than to have turned the Germans out of Italy. Within a few hours, however, it became clear that the Italian troops had

[1] Many of these, at a later stage, were caught and imprisoned. Some of the bravest — including several women — were shot immediately. Others were tortured in the prisons of Via Tasso and finally executed in the massacre of the Fosse Ardeatine.

received no orders: in spite of sporadic fighting -- notably by the Piave Division and the Granatieri — the Germans became the masters of the situation. Confronted with the threat of the bombing of the undefended population, Count Calvi di Bergolo (the King's son-in-law who had taken charge) accepted the German conditions — and so they once again entered Rome, as masters. They then, having possessed themselves of the Italian ciphers, issued orders of surrender all over the country — and thus became once again the rulers of Italy.

Yesterday Antonio talked with Marshal Caviglia who had come to Rome for two days. Antonio asked him what, in his opinion, an Italian could do at this moment for his country. 'What life are you leading?' asked the Marshal. 'A peasant's,' replied Antonio. 'So am I — there's nothing we can do but wait.'

November 24th

Return from a week in Florence, having gone there by car. The roads empty and peaceful. Occasional filled-in holes by the roadside show where mines have already been laid by the Germans. The larger bridges of Florence (though not the Ponte Vecchio) have also been mined — as well as the electric plants, gasworks and telephone. The town itself seems, at first glance — except for the German troops — almost normal. It is only after a day or two, when one has begun to talk to people, that one realizes the extent of the underlying apprehension. The new Italian S.S. — formed on the German model, but apparently chiefly consisting of irresponsible boys of seventeen and eighteen (some, according to rumour, taken from the boys' reformatory, the *Minorenni Corrigendi*) has already got to work; at night, after the curfew, its members amuse themselves by a lavish use of their revolvers and hand-grenades. Moreover they have proceded to numerous arrests — some on the charge of having given assistance to British prisoners, but some merely on vague unspecified charges — so that no anti-Fascist can feel safe. The arrests generally take place in the early morning, when the victims are in bed, and their families are left in complete ignorance of where they have been taken. The questioning is often brutal and prolonged. Sometimes, if the right strings have been pulled by their friends, the arrested are let out after a few days — sometimes they disappear completely. The complete capriciousness in the choice of victims (since many well-known anti-Fascists are still at liberty, while some obscure citizens, innocent of every political activity, are under arrest) produces a peculiar uneasiness — and there are few houses where a ring at the bell, after dark, does not cause alarm.

During my visit several acquaintances, who belonged to an association for helping British prisoners (guiding them in the hills from one band to another, and furnishing them with clothes and arms), were suddenly arrested — betrayed by a spy to whom they had idiotically entrusted the driving of an ambulance in which some of the prisoners had been hidden. Consequently all the members of the organization whom this spy happened to encounter are now under arrest — and the others are afraid that their names may be given away too. Among those arrested are several whose share in the work was very slight and whose motives were unpolitical — kindly, naive people, with English connections or friends, who wanted to 'help the boys' — and scarcely even realized the danger they were running. One elderly man, whose only share was to allow some of the clothes to be deposited in his house, has suffered a most brutal examination — after a night in the punishment cell — which is so narrow and low that one can neither stand up nor sit in it, but merely squat. His wife came to us, begging for candles, since all his life the poor man has been afraid of the dark. One little boy of twelve, who had helped his mother in guiding the prisoners in the hills, on going one day to his aunt's house, opened the door to find an S.S. man standing there, who pointed his revolver at him, and took him in charge. Eventually he was allowed to go home, where he reported all that had occurred, and his aunt's arrest, with complete self control and clarity — only that night, as he was going to bed, his mother noticed that his pants were moist. He blushed. 'When that man pointed his revolver at me, I couldn't help it!'

While the S.S. are thus engaged, the Germans are continuing the rounding-up of all the Jews. All who can have escaped to the country, or are hiding in friends' houses — but many have been discovered. Even those who were lying in bed in hospital, and some old men and women of over seventy, were hunted down, while the houses of those who had previously been left alone have been burned or looted.

And now a new cloud hangs over the city: to-morrow is the last day on which the young recruits of the 1924 and 1925 classes must report themselves to the Fascist Republican Army. Many, of all social classes, will not go — but now the threat is that their family will be arrested in their stead. Some are in hiding in the country, some have got faked doctor's certificates — some are already on their way to join the Allies. But what will happen to their relatives, no one yet knows. O. (a colonel in the Air Force, who has joined the Germans) said that some 'examples' are to be made, as a warning to the rest — and told me the following story. An officer in the Navy, who had been compelled to sign the declaration by which all officers who happened to be in Rome after September 8th undertook to remain at the disposal of the Fascist Government, had failed to report and was in hiding in his own house. The Germans, knowing that he was there, went to fetch him. His wife opened the door — no, she said, her husband was away; she did not know where he was. As she was talking to them her little boy came into the room. 'Very well. Your husband won't report himself. We'll take the boy instead.' The father, who was hiding in the next room, heard them, came out and gave himself up — and was shot. With stories such as these in their minds, the new recruits are awaiting their turn.

I asked O. about the fate of the Italian prisoners in Germany. 'Those belonging to the Air Force are all right,' he said triumphantly. 'We've succeeded in getting them all back here.' 'You mean,' I said, 'all those who have agreed to join the new Fascist Army?' — 'Well, naturally' — 'And the others?' He shrugged. 'I don't know.'

Beside such human tragedies as these, it is impossible to attach much importance to the fact that our house, the Villa Medici, together with most of the other villas on the Fiesole hill, has been requisitioned by the German Staff. I try, however, to pull various strings to save it, on the grounds of its historic interest and beauty — but fail completely, only succeeding in obtaining permission to remove the most valuable furniture. When I arrive to sort the furniture the first lorry-full of German soldiers has already arrived, and are installing a telephone in the old chapel. They are perfectly civil and ask for one piece of furniture only: the piano. 'One of our officers,' they say, '*ist ein berühmter Komponist*. He has composed an opera about Napoleon!' I agree — and receive permission in return to shut up the drawing-room, with its eighteenth-century Chinese wallpaper. They also let me take away the linen, glass and china — all of which, in many similar cases, have been requisitioned. As I go from one familiar room to another — all now full of German soldiers — I have a strong presentiment that this is the end of something: of this house, of a whole way of living. It will never be the same again.

During my week in Florence we had five or six alarms — but no one pays much attention to them, except as an inconvenient interruption to whatever one happens to be doing. So profound is the Florentine conviction that the Allies mean no harm that when at Pontassieve several ill-aimed bombs missed the station entirely and fell in the midst of the little town, the population merely remarked that they must have been German planes![1]

The bulk of hatred, however, which is gradually accumulating against the Fascists is formidable — and may find expression in a terrible manner, when the time comes. Already in the Romagna

[1] A little later this little town was almost entirely destroyed by Allied bombs. When I went to visit it, on a Red Cross inspection tour in the spring of 1945, it was still in ruins and over nine hundred families were homeless, scattered in the surrounding farms.

and Emilia — where, at all times, political feeling runs high and violence comes easily — there have been episodes of revenge. At Ferrara the head of the Fascists has been assassinated; at Mercatale, a small village in the Romagna, a Fascist factor was shot by a group of partisans who came to fetch him in his house, stole his horse and some wheat, and left his corpse in a farmhouse with a bullet through his head. Throughout the Romagna and Emilia, arms are hidden in cellars and farms — some of them brought back by officers from Jugoslavia and smuggled down the Po in barges by night. Jews or anti-Fascists who have as yet escaped arrest have bought German uniforms (from Austrian deserters) and propose to make use of them when the retreat takes place for their own private revenge.

Most of the Republican Fascists (at least in this part of the world) are fully aware of the hatred they have aroused, and openly declare their intention, when the Germans retreat north-wards, of going with them.

E., coming from Bologna, says that a large part of the town is now deserted — and that the part of the population which is still there is so much alarmed that the only streets in which anyone is to be seen are those which possess air-raid shelters. Alarms every day, and frequent small incursions. German troops every-where. In their own village, Pianoro, a German chaplain — in uniform — says Mass alternatively with the parish priest — who does not hesitate to express his opinions (in Latin) to his colleague. Pointing at the swastika on the Chaplain's uniform, *Crux diabolo*, he said. The Chaplain, glancing at the giggling choir-boys, answered non-committally, *Crux Hitleri*. Then, as the choir-boys went out, he added in a lower voice, *Mala bestia*.

From this village long columns of lorries start up the Futa Pass. 'All day the columns go past,' writes E., 'rumbling and puffing up the hill — a sound which I shall always associate with this long season of anguish. Even when it stops it still goes on in my ears, and sometimes at night I wake up because I've heard it again in my sleep. Poor unhappy humanity, travelling and struggling and arriving nowhere – poor *figli di mamma* rumbling along the roads towards their death.'

November 25th

   To-day is the last day on which the 1925 recruits must report themselves. Many of them have attempted a simple ruse: they have reported at their local Commune, have had their papers and have been given a ticket for the town where they must report, and have set off – and then, on their way to the station, have scattered and disappeared. Their families accordingly can swear that their sons went off to report themselves and that they have not seen them again – while of course knowing perfectly well where the boys are in hiding. It seems, however, unlikely that so simple a device will work – especially as some of the boys have not been able to resist coming home again for a last glimpse of their families. Among them is Adino, the son of Gigi, our gardener – who returned to his family last night and spent the day hidden in our garden. Gigi, when I pointed out that the boy's return was very unwise, suddenly broke down completely and sobbed. To-night after dusk Gigi will take him to another farm, belonging to a relation, where he is to be hidden – and then will return here, to await the consequences.

   Chiusi was bombed severely at one p.m., the bombs just missing the railway lines, and hitting the station buffet and some adjoining houses. Sixteen or seventeen dead. The Germans must have received some warning, as they removed all troops from the vicinity of the station only that morning – but did not see fit to warn the civilian population.

November 26th

   At Campiglia the recruits of the 1925 class were rounded up yesterday by the local Carabinieri. At Pienza, the fathers of the young men who have failed to report have been taken by the

Carabinieri and told that not only will they be kept in prison, but that the ration cards of the whole family will be taken away, until the boys turn up. At Chianciano a lorry-full of German soldiers, led by the local Fascist, N., went to a farm and arrested the father of the missing recruit — whereupon at the last moment, as the lorry was driving off, the boy ran out and took his father's place. Now we are expecting a similar visit here, to Adino's father and some of the farms. The feelings with which N. is regarded by the whole local population can easily be imagined — but, indeed, the hatred and contempt which everyone, of every class, feels for the Republican Fascists, the *Repubblichini*, is such that, by comparison, the Germans seem angels of light.

November 27th

Daily the procession continues of the fugitives, the homeless, the old and the hungry. To-day, in a single morning, I have interviewed the following:

(1) Three fugitive Italian soldiers, who, having walked all the way from France to south of Rome, were unable to get through the German lines, and now — returning here, hope to cut across the mountains by Todi towards the Adriatic coast, and then get through to join the Allies. They don't need food or shelter — but only warm clothes, a pair of boots and a look at a map.

(2) Two other fugitives, Italian airmen from Albania — one suffering from bronchitis — who have already been captured twice by the Germans and have now walked down from Vicenza. They have given up all hope of getting through the lines, and beg to be allowed to stay on here and work, until the Germans retreat. We find a place for them at one of our farms.

(3) Four of the British p.o.w.s from our own camp who (unknown to us) have been living all this time in a cave not far from here, fed by the farmers. Now one of them has hurt his leg and the others have come to ask for bandages, warm clothes, and some books. Where are the Allies? they ask, and when will the war

end? We provide what they need – except, alas, a satisfactory answer to their questions.

(4) More families of evacuees – one from Naples, one from Palermo and a woman from French Morocco – who have walked up from Chianciano. All people who originally had some little means of their own, but now have exhausted them. The Moroccan woman, moreover (after an examination at our *ambulatorio*) proves to be seriously ill with pernicious anaemia – and must. be sent to the Siena hospital. They all want to know whether it is possible for them to get through the German lines to southern Italy. I can only advise them to give up the plan and wait.

(5) A destitute old woman from Chianciano, with five small grandchildren. They all need shoes and clothes.

And so, day after day, it goes on – an unending stream of human suffering. And it will yet be worse.

November 28th

Antonio returns from Florence with the news that the Jew-hunt still continues. Last night they searched even the convents, hunting out and capturing the last poor wretches who had taken refuge there, including even a two-months' baby, which had been deserted by its panic-stricken mother. A new law has now declared all Jews to be enemy aliens, and their property, consequently, is confiscated, while they themselves are being deported, in sealed vans, to 'concentration camps'. Some will not arrive there. When the closed vans of one train which left Rome on Friday were not opened until Tuesday at Padova, one of them contained the corpse of an old man, another a new-born baby. No one was allowed to get out, and the train went on to Germany.

Every Italian I have met, irrespective of political opinion, is horrified and disgusted by this brutality – which is equalled by that of the new Republican police. At Palazzo Braschi (their headquarters in Rome) young men armed with whips stand about openly in the courtyard. We are being governed by the dregs of the nation — and their brutality is so capricious that no one can feel certain that he will be safe to-morrow.

November 29th

Two exhausted Italian soldiers turn up at night at the clinic — one with a temperature of forty degrees Centigrade. Both have escaped from a German concentration camp near Mantova and are utterly terrified and worn out. They drop asleep on a wooden bench the minute they sit down on it — and we put them straight to bed.

November 30th

The 1925 recruits — seeing their parents threatened with imprisonment, and the whole family with the loss of their ration cards — have mostly decided to report themselves. Only a few, in the most lonely farms, are still hidden. To-day in Siena the streets are filled with columns of young recruits, marshalled by Fascist officers, marching glumly to the station. They will hardly form a very satisfactory army.

Lunch at Siena with a young man (an officer of the Pinerolo military school) who has escaped from a train, which was taking him as a prisoner to Germany, by lowering himself under the axles and remaining motionless between the rails as the full length of the train passed over his body. When the train had passed and he became visible he was machine-gunned by the police on the train, but miraculously escaped being hit.

December 2nd

One of the two soldiers who arrived three days ago is now recovered and we send him to pick olives in one of our farms. The other is much better, but suffering from shock. He wanders about the clinic at night in his sleep, crying, 'Mamma! Mamma! They're going to arrest me!' and saying that he must find a bicycle to escape from the Germans. Both he and his companion are from Calabria — peasants with very little to say for themselves, and a look of bewildered, animal fear in their eyes.

December 4th

In the late afternoon I am told that a *signorina* wants to see me. A fair young woman, in towny but muddy clothes, comes in and immediately breaks down, crying and trembling. 'I don't know how to begin' — 'Begin at the beginning', I suggest. 'Where do you come from? What is your name?' — 'That's the trouble — our name is X!' Light dawns on me, and then the rest of the story pours out. She and her father and mother — all Jewish — who had come to Chianciano for the cure, gradually found their position in the pension untenable — and two days ago, having received a warning, ran away, spending the first night in a convent and last night in our woods. Her clothes, indeed, are muddy and she seems utterly exhausted. 'You are our last hope — for God's sake take us in, hide us.' Her father and mother, whom she has left hidden in a room in the clinic, give me more details — including the danger incurred by their brother who was an employee of an Anglo-Italian Society in London. They have been Catholics since 1913 — but that, they well know, will not save them. We consult as to what can be done for them, and meanwhile put them up for the night.

December 6th

Antonio spends the day in driving from one village to another, trying to find a safe shelter for the X.s. At last, through the Bishop of Pienza, a hiding-place is found for them in a remote convent — and we take them there.

December 7th

Start evening classes for the elder refugee children, who have got beyond the elementary school stage: V. teaches them mathematics, physics and science; Signorina G., Italian and history; I, English and Latin. Life is returning to the medieval pattern: as the outside world is more and more cut off, we must learn, not only to produce our own food and spin and weave our own wool — but to provide teaching for the children, nursing for the sick, and shelter for the passer-by.

December 10th

Antonio returns from Florence, where arrests still continue and everyone is exceedingly jumpy. The Republican S.S. has instituted a reign of terror. The house near San Gallo, where the questioning takes place, and from which moans and screams are heard by the passer-by, is now called the *Villa Triste*. Personal vendettas or mere capriciousness lie beneath many of the arrests — as well as remarkable carelessness. One unfortunate old Sienese landowner of seventy was fetched one day by some young Fascist hooligans, beaten and tortured at the *Villa Triste* to extract an admission that he was involved in a Communist plot of which he knew nothing, and finally put in prison. When at last his family succeeded in speaking to the Questore, and inquired what charge there was against him, they were told that his name had been found on a list of addresses in the pocket of a Communist: 'Look, Francesco B.' — 'But *his* name is Giuseppe!' protested his family — and so at last the poor old man was set free.

December 15th

Two other fugitives turn up — an old Jew from Siena and his son. Both of them, clad in the most unsuitable of town clothes and thin shoes, are shivering with cold and terror. The father, the owner of an antique shop, produces from an inner pocket, drawing me aside, a little carved ivory Renaissance figure which he wishes to exchange for food and warm clothing. We supply the latter, and suggest that he should keep the figure for future needs. He and his son wish to walk through the German lines to Naples — and to all our dissuasions (since it is clear that the old man, who suffers from heart-disease, will die upon the way) they only reply — 'We have no choice. We must.' After a rest and some food they start up the hill in the snow, the old man groaning a little as he leans on his son's shoulder.

December 22nd

Kind friends send messages to warn me of a law by which all English and American women are to be interned in concentration camps, and advise me to look for a hiding-place. But where? and if I were away, Antonio would almost certainly be taken in my stead. It seems more sensible just to go on with daily life, which at the moment consists chiefly of tying up Christmas parcels for our refugee children and for the hospital. There are two trees to decorate, too, and layettes to finish for new-born babies in the Montepulciano hospital — where many expectant mothers have been evacuated from Grosseto or Livorno.

December 23rd

Half of one's Roman acquaintances are in hiding (some in the country, some in convents, some in segregated rooms of friends' houses) and those who are still at liberty to-day are not certain whether they will be to-morrow. One afternoon in Rome, for instance, a bomb burst in front of the Hotel Flora — whereupon S.S. men sprang up out of the ground, and everyone who happened to be walking down the Via Veneto (over two hundred people, including the Spanish Ambassador) were promptly arrested. Sniping of Germans and of Fascist officials continues — and no buses, trams or even bicycles are allowed after dusk — so that at five p.m. the whole life of the town comes to an end. But all night the streets resound with the reports of machine-guns and hand-grenades.

The food situation in the city is becoming more and more serious. Unlimited meat, vegetables, etc., can still be bought at preposterous 'black market' prices, but are practically unprocurable by the poor, and every day the discontent increases. Unfortunately faith in the Allies' promises is also gradually decreasing — and the only Party which is daily growing stronger is the Communist. Of Mussolini no one now speaks and it is said that he himself, on being asked to make a speech on the wireless on October 28th, replied: 'What can a dead man say to a nation of corpses?'

Christmas Day

The Pope's Christmas Eve homily had a despairing ring, as if he himself knew all too well that his appeal for peace to men of goodwill would fall upon ears deaf to any interpretation of right and justice but their own. Almost desperate, too, was his appeal for better international understanding, based on a universal human solidarity. But indeed of this there has been (certainly here, and I believe almost everywhere) a reawakening. In church this morning as I looked round I saw, among the usual Christmas congregation from the farms and the *fattoria*, the large group of refugee children from Genoa and Turin, rosy-cheeked and plump and excited; the Calabrian and Sicilian soldiers who are working in the farms; the Egyptian boy from the G.I.L.E.; all those who have found refuge here — and coming out I felt, in the familiar exchange of Christmas greetings, a bond of deep understanding born of common trouble, anxieties and hopes such as I never have felt before. And in the attitude of the farmers to all the homeless passers-by (whether Italian soldiers or British prisoners, whether Gentile or Jew) there is a spontaneous, unfailing charity and hospitality. Even now that the risks have increased — since the police are supposed to be rounding up the boys of the 1925 class – there is no farm which would refuse them shelter; and to-day I noticed that each one of the soldiers who are living here was wearing at least one warm garment given off their backs by their hosts.

Yesterday we took a small Christmas tree to the Montepulciano hospital for the sick children; to-day we had a tree and a party for Benedetta and the refugee children here. The older girls danced and recited, they all sang *Stille Nacht* and *Tu scendi dalle stelle* – and Antonio made a magnificent Father Christmas with a flowing white beard, fur coat and cossack cap. For an hour or so it seemed like any other Christmas. But then the telephone rang: the Chianciano policeman issued a warning that Adino must report himself to-morrow morning, or the police would come to arrest his father, Gigi. Adino promptly disappears.

Turning on the radio in the evening, we hear of the bombing of Pistoia and Pisa.

December 27th

Wait all day for the police to fetch Gigi – who, in preparation for prison, had changed into his best shirt. But no one came. A few hours later we hear that the order to arrest parents in place of their sons has (for this province, at any rate) been revoked.

December 28th

Coming downstairs this morning, I am greeted by the now familiar information: 'There are some Germans in the *fattoria* courtyard – and an English prisoner in the garden.' I hastily put the latter into the little room by the garden door where I do the flowers, and (while Antonio is dealing with the Germans) listen to his story. He was originally, he says, in a camp near Trento, and has already twice been recaptured: the first time by the Germans, from whom he escaped near Trento; the second time by the Fascist militia who put him in the barracks at Arezzo — from which he escaped during an air-raid. He then found refuge with a family near Sinalunga — but yesterday someone gave him away, the police turned up, and the friend who was with him was arrested, while he himself only got away by the skin of his teeth. 'They were father and mother to me,' he said of the family which had sheltered him, and his chief anxiety was lest they should now be in danger. It was difficult to know what to advise him, since many men who have tried it have told us that it is now impossible to get through the German lines, and that in the mountains south of Rome many prisoners have been rounded up. But he was determined to attempt it and, after consulting a map, he wearily set out.

December 31st

Return from two days in Florence. On the surface it is quieter than a few weeks ago. The Fascist S.S. are less active, and their leader, whose singularly inappropriate name is Carità, has been removed. During his rule, however, the number of arrests, followed by torture, was sufficiently large. Among his victims was a little hairdresser (of pro-Allied sympathies) whose shop was frequented by some ladies who had helped British prisoners, or merely chattered about them. He was tortured to supply a list of their names, but remained silent — and was finally taken to the prison of Le Murate in such a condition that the Governor refused to take him in, and sent him off to the hospital instead.

The rounding-up of the Jews appears now to be completed — though no doubt many unfortunate women and children are still hidden. The Archbishop of Florence, Cardinal della Costa, has taken a courageous stand. When some of his nuns were arrested, in consequence of having given shelter to some Jewish women in their convent, the Cardinal, putting on his full panoply, went straight to the German Command. 'I have come to you,' he said, 'because I believe you, as soldiers, to be people who recognize authority and hierarchy — and who do not make subordinates responsible for merely carrying out orders. The order to give shelter to those unfortunate Jewish women was given by me: therefore I request you to free the nuns, who have merely carried out orders, and to arrest me in their stead.' The German immediately gave orders for the nuns to be freed, but permitted himself to state his surprise that a man like the Cardinal should take under his protection such people as the Jews, the scum of Europe, responsible for all the evils of the present day. The Cardinal did not enter upon the controversy. 'I look upon them,' he said, 'merely as persecuted human beings; as such it is my Christian duty to help and defend them. One day,' he gave himself the pleasure of adding, 'perhaps not far off, *you* will be persecuted: and then I shall defend you!'

1944

1944

January 1st

The first severe snowfall. We have been completely cut off — the road to both Montepulciano and Chianciano impassable — no post, no light, and consequently no radio. A telephone call yesterday told me that a workman had arrived at Chiusi from Turin at two a.m., with his two little girls, on their way back to La Foce. The eldest of them, Nella, had been taken back to her home in Turin by her mother (who could not bear the separation from her) a few weeks ago — but since then Turin has been bombed again, and now the father has come down to implore me not only to take Nella back, but also her little sister. There was no means of fetching them, the motor-buses had been requisitioned by the Germans — and they could find neither food nor shelter in the half-destroyed station. After several hours and much distracted telephoning I succeeded in getting the children taken in by the nuns at the Chiusi orphanage. To-day, at last, a car has brought them as far as Chianciano, and they have walked the last four miles through the snow. In Turin conditions are very bad. No oil and no fats have been available for over three months. The bombing continues. Many of the war factories have now been destroyed: and there are continual strikes in those which are still working. When the strike is general there are few consequences; but when any single factory strikes alone, the retort is simply to shoot a tenth of the workmen. Meanwhile the partisan bands in the mountains are constantly being reinforced, and receive clothing and arms from the factories, and food from many of the landowners.

January 13th

After a grotesque and brutal trial, eighteen out of the nineteen members of the Great Council who voted against

Mussolini were yesterday condemned to death at Verona. The five who have been captured — Ciano, De Bono, Marinelli, Gottardi and Pareschi — were shot this morning. The newspaper reports of the trial render all comment superfluous. Ciano (who had escaped to Germany and had been sent back to Italy on the clear understanding that his life would be spared) and De Bono were equally certain, until the actual reading of their sentences, that they would be acquitted — De Bono having even written from prison to his family to get his room ready as he would be coming home at once.

January 14th
Anatole France, in his old age, intended to write a novel, of which the title was to be *Les autels de la peur*. The Altars of Fear — could a better title be found for an account of our times?

January 15th
Go to Florence for three days, and on my return find two disquieting pieces of news: one of the refugee children, Maria, has got scarlet fever, and a thousand German paratroops are arriving at Chianciano. Moreover, the vice-Mayor of Chianciano informs me that the Capo della Provincia has decided to quarter them here and at the Castelluccio, turning us all out. After twenty-four hours of anxiety, however, we hear that the Germans have preferred to occupy all the Chianciano hotels. Nevertheless, in view of the probability of the arrival of other troops, we begin to pack up our best furniture, mattresses, books, etc. and send them in ox-carts to remote farms.

January 18th
Rumours of imminent Allied landings; the bombing of railway-lines and junctions intensified throughout central Italy.

Nevertheless, Antonio, returning from Bolgheri, reports that the German Command in the Pisa-Grosseto area is confident that there will *not* be a landing there. The port of Livorno has been blown up and the town evacuated, but the rest of the coast is completely undefended.

January 19th

The paratroops at Chianciano have come from Cassino, and are here to recuperate and train new recruits from Germany before returning to the front. The Germans are a formidable lot of veterans, from the Russian front and Crete, commanded by a major of sixty-five. Their interpreter (who comes up here with one of the officers, to requisition oil, wine, sheep, etc.) says that frequently the maintenance of discipline has to be enforced by their officers with a revolver. Their rations from Germany are not arriving regularly (no wonder, after the continual bombing), and they see no reason why sheep, pigs and geese from the local farms should not replace them. Occasionally, too, when they are drunk, there is trouble in the village, where they bang at the doors at night, shouting, 'Out with the women!'

The nerves of the Chiancianesi, already considerably shaken, are not improved by such incidents, nor by the troops' A.R.P. drill. Shelters have been hastily built, and in these a considerable part of the population (many of whom are evacuated from Naples or Messina, where they have already been severely bombed) spend each night, as yet quite unnecessarily. Several families have already arrived at our farms, bringing their bedding with them, and have demanded, rather than requested, to be taken in. And this morning three terrified old ladies, refugees from Naples, drove up to see me to ask for shelter. Far too urban, in their high heels and moth-eaten furs, for any farm-house, but penniless, since for months they have received no money from home and are living on the evacuees' allowance of eight lire a day, they constitute a difficult problem — but I hope I have succeeded in finding them rooms in an, as yet, fairly safe village some miles away. Meanwhile the bombing continues, and now both the Siena-Chiusi and the Florence-Chiusi lines are cut (at Poggibonsi, Foiano, and Arezzo) so that we are completely cut off from the north. The B.B.C. states that the Pisa-Rome line is also cut, so that now the only railway line in the country still working is that along the Adriatic coast.

Maria, the child with scarlet fever, is dangerously ill. None of the others have yet developed it.

January 20th

Allied prisoners are beginning to come through again, three yesterday, two to-day. The farmers who have given them shelter until now are beginning to be nervous, as the number of Fascist militia-men in the district is increasing, and there have been several arrests of prisoners and of the peasants who had hidden them. The latter will be shot. The prisoners need warm clothing, blankets, a ground-sheet for sleeping out in the woods (the nights are bitter) and, most of all, information. What way shall they go? and where are the Allies? We supply all that we can, but warn them that getting through the lines at Cassino is now practically impossible. Only a few days ago one of our own British prisoners, who had nearly got to Cassino, was caught there, poor devil, and succeeded in sending us a message as he passed through Chianciano on his way up to Germany. One of his companions, while the prisoners got out to get a drink, managed to hide under a bench in the waiting-room: the porters pretended not to see him, and when the train went off he escaped across country. But it's a hell of a life for them now, and no one has more cause than they to regret the Allies' slow progress. In these last few days, however, there appears to have been a much more determined attack on the Garigliano and there is a general expectation of some fresh event.

January 22nd

The news has come: this morning Allied troops landed at Nettuno, thirty miles south of Rome.

January 23rd

The landings continue, so far with only slight German opposition, but they are said to be massing for a counter-attack. The paratroops at Chianciano have left, and all last night long columns of German lorries were rumbling down the Via Cassia.

Meanwhile we have our local problems to deal with. The Mayor telephones that a German officer will be coming up shortly to inspect the Castelluccio and this house, with a view to quartering about a hundred soldiers there, and the Maresciallo of Pienza comes over to inform us that the Colonel of the Fascist Militia in Siena has ordered him to keep us under special surveillance as suspect persons, guilty of having given funds to the partisans and of inciting our peasants not to report for military service. We are even supposed to have paid the sum of fifty lire to each man who fails to report! The Maresciallo himself, a very decent fellow of the old school, has accordingly come straight to Antonio to warn him. He confides to us that he himself has not as yet taken the oath of obedience to the Republican Government; if he is asked to do so, he will resign. Throughout the country the Carabinieri have taken a similar stand: seventy per cent of the officers and ninety per cent of the N.C.O.s preferring to resign from the Service rather than take the oath. Wherever they still remain they stand for stability, decency and order.

January 24th

The German officer turns up: a parachutist, covered with medals of both this war and the last, in which he served as a volunteer at the age of sixteen. He inspects the Castelluccio, is unfortunately delighted with it, and a notice, stating that the castle has been requisitioned, is placed on the door. Mercifully our own house is not required — as yet.

In the afternoon we walk up to Pietraporciana — a lonely farm on a hill-top at the top of our property — to see if we could take all the children there, if we are turned out. There would be thirty-six of us.

January 26th

Spend the day sorting furniture and books to be hidden in outlying farms. Schwester Marie, the babies' charming Swiss nurse, who was to have returned home at this time, decides to stay on with us and see us through, in view of the possibility of our being arrested and the children left alone. Our relief is very great, but she may soon be completely cut off from her home.

Antonio returns from a day at Siena, having met long German columns on their way to Rome. An acquaintance had just arrived from Rome, in a car which was machine-gunned on the way, and reported that the water system in Rome has now been mended, but that there is much anxiety about food, as all the roads leading to the city are now blocked. A 'state of emergency' is to be declared there this afternoon.

January 28th

Move the best furniture out of the Castelluccio before the Germans arrive. Walking back, notice a man following us in the woods. We stop and he comes up: he is a South African p.o.w., needing information and food. We advise him to push on in the direction of Bolsena, avoiding the main roads, and await events there.

A lady from Chianciano arrives, asking for a room for her invalid daughter and a nurse — which I am obliged to refuse as the house is already filled by the refugee children. She clearly does not believe me. Half an hour later an officer of the Fascist militia turns up — the worst type of 'gerarca' — covered with medals, conceited and bullying. He has run away from Rome with all his family (in a large car, with a motor-bicycle preceding him) and requires for their accommodation nothing less than the whole of the Castelluccio. Take some pleasure in informing him that it has already been taken by the Germans and that he will find their label on the door.

After dark a family of six arrive on foot from Chiusi asking for beds for the night. We put them up as best we can: father, mother, uncles, and three children. They come from a village near Cassino, have lost everything they possess, and have come to Tuscany to pick up their two little girls, who were at school at Castel Fiorentino, and to-morrow another child at Montalcino. The wife is a Frenchwoman, gay and tidy in spite of her extreme fatigue and the high-heeled *chaussures de ville*, which are causing her agony. I provide shoes for her, and to-morrow (since there are no trains) they will all go, on foot, to Montalcino and thence to Siena and Florence — where they hope to get a train to the Val d'Aosta, their home. They say that all the land round Cassino is flooded. So indeed (for fear of Allied landings) is the whole of the great Ferrara *bonifica*, and also five thousand hectares near Ravenna, and the Ostia *bonifica* near Rome — all land recently reclaimed which is thus again becoming a swamp. Moreover, all the machinery has been taken away to Germany. Thus all that was good in the work of the last few years is being destroyed; what is bad is still with us.

January 29th
The bombing of central Italy is increasing. Within the last three days Orvieto, Orte, Terni, Arezzo, Foiano, Siena, Poggibonsi, Pontedera, Pontassieve, have all again been bombed. Yesterday a train, carrying Allied prisoners and civilians evacuated from Rome, was hit on the bridge of Alerona near Chiusi. The

arches of the bridge were also hit, and some of the carriages plunged into the river: there were over four hundred dead and wounded. Such incidents, however horrible, are a part of war. But the almost total destruction of a little town like Arezzo, including the districts furthest away from the railway — and of country churches, like the Convento dell'Osservanza outside Siena — these, and the machine-gunning of the civilian population, cannot easily be explained. It is difficult to believe that public opinion in England, if fully informed, would approve of all this.

January 30th

A German interpreter, who has come up to the farm to buy oil, complains that after the bombing of the bridge at Alerona, when some of the wounded were brought to the hospital of Chiusi, the population brought water and wine to the British wounded, utterly disregarding the Germans.

Hear that a small band of British and American prisoners is hidden in the woods above Spineta, living in a charcoal-burner's hut. One of them has come down by parachute, and they have a radio-transmitter; some of their supplies are brought to them by plane.

February 3rd

Our radios are blocked by order of the Fascist Government. We are given a choice between the Rome and Florence stations, and since the latter includes the German news and concerts from Vienna we choose this. We also conceal two smaller radios in the nursery and in my bedroom, and continue to listen to the B.B.C. as before.

Drive to Florence, starting at six a.m. to avoid machine-gunning or bombing on the way. Everything perfectly quiet and normal on the road, and we only meet a few German lorries beyond Siena. At Poggibonsi the destruction caused by the second air-raid is even greater than that caused by the first; this time the station has been hit, but also most of the town and some farms outside. The streets are deserted. In Florence the hotel is filled by Germans, Fascist officers and plain-clothes policemen; large German lorries stand before the door, and cars continually drive up, with people feverishly hurrying away from Rome or towards it – according to their circumstances and their political opinions.

February 4th
The atmosphere is extremely tense. The hall of the hotel is like a police station in an operetta, in which the frequent irruptions of large bodies of police suggest to the innocent observer the arrest of some criminal, but, in fact, generally merely herald the arrival of some member of the Government. Last night two old Italian generals, who had fled from Rome and had attempted to spend the night here without showing their papers, were arrested by the Germans during the night. People who have friends in Rome telephone to them (by means of large bribes to the telephone girls) on the German lines in the hotel. Their conversations are very curious and elliptical. Arrivals from Rome say that it is now expected that the Germans *will* defend the city. The Pope has told his parish priests to warn their congregations that his efforts to obtain promises safeguarding the city, on either side, have failed completely. Here in Florence the German military attitude has considerably altered – not perhaps unnaturally – since the attempt on the lives of German officers last week (bombs thrown in the Excelsior hotel and at the station), and though the curfew instituted a few days ago has now again been removed, the amenities which previously existed have come to an end. The town is placarded with revolting photographs of corpses in the snow, said to have been found in a ditch near Vines in Croatia. The photographs bear the captions: 'A Second Katyn' and 'Anglo-Russian-American Civilization'.

There have been some more attempts against the lives of Fascist officials, and several officers and militiamen have been killed. And now, of course, there will be reprisals similar to those last month when — after the murder of the Fascist Colonel Gobbi — five anti-Fascists who happened to be in prison, and who had nothing whatever to do with the crime, were immediately shot. So long, however, as these incidents only concern the Fascists and their opponents, the Germans show no interest in the matter.

The Gh.s arrive from Bolgheri, on the coast near Livorno. Their house and the houses of the owners of neighbouring properties have now all got Germans quartered in them. The machine-gunning on the roads from Allied planes is not agreeable; not only is any car upon the road attacked, but a woman and children have been fired upon on the beach, and old Count G. in the middle of a paddock.

February 5th

A good deal of firing during the night. Generally it is merely the younger Fascists letting off pistols for fun (but occasionally hitting someone) — but last night a militiaman, who was leaning on the embankment of the Arno looking at the river, received two revolver bullets in his neck from a man passing by on a bicycle. The oddest story circulating in Florence is that a meeting took place in the Grand Hotel a few days ago between the German military and civil authorities to discuss, in cold blood, whether or not the city (when the time comes to retreat) shall be sacked. The Consul and other civilian officials were said to be against the looting, the soldiers in favour. The ultimate decision is not known, but it is certain that, at the present rate, there won't be much left to be sacked, as all that is left in the shops is systematically being taken off to Germany.[1] Ugolini, for instance,

---

[1] I had not allowed for Florentine ingenuity. A great deal was saved and successfully hidden — to reappear in the shops immediately after the Allies' arrival.

told me that in the last few days ninety-six thousand lire worth of woollen goods has been removed from his shop — and as he spoke a large lorry was going down Via Tornabuoni, collecting goods from each shop in turn. Some of these goods are, theoretically, paid for — with enormous quantities of paper money, specially printed in the Vienna Mint, of which every German soldier carries great rolls in his belt.

February 9th

Stray Allied prisoners continue to come by — two yesterday, a French-Canadian and an Englishman, and one, a boy from Inverness, to-day. The first two had jumped out of the bombed train at Alerona, and the Canadian had been hit on the shoulder by falling stones and fragments of the destroyed carriages: the shoulder was badly bruised and sprained, but not fractured. The nurse and I took some bandages into the woods and tied him up — and he and his companion set off again in search of friends nearby. The young Scotsman, who has been caught and has escaped again no less than three times since the armistice, was bound for Anzio: he wanted some news and a shirt. We now generally advise such travellers to hang about in the wild wooded country between San Casciano and Bolsena until their troops arrive. But when will that be? The news from the beach-head is increasingly discouraging. The area occupied by the Allies is now only ten miles long, and is continually under fire from the Germans, who are said to have brought down nine divisions to this district.

February 13th

Mr. Churchill declares that 'while all battles, as they approach their decisive phase, are anxious', he feels 'no especial anxiety' about the Anzio battle. I wish I could share his feelings.

It is odd how used one can become to uncertainty for the future, to a complete planlessness, even in one's most private mind. What we shall do and be, and whether we shall, in a few months' time, have any home or possessions, or indeed our lives, is so clearly dependent on events outside our own control as to be almost restful. For of course everyone else is in the same boat. Refugees from southern Italy bring tragic tales of the results of the 'scorched earth' policy, carried out by the Germans in their leisurely retreat. Not only the small towns, but the farms and the crops have been destroyed — in addition, of course, to the havoc already brought by bombing. There is no reason to think that central Italy will be spared a similar fate — the only uncertainty left to each of us being whether or not we shall happen to be on the road of the advancing or retreating armies. Our friends the Caetani, whose home is at Ninfa, in the thick of the present battle, and the Senni family, who live on the road between Grottaferrata and Rome next to a large airport, are at any rate already in the thick of it. Those of us who live farther north are still uncertain of our fate. The Gh.s, living on the coast thirty-seven miles from Livorno, will be obliged to leave their house (like all the rest of the civilian population) if there should be a landing on the Tuscan coast; meanwhile they already have German officers in the house, cannons in the garden, and troops in the village. E., whose house is situated just above a tunnel between the main road and the railway from Florence to Bologna, is in an equally precarious position. So is everyone who happens to live near a railway (even in as small a town as Poggibonsi) or on a main road. Nevertheless, practically all landowners have chosen to remain on their properties until they are actually bombed or turned out, together with their peasants, who have no other choice. Most of us have buried our jewels and papers, walled up some reserves of wheat, potatoes, oil and wine, and hidden some of our best furniture, books and clothes in the more remote farm-houses, and now are sitting tight. In our particular case, if ever we are forced to move, we shall have with us, in addition to our own two small children, the twenty-three refugee children, including a five-months-old baby — no simple matter either to transport or feed.

Meanwhile daily life holds nothing worse than isolation and boredom. For the last three days we have been snowed up, and can reach neither Montepulciano nor Chianciano: the telephone is broken, and we have often no letters or papers for five or six days together. No trains are running either on the Arezzo-Chiusi or Siena-Chiusi line, and Chianciano's only link with the rest of the world is a bus to Siena three times a week. So we build snow castles with the children, go for long walks, try to feed and clothe the people who come to us for help, listen to the radio (but much less than one would expect, and with an odd indifference, even when the news is such as is likely to be vital to us), re-read all our old books — and wait.

I have spoken of the immediate hazards: the more remote ones are of course even greater. Though each one of us in his inmost heart believes that he and his family will survive (through some privilege which we certainly could not account for) certainly no one can make a guess as to what his future life will be. Shall we have any money left, or work for a bare living? In what sort of a world will our children be brought up? What should we teach them to prepare them? Can any peace or order be restored again in this unhappy, impoverished and divided land? And when those who, like myself, have relations and friends in other countries, are able to hear from them again, what news will we receive? Three weeks ago — after four months of silence and anxiety — I received the news of my mother's death in Switzerland, eighteen days after the event — in a letter from a stranger which had been smuggled across the frontier. When letters begin again, how many other such pieces of news shall we all receive? Which of our close friends and relations are already dead, or will die before we meet them again? And, even among those who survive, what barriers of constraint and unfamiliarity will have arisen in these years — not only of physical separation, but of experience unshared, of differing feelings and opinions? What ties will survive that strain?

February 15th

Yesterday the Abbey of Monte Cassino, fourteen centuries old, was destroyed by Allied bombs — to the accompaniment of a flood of radio propaganda from both sides. The Allies state that they refrained from damaging the Abbey until the Germans began to use it as an armed fortress; the Germans deny it. The Abbot states that German soldiers came out of the ruins; the Germans, that the Abbot, some of the monks, and many refugee women and children from the town below, were still there. Most of the precious library has been saved.

February 16th

Yesterday and to-day Rome has been bombed by the Allies — in order to obstruct the passage of German troops. Radio Roma states that there has also been machine-gunning of the civilian population, including three cars from the Vatican on their way to the bombed quarter. Three days ago the great villa at Castelgandolfo adjoining the Pope's palace, which was filled with refugee women and children, was hit by Allied bombs. The radio controversy about Cassino continues, the pot calling the kettle black. What appears to be true, from a statement signed by the Abbot himself, is that twenty monks and about a hundred and eighty civilians perished in the ruins.

Two other prisoners who have escaped from the bombed train at Alerona were waiting for me in the wood this morning. They are two Americans, who have been living for three days in one of our farms where their uniforms are being dyed: and now they are planning either to go to the coast and 'somehow' get a boat to Corsica, or else to walk up to Piemonte and get into France across the Alps. I point out the difficulties of both courses, and they decide to go south instead. They belong to the Eighth Army, and were captured at Venafro.

February 17th
To-day a new sort of fugitive has turned up: three Austrian soldiers who have deserted from the German Army at Anzio and are trying to get home. One is still in uniform: the other two have their uniforms in a bag, and put them on whenever they travel by train, changing into civilian clothes when tramping. Their chances of getting home seem very poor, and if taken they will of course be shot. I show them a map and give them some food. Antonio, who knows German much better than I do, says that only one of them is an Austrian. If the German front breaks we shall no doubt see many others like them; but will it break? To-day there is news of fiercer fighting on both sides; perhaps it is to be the 'decisive battle' which we are all awaiting. All night we hear German planes flying overhead.

February 18th
Bring back a ten-days-old baby from the Montepulciano hospital: Giovannino. His mother is suffering from septicaemia and cannot nurse him, and (owing to the general lack of food and the number of refugees at Montepulciano) it is impossible to find either a wet-nurse or cow's milk. So we have brought him back here and have made him a cradle in a large basket in the nursery. He is a miserable little scrap, with sores on his legs and in his mouth from starvation, and I only trust that we may be able to save him. Schwester Marie is being angelic about all the extra work, saying (as indeed is true) that it is as much war work as any other.[1]

[1] The child survived; it is still living with us, his mother having died.

February 19th

Bad news yesterday. The Fascist Government — presumably under pressure from the Germans — orders that recruits of the 1922, '23, '24 and '25 classes, called to the colours, who do not report within a fortnight will immediately be shot. The sentence will be executed on the spot where they are captured, or at their own home. Moreover, a police circular (of which a copy has been sent us by the Maresciallo of Pienza) states that all landowners who shelter, or allow their peasants to conceal, recruits of these classes on their property, will be considered directly responsible.

February 20th

The fighting on the Anzio beach-head continues, each side having brought up heavy artillery. The situation appears to be unchanged — the advantage, if any, being to the Germans. More of their planes fly over us in the night.

A young man who has just come back from Rome says that fresh material for labour-camps in Germany is being collected in the following manner: Fascist or S.S. troops appear suddenly in one of the main streets, cut off a section, and arrest all the men in that section between the ages of sixteen and fifty-five. They are marched off (without even being allowed to send a message home) and never seen again.

February 22nd

Go for the day to Montepulciano and help to serve lunch at the communal kitchen started by Bracci, the Mayor, at which four hundred people are given lunch daily in two shifts. They usually get soup or macaroni, followed by vegetables or chestnuts, with a piece of bread of fifty grammes, and meat once or twice a week — all for half a lira — and a glass of wine for an extra half lira. To-day, being Shrove Tuesday, there was a slice (smallish) of roast beef in a plate of macaroni, followed by a small slab of chestnut-cake — and a glass of wine free. All this in addition to the usual scanty food ration, which thus remains available for the evening meal. The food was well cooked and hot, the rooms clean and cheerful. Everyone who has applied — whether evacuees or the poor of the district — has been admitted. An admirable enterprise.

Hear Churchill's speech to the House. The part referring to Italy will be heard here with feelings not unmixed. No one can view with indifference the prospect of the rest of Italy suffering the same fate as the district between Naples and Rome. Nor is it exactly comforting to hear the references to 'Hitler's intention' of making Rome a second Stalingrad.

February 27th

A peasant from a remote farm on Monte Amiata, Fonte Lippi, came to see me, bringing with him a letter from three of our p.o.w.s, who (after having lived for four months hidden in this man's farm) set off in January to try to rejoin their own troops. There were four of them, but when they got near to Cassino one of them was captured, and the other three have now returned, worn-out and ragged, to the same farm. Their note says: 'We realize that this man has robbed himself and his family to keep us,' and begs me to help him in any way that I can. The peasant's story is remarkable. He took in these four Englishmen at the beginning of October, when they were obliged to leave here, and fed and housed them — disregarding the danger as well as the expense — for over three months. Then the Fascist militia of Radicofani (having been warned by a spy) came to search his house and threatened to shoot him for harbouring enemy aliens. They came in the middle of the night and turned the house upside down, but *della brava gente* (some good folk) had given the warning two hours before, and the prisoners had escaped into the woods in time — returning again to the farm the next day. 'We just couldn't turn them out,' said their host. 'They had become a part of the family — and when at last they left, my old woman and the children cried.' But meanwhile they had eaten up all the family's flour — everyone was going short — and at last, in January, they had set off — only to return again a fortnight ago. The farmer went to his landlord to ask for some more wheat, but he refused, saying that he knew it was needed because the man had helped Allied prisoners. 'So much the worse for you.' The Englishmen have tried to join up with one of the bands on Monte Amiata, but their leader has told them to stay where they were for the present, as he too is short of food. (All the hopes of these bands are set on another Allied landing nearer here.) Finally, in despair, the peasant has come to us. He has also provided the Englishmen with clothes, at his own expense, and all he is asking for it is some wheat so that his family will not go hungry, and, if possible, some boots for his guests. We are providing the wheat (two quintals) — which will be taken down to the valley at night in the cart of one of our farmers who can be trusted — and there transferred to this man's ox-cart. Boots are as unprocurable as the crown jewels, but I have sent Antonio's last pair of shoes, some socks, cigarettes, books and playing-cards (for the men do not now dare to stir out of the house) and some money.

Surely this is a very creditable story. Much has been said in these times (and not least by the Italians themselves) about Italian cowardice and Italian treachery. But here is a man (and there are hundreds of others like him) who has run the risk of being shot, who has shared his family's food to the last crumb, and who has lodged, clothed and protected four strangers for over three months — and who now proposes continuing to do so, while perfectly aware of all the risks that he is running. What is this, if not courage and loyalty?

February 28th
Receive a bundle of letters from Rome. Life there — a month after the Allies' landing at Nettuno — is not agreeable.

German troops pass through the centre of the city (lorries, tanks and guns) from Piazza del Popolo down the Corso — the road of all the great invasions of the past. Allied planes circle over unceasingly, frequent dog-fights take place, but bombing, so far, has been limited to the outskirts of the city and the quarters near the stations. The bombing of the Castelli, however (Frascati, Castelgandolfo, Velletri, etc.), has been very bad.

The peasants of the Ostia *bonifica*, which has been flooded, suddenly appeared in town with five hundred cattle, and are camping in huts in Villa Glori, together with the children from the Frascati nursery-school, while C.A. struggles to find food for both men and cattle. At Frascati the survivors — about three hundred and sixty people — live day and night in the shelter beneath Villa Aldobrandini, only coming out for two hours between five and seven to bake their bread. At Villa Senni, near Grottaferrata, the house is occupied by Germans, but the daughters of the house have refused to leave it and sleep in a cave on the property, together with about thirty peasants and some cattle. In Rome the streets are full of pitiful sights — refugees wandering in the streets, without food or shelter, and sleeping at night under the bridges or in the tunnel. Food is still obtainable by the rich, but at preposterous prices: a few communal kitchens have been started for the rest of the population (notably by the Vatican) but too few and too late. In the first days after the Allied landing many pro-Allies (certain that in a few days their friends would have arrived) took an active part in manning bridges or other preparations, or merely expressed their hopes with injudicious freedom: now many of them are under arrest or in hiding — or already executed. Most tragic was the fate of the patriot bands, who had for months been waiting for their chance in the woods and hills, and who succeeded (on the second day after the landing) in taking Velletri, hourly expecting the Allied forces to join up with them. But the Germans arrived in their stead and the patriots were wiped out.

A friend writes: 'The other evening I heard on the radio the

147

account of Monte Cassino's destruction, told by the Abbot, an old man of eighty. Without a single adjective, quietly, in a tired and saddened tone, he told the story as if it had happened a hundred years ago. It was terribly moving and I can hardly imagine what the Benedictines from that monastery, now scattered all over the world, must have felt in hearing that quiet, heartfelt account of the end of that source of civilization — now, after fourteen centuries of religious life, buried for ever.'

February 29th

A young officer — a shy, silent, melancholy Sardinian — has turned up with a letter from Don Remo — the parish priest of Sinalunga, asking us to give him shelter. His papers are in order (he is of the 1919 class) but he is very jumpy and restless — clearly suffering from shock, after having been through both the Russian and the Sicilian campaigns. We offer to take him in here, but he prefers to go to one of the farms.

March 2nd

The Sicilian boy has gone off; he must get through the lines at once, he says, and join the Allies. We point out that he has now practically no chance of getting through. But he won't listen: 'Justice is on the other side,' he says. 'I've got to get through to them.' We tell him that if he fails he can come back to us, and I give him a note for G. — a member of the Resistance movement in Rome. 'This is to introduce a friend of ours, who has been staying here and wants to meet Vittoria' (England). He goes off through the woods in his shabby overcoat and worn-out shoes, a paper bundle over his shoulder.

March 3rd

Letter from a friend near Livorno. The strip of land along the coast is now being flooded, and there are German troops everywhere. (Six months ago there was no one.) There is a good deal of bombing of towns and villages on the railway, and also much indiscriminate machine-gunning on the roads. 'What will be left of this wretched country?' a friend writes to me to-day. 'Perhaps a few isolated houses in the woods or hills — all the rest destroyed. I don't believe that the wars of the past, even with the pestilence and famine that they brought, were as destructive as this one. First we fought to save Africa, then Italy and her islands, then the peninsula, then each province in turn; then we struggled to keep our cars and our freedom of movement, then our houses and those we love — and no doubt we shall soon be thankful merely to save our skins.'

March 4th

The Italian Republican Government still economically makes use of the old stamps with the King's head, but has stamped on them an emblem of the *Fascio* which half obliterates the King's face.

The Germans are launching another violent counter-attack (the third) on the Anzio front.

March 6th

To-morrow is the last day on which the recruits of the 1922-25 classes can join up; then the savage penalties will come into action. Not one of our farmers is going: but on driving yesterday to S. Angelo, on the other side of the valley, we discovered that, on the contrary, all the young men in that district have joined up. This will enable the Fascists to concentrate on the districts where there are most defaulters, and to 'make an example' of as many as they please. It is the old story, in this country, of lack of unity. (I am reminded of the state of things in Ireland in my childhood.) The same thing has just happened with the general strike, organized by the Communist, Socialist and Demo-Christian Parties as a protest against the penalties threatened by the Government for the young men who do not join up – and also, in some districts, against the lack of sufficient food for the workmen. The strike, which was intended to include all the workers of the German occupied territory, began on March 1st. According to Radio Roma it included a quarter of a million workers (one hundred and twenty thousand in Milan, thirty thousand in Turin and twelve thousand in Florence); according to the B.B.C., about five times as many. What is certain is that it was not the universal protest which was intended – and that the numbers of the strikers, in many cities, were small enough to permit the Government to inflict severe punishment on those who were courageous enough to take part.

March 9th

Antonio returns from Florence, where the atmosphere is not agreeable. Arrests continue, and he himself, while sitting quietly in a café, was caught in a German round-up. On showing his papers he was left in peace, but he saw the lorry of the less fortunate captives – both men and women – making its way down via Tornabuoni.

March 10th

The first mild spring day, Rome and Florence are both bombed, the latter severely, for the first time – also the station of Orvieto.

The peasant who is sheltering the three Englishmen comes back again. They are leaving, he says, to-night: and he asks for money to provide them with boots. A Mexican lieutenant (*la vedesse che degna persona!*),[1] who is now commanding one of the bands on Monte Amiata, came last night to fetch them – and though they are sad to leave and their hosts to see them go, there is no other choice, as this morning some Republican militia-

[1] 'You should see what a stout fellow.'

men have come down from Radicofani to search those woods for p.o.w.s and deserters. The band to which his guests are going, the farmer says, is already several thousand strong, with both Italian and Allied officers. If this is true, there will be some 'activity' in this district before long.

March 11th

The first signs of it have already appeared. Yesterday at dusk the fattore's boy came to tell his father that two men with muskets were hanging about the wood, just above the clinic. When the fattore went to investigate the men made no bones about their intentions: they were lying in wait for one of the forestry militiamen (who has made himself hated in the district) 'to bump him off'. The fattore protested that it was hardly tactful to do this at our front door — and after a while the men went off, saying they'd have another shot later on. In the evening we heard that four other armed men had been waiting near by, and that they all belong to a local band led by a young Jugoslav officer, who has been living all this winter on one of our farms.

Antonio meets an officer who (having gone over to the Republican Party) has returned from imprisonment in Germany, in the officers' camp at Przemysl. The conditions there, he said, were very bad, and the scarcity of food such that towards the end of the time he hardly had the strength to stand upright. (A report of the International Red Cross after inspecting these camps says that the food ration is the following: three hundred grs. of bread, to be divided in the three meals; a herb tea for breakfast; two boiled potatoes for lunch; two more for supper. That is all.) As soon, however, as he had agreed to join the Republican Party he was moved to another camp near Berlin, where conditions are entirely different and the food is the same as that given to the German officers. Those prisoners who have not gone over, however, still remain in Poland — and are presumably still starving.

Antonio also accidentally meets, at a lonely house some way away, a young German sergeant, whom (from the confused story he tells) he suspects of having deserted from Anzio. He is all to pieces, and says that it is hell there.

March 12*th*

A friend writes from Rome: 'The third Sunday in Lent: where shall we be before Passion Sunday? During air-raids I say to myself the Ninetieth Psalm: *Non timebis a timore nocturno, a sagitta volante in die, ab incurso et demonio meridiano.*'

Hear the broadcast of the Pope's Benediction of the faithful in Piazza San Pietro — a crowd chiefly composed of the homeless and starving refugees who have now flocked into the city. It was a short address, without any political flavour: an admission of the Pope's inability to stop or mitigate the horrors of war even within his own city, a final appeal to the rulers on both sides — and, to the congregation before him, a repetition of the well-known words of Christian consolation: 'Come unto me, all ye that are weary and heavy-laden.' Perhaps never, in all the history of suffering humanity, have these words been spoken to so great an assembly of the homeless, the penniless and the bereft. And when, the address ended, the Pope paused a moment before the Benediction, from thousands of throats came a cry of supplication, unforgettable by anyone who heard it — a cry which sounded like an echo of all the suffering that is torturing the world: 'Give us peace; oh, give us peace.'

March 14*th*

The local news is grim. Three young recruits who had failed to report have been shot in Siena, in the presence of their comrades, as 'an example'. At Piancastagnaio two partisans, who were caught in the woods, have been shot on the spot, and their corpses were hung at the gates of the city. In Florence the whole treasure of the Florentine synagogue — worth several millions and containing, besides wonderful silver work and brocades, the Holy Books of the congregation — has been found by members of the Political Bureau of the National Republican Guard in farm-houses near Fiesole and Prato, and has immediately been 'confiscated'.

Antonio sent for the young Jugoslav officer who is living in one of our farms and is said to be leading a band of local partisans; the young man, whose name is Larig, says that he has got about a hundred and twenty men, scattered in various farms — but denies that it was they who intended to kill the militiaman at our front door. He now intends, he says, to take all his men in small parties to join the partisan band on Monte Amiata, and the first party will start to-night. But they need wheat and oil, boots and clothes; will we help?

March 15th

Yesterday evening, after dusk, shadowy figures were lurking in our hedges and ditches: the new recruits of the partisans crossing the valley on their way to Monte Amiata. During the night the house of the forestry militiaman — which stands alone in the valley — was surrounded by thirty armed men, who then entered and captured its two inhabitants — confining themselves, however, this time, to threats and to taking off all the men's clothes, leaving them naked.

March 17th

Antonio returns at two a.m. from Rome, having met on the road German columns and tanks going north. The centre of the town, he reports, looks much the same as usual: all the bombing has been in the suburbs and near the stations. The chief trouble is the lack of water, which is now cut off from private houses but mercifully still remains in some of the public fountains. Long queues stand before them all day, and hand-carts go from house to house selling flasks of water at prices which once would have seemed dear for wine. No gas anywhere, and coal for cooking unprocurable. No light in some parts of the town. No motor-buses, but still some trams. But the really tragic problem is that of the refugees. There are now over a million of them in the city — evacuees from the bombed Castelli and from the coastal towns, and earlier refugees from southern Italy, who had gone farther north, and after the Anzio landing hurried down to Rome again 'so as to get home sooner' — as well as many anti-Fascists, who wish to get into touch with the Allies as quickly as possible. Most of them have not even got food-cards and cannot apply for them, since officially they are not there. So they mostly live in the suburbs, going into the centre of the town during the bombing hours, and living on a starvation allowance at the public kitchens. The Vatican is doing what it can and half a million bowls of soup have been distributed this last month by the *Circolo di S. Pietro* alone — but it is far from meeting the need.

A member of the German Secret Service in Rome tells a friend of ours that Rome will *not* be defended, inside the city. The Germans have given up all hope of throwing back the Allies into the sea at Anzio, and are accordingly removing some of their best troops from this front. They will continue their defences round Rome for the present, but if or when the Allies break through at Cassino, will withdraw above Florence, forming their defence line along the Apennines, from Spezia to Rimini. (This is good news for us in Tuscany.) And there — so far as the Italian front is concerned — they expect to remain for the rest of the war.

March 21st

Three days in Florence, seeing friends and doing some shopping — with some difficulty, as the shops have been combed by the Germans and lack even the most necessary things, such as baby's diapers and children's vests and jerseys. Moreover, there are two or three air-raid warnings a day, during which the shops are shut and the life of the town is held up. Most people do not take refuge in shelters, but merely go to the centre of the town — where the more devout congregate in the Duomo, and the more frivolous in the Lungarno or on the benches of Palazzo Strozzi. Last Saturday's bombing was confined to the Rifredi station, the factories round it (a large engine-depot was hit, destroying thirty-six engines) and some villas containing German Commands. But unfortunately one of these — which had previously held Germans — now contains the patients of the children's hospital, which has been moved out there for greater safety, and there were many casualties — a tragic business. Except for the alarms, and for a certain amount of shooting under one's windows at night, daily life seemed fairly normal — but everyone is strained and vaguely expecting some new move: and several of the defaulters of the 1922-25 classes have been executed.

March 22nd

Return home. The Poggibonsi and the Valdarno roads are now both cut (bridges on them bombed this morning) but the Chianti hill road is still clear, and full of German lorries which have also discovered this route.

On arriving, after dark, I find two strange young men hanging about the garden, and two others arguing indoors with Antonio. It appears that yesterday an unknown young man appeared on a bicycle and handed to Antonio an illiterate intimidatory letter, ostensibly from a group of partisans, containing a request for an immediate gift of eighty thousand lire. Antonio told him to get out. Then this evening these two others turned up, also with requests for money to help the partisans. Antonio said that he would consider helping them if they could show any proof that they really were partisans — whereupon his guests turned upon each other with eloquent mutual accusations of dishonesty. Finally they went off — and we are now expecting the arrival of other envoys.

March 24th

Last night about a hundred and fifty partisans slept in some of our farms, about a mile away. They turned up in the morning with sacks of flour, baked their bread in the farmer's oven, and then borrowed his cart to take the loaves away. They had plenty of oil with them (presumably taken from some farm) and a certain amount of tinned food, mostly peaches. Later on in the day, when some German lorries drove up here to fetch some wine, the partisans thought that they were looking for them and prepared an ambush on the hill with machine guns — but the lorries drove back to Chianciano, unaware of their narrow escape. It looks as if our local guerrilla were beginning.

March 25th

The district nurse (who spends her time tramping from farm to farm, as a severe epidemic of pneumonia — a sort of Spanish influenza — has broken out) reports that at one of our farms, the Sassaia, there are two boys of the 1924 class in bed, dangerously ill with pneumonia — one the farmer's son, who had joined the partisans, and the other a boy from Bergamo, who knocked one night at the farm for shelter, already very ill. We send them some warm clothes, medicines, milk and food, and the nurse will look after them as best she can. The boy from Bergamo ought to be moved to the clinic for proper nursing, but we dare not do so for fear of being caught.

The Swiss radio informs us that yesterday in Rome, at a celebration of the twenty-fifth anniversary of the foundation of the Fascist Party, a bomb was thrown by partisans in via Rasella, killing thirty-two German officers and men. The reprisal was swift: a proclamation declaring that for every German killed, ten hostages ('to be selected in those circles which are *presumably* responsible for the crime') will be shot.

March 26th

A letter from Rome, received a few days ago, affirms that the Allies 'will arrive' (it does not specify where) before the end of the month. The partisan bands in this district now include many groups which have come down here from farther north, and there are continual rumours of a fresh landing near by — while certainly the bombing of railways and roads has, within the last few days, been intensified. But there have been so many false alarms before that it is difficult not to be sceptical.

March 27th

Find on my breakfast tray a note from the nurse: 'Have got a man here with a bullet through his shoulder, who killed a Fascist last night. What shall I do with him?' Hastily go down to the clinic, and find there three young partisans, all armed, and one with his arm in a sling. One of them is Larig, whom increasingly we do not trust. (Indeed he has hinted that he would be willing to play a double game and act as a spy for the Germans if they should make it worth his while.) The wounded partisan states that last night he and some friends broke into an inn to try and rescue a friend of the 1925 class who had been captured by the Fascist militia. Everyone appears to have fired indiscriminately in a small room; one Fascist was killed, and two others wounded. After his wound has been dressed, the young man goes off to one of our farms, arranging to return after dark for further dressings. Larig, in an attempt to persuade us to give him more food and money, states that an 'English and an Italian general' were 'in these parts' last night, but when pressed, wriggles out of it. A very fishy customer.

At night, as Antonio opens the window before going to bed, a bullet whizzes by — quite close, but presumably not aimed at him. All these young men appear to be very 'easy on the trigger'. (This does not, of course, necessarily mean that they would fight well.)

March 28th

A continual stream of partisans is still passing by, as well as many young soldiers who have escaped from a German labour camp near Orvieto, and are trying to get back to their homes in the north. Six of them turn up this evening, receive food and some clothes, and spend the night in one of the stables. Earlier in the day, two Englishmen turned up — both from Newcastle — who were in a camp near Verona at the time of the armistice. They have twice tried to get through the German lines, and have twice been captured and escaped again. They are particularly cheerful, resourceful young men. At one time, they said, they belonged to a small band of seventy partisans near Florence, but didn't think much of it. I tell them of the partisans near here, and they think they will try to join them, but when I say they are beginning to help themselves to what they need, say firmly: 'We shouldn't like that.' Send them on, however, to Fonte Lippi, where they can see and decide for themselves.

March 29th

Monday's incident is likely to have a tiresome sequel. Yesterday afternoon a note was brought me, warning me that the Carabinieri of Montepulciano have been informed that the wounded partisan has taken shelter in our clinic — and that they propose to come and arrest him to-morrow. Antonio is away in Siena, so I send the fattore off to warn the farms. Discover that the story was given away by the nurse's small niece, who chattered to another child, 'We've got a wounded patriot in the house!' And so the story spread — and now we may expect trouble. After Antonio's return we hold a council of war, and instruct the nurse *not* to deny having dressed the man's wound, but to point out that, as he was accompanied by two armed men, she had no choice but to do what she was told. She is to add that he left as soon as the wound was dressed, saying that he was leaving the district. (The young man, meanwhile, is hidden in one of our farms, where the nurse is continuing to dress his wound.)

March 30th

Spent yesterday evening in expectation of a Fascist visit — but, as nobody has come, Antonio decided this morning to take the bull by the horns and went off to Montepulciano to call on the captain of the Carabinieri. A curious conversation then ensued, in which the captain fully agreed that there was nothing else that we could have done about the wounded partisan. '*I* certainly can't protect you,' he remarked, 'you must manage as best you can.' Antonio pointed out that he would probably receive further demands from the partisans for wheat, oil, etc., and that he would be obliged to grant them — and this, too, the captain agreed was inevitable.

Meanwhile we continue to have many self-invited guests. This morning I met two American prisoners just outside the house. And this afternoon, walking up our private wood-path to the chapel, Antonio heard some rustling in the bushes, and found a party of fifteen men, armed with a tommy-gun and muskets, and three of them wearing the Communist Red Star — lying in wait, they said, 'for anyone who comes to make trouble'. Antonio had an amicable conversation with them, suggesting that it is better to avoid unnecessary bloodshed — and then left them there.

March 31st

The partisans are now guarding all the roads which lead to this part of the world. The Carabinieri got as far as Casalvento and then turned back, having been warned. Most of them, indeed, are on excellent terms with the partisans, who only fire upon the Fascist militiamen. But now it appears that the Republican Government is proposing to order the Carabinieri to wear the same uniform as the militiamen — and if this is carried out, most of the Carabinieri will desert and join the partisans.

April 3rd

This morning a party of armed partisans came into our little school, took down the portrait of Mussolini (which, by law, the teachers are obliged to have there) and then, going up to the teacher's house, searched it for arms and ammunition. Since they did not come to our house, nor into the farm or the clinic, it is clear that the intention was merely to frighten the teacher, the only 'republican' on the place. Subsequently they pinned up the Duce's picture on a wall and shot at it. A childish performance — but one that has succeeded in frightening the teacher.

April 4th

To Siena for the day. Hear that the Carabinieri of both Campiglia and Castiglion d'Orcia have been disarmed by the partisans, and that a militiaman on duty with the Carabinieri was ordered to dig his own grave. When the wretched man had done so the partisans told him that this time they would only put his hat in the grave, but that next time he ventured out he would follow it. He is now in bed, with a high temperature.

Not far away another large farm was broken into by a band, who removed one hundred and fifty thousand lire as well as twelve pairs of sheets and some food. More and more (as in this case) the partisans are resorting to looting — a fact which is bitterly deplored both by the genuine patriots among them, and by the timid, but perfectly honest, peasant boys who have joined them merely to avoid their army service.

April 5th

A woman, in a great state of dismay, comes running from Pianoia to warn us that lorries containing eight hundred Fascists (more likely eighty) from Siena have gone to attack the partisans at Montichiello, about five miles away, and may come on here.

Spend the morning in expectation, but no one turns up but a charming, gentle and footsore South African prisoner – in need of some food, some socks and a toothbrush. As it does not seem very safe for him to linger near the house to-day I take these things up to him in the woods, and sit talking to him for some time, listening to the firing from Montichiello, and discussing what he shall do next. He tells us that at one time he joined one of the partisan bands himself but left when he discovered that they were going in for robbery. While I was talking to him, the firing appeared to be getting nearer – so he puts his boots on again, and sets off in the opposite direction.[1] We then hear that the Fascists, who are now said to be about three hundred, surrounded a neighbour's house early in the morning, and searched it for prisoners or partisans – and that now a 'battle' is in progress round Montichiello. The sporadic firing goes on until sundown.

April 6th

Poor Corrado – the boy at the Sassaia who came home with pneumonia after a few weeks in the woods as a partisan – has died, and five other people in the same house are seriously ill. It appears to be a form of Spanish 'flu', ending in pneumonia, and there are about eighty cases of it on the place. To-night we have been to the boy's funeral, a tragic business, with his mother keening over the grave. As we waited at Palazzolo for the funeral

[1] After his return to South Africa he wrote a charming letter of thanks: 'You may remember a foot-sore prisoner turning up one midday at La Foce – one among the many you helped – and receiving sundry items of assistance from you and your husband, including ointment for his feet and a route of the way to Laterina. It was the afternoon that the Fascists turned up from Siena and attacked the local partisans, and perhaps you may remember in what a hurry I had to leave when the shooting started in the hills surrounding your home – in such a hurry that I ran off with your pencil – which I fear I cannot return. I shall never forget how grateful I was for the socks you gave me; in a few days my feet healed completely . . . I stayed at Laterina until Cassino fell two months later, then pushed south with a Tommy who had called at your place the day after my visit. We wanted to call in again, but your contadini warned us that Jerry had got in first, so we went regretfully by . . . The kindness of the Italian people I shall never forget. They could not do enough for us who were wandering around waiting for the Allies . . . When I went home, I regretfully said farewell to the country that had meant so much to me. . . .'

procession to come walking up the country road, a party of about twenty partisans, with pistols stuck in their belts and guns over shoulders, looking for all the world like brigands in a melodrama, suddenly appeared over the crest of the hill — then, on seeing the funeral procession approaching, settled down to wait under the pines. Later on, when we had gone home, they came down and laid some flowers on their comrade's grave.

April 10*th*

Hear further details of the 'battle of Montichiello'. It appears to have been in the best medieval tradition — the partisans having taken up their position behind the old walls of the little city, the Fascists attacking. There were about two hundred and fifty Fascists, and a hundred and twenty partisans. The local population took an active part, the younger women helping the partisans with the loading, the old ones bringing in *coppie d'ova* (couples of eggs) to refresh the combatants. The partisans' popularity was no doubt partly due to the fact that on the preceding day — having stopped a lorry of the government food supplies laden with wheat — they had proceeded to distribute the wheat, in the manner of Robin Hood, to the population. The Fascists, on the other hand, arrived at a small farm without any rations, and commandeered food for all their men. After eleven hours' fighting, when the Fascists were already disheartened, the partisans made a sally down the hill — the women on the ramparts shouting, *forza, ragazzi!*[1] — and the Fascists ignominiously turned tail and fled, leaving some of their arms behind them. Then they climbed into their lorries and drove back to Siena — and the partisans, in their turn, made good their retreat during the night on Monte Amiata. Only two of them were killed — one during the fighting, and one wretched peasant boy, who, having gone home with toothache, was caught by the Fascists in the very act of trying to get rid of his hand-grenade in a field, and was shot on

[1] 'Go on, boys!'

the spot. The Fascist losses it is impossible to estimate, since they took their dead and wounded away with them.

On the next morning – Good Friday – the population of Montichiello was awakened by a battering at their doors: German troops from Chianciano (summoned by telephone by the retreating Fascists) entered the town, turned all the population out of doors, and searched every house – without finding a single rebel or a single gun. On the Saturday a further party of about thirty Fascists, together with five lorry-loads of Germans, attempted a mopping-up in the valley, but only succeeded in killing one blameless old peasant whose cart had been requisitioned by the partisans.

April 11th

Three old friends arrive: Bert, the cook of the p.o.w.s at the Castelluccio, with two of his companions – the purpose of their call being to get their boots resoled! They have been asked to supper on Easter Day, they tell us, in one of our farms – and then will come back here to pick up their boots, and will move farther south again. I provide them with tennis shoes of Antonio's to wear meanwhile, and take their boots down to our farm cobbler, who can hardly fail to recognize the British Army boots, but asks no questions and sets to work. For a short time, they say, they joined one of the bands on Monte Amiata (about four thousand strong, under the command of an officer in the Indian Army), but a Fascist punitive expedition in that district has caused them to move on.

April 12th

To-day I have received a visit from two other Englishmen, whom I found sitting in deck-chairs in my garden! I suggest that we should move up to a more secluded spot in the woods and there we have an agreeable conversation. Both educated men, who have now been prisoners in Italy for nearly three years, they speak of recent events ('from a worm's eye view', as they say themselves) with great moderation and good sense. They are only too well aware of the change in feeling here in the last few months — caused partly by the indiscriminate bombing, but even more by the Allies' dilatoriness. 'Do you realize,' they say, 'that for the last fifty miles everyone whom we have asked for help has sent us on to you? Hadn't you better be careful?' They are, however, unable to suggest what form such carefulness should take — and as we are sitting talking, at the edge of a pine wood over the brow of the hill, I become aware that someone is standing behind us — a ragged, unshaven figure, watching us in silence. I hastily get up, my mind full of the tales of Fascist spies, and go towards him — only to observe, to my intense relief, that he is wearing Antonio's tennis shoes! He is one of Bert's friends — and with great relief I take back the news to the other p.o.w.s, who have meanwhile moved off into a thicket. 'What a life you do lead!' — they remark, and we part with mutual expressions of good will.

April 13th
  Take Benedetta up the hill (where there is a good meeting-place for such encounters, away from the farm and the road) to say good-bye to Bert and his friends, whose boots are now mended. Benedetta says 'Humpty-Dumpty' to them. 'Nice to hear a kiddy speaking English out here,' says Bert.
  Talk to a young partisan at one of our farms. He is much concerned, as are his comrades, with the problem of Larig — who took no part in the Montichiello fighting, is drinking the wine and selling the foodstuffs entrusted to him, and who they are afraid may give them all away. Moreover, he has seduced a girl of sixteen, the daughter of one of the workmen on the place, and is trying to get her to run away with him.
  His former comrades are proposing to take the law into their own hands, and get rid of him.

April 14th

Drive down to Sassaia with the children to see the mother of Corrado — the boy who died last Thursday. The whole family are in a pitiful state, having all caught the fever, too. Their kindness is really amazing. When Corrado was at his worst, and most of the rest of the family ill, they yet managed to take in another young partisan of the same age — a complete stranger — and nurse him back to health, and when they spoke of it, they said their only regret was that they had not been able to take in two of the British prisoners who stayed with them before. 'But they've promised to come for a visit, after the war.' At the next farm, Olmaia, I find yet another stray young man in bed with bronchitis. He has run away from a German labour camp near Orvieto. Five of his companions — all from the same camp — are digging the vineyard in return for their lunch and supper, and will proceed to-morrow on their long tramp to their home, Bergamo.

As we are walking down the hill with the children we hear a loud explosion quite near, followed by many smaller ones — and then fourteen small fighters fly over our heads, very low. Remembering all the stories about machine-gunning, I wonder whether to make the children lie down in a ditch — but decide to chance it, and Benedetta looks up and says, 'How nice and near they are to-day!'

When we get home we hear that a German munition-dump near Chianciano has been hit — with a good many casualties, mostly among the workmen. We also find three Italian deserters sitting in the courtyard still in uniform. One of them has hurt his ankle and can't go on. Take him to the clinic to be tied up, and find lodgings for the night for the other two.

April 15th

A letter from Rome. Life there is increasingly difficult and expensive. No list has been published of the three hundred and twenty hostages shot in reprisal for the bomb which killed thirty-two Germans — and consequently all those whose friends or relations are in prison cannot discover whether they are alive or dead. Arrests continue, on a variety of pretexts, and no one knows on whom the next blow may fall. Bombing is only in the outskirts, but the air-raid warnings are very frequent, and guns can be heard in the distance from the Anzio front. Every day the Romans say, 'To-day something will happen', every day drags on, without any change.

April 16th

In Florence, Prof. Gentile is murdered — shot in his car as he was driving up the via del Salviatino one evening. He was head of the new *Accademia*, and the intellectual apostle of Fascism — guilty, in many people's view, of *la trahison des clercs*, but a sincere and honest man. It is a mean and despicable crime, worthy of those committed on the other side, and an instance of the blind party hatred by which this unhappy country is torn. One is reminded of Dostoevski's comment on his own country. '*Mon avis à moi, c'est qu'en notre temps on ne sait plus du tout qui estimer en Russie. Et convenez que c'est une affreuse calamité, pour un pays, de ne plus savoir qui estimer.*'

April 17th

Spend the morning trying to alter the date of birth on the identity card of a young deserter who turned up this morning and firmly requested this service — with the same confidence with which others have asked for a clean shirt or some food. It is much more difficult to do than one would think, even though the type of my machine is fortunately of the same size as that used in his document, the difficulty being to put the new figure precisely in line with the others. And clumsiness is lent to one's fingers by the thought that the boy's life may hang on its being done well.

Antonio comes to tell me that the leaders of the local band are going to-morrow night to meet 'a general' who has come up from Rome to organize them. They certainly need it.

April 19th

To Siena to-day, leaving at six a.m. to avoid the Allied planes. See on the road many burned-up lorries and cars, and arrive in Siena just twenty minutes before the first air-raid. Air-raid warnings continue steadily all through the day until five p.m., and during them the shops are closed, so that it is difficult to get one's shopping done. We leave at seven p.m., when the obligingly punctual planes are supposed to have left, and get home without incident. Yesterday, however, the little old horse-bus with orange curtains was machine-gunned on that road near Buonconvento, and three people were killed. Our school-teacher, too, was machine-gunned, driving in a pony-cart on a country road, and only escaped by throwing herself down in a ditch.

April 20th

F.G. writes that the Maremma is now full of Kalmuks, volunteers from Astrakan, Kirghis, etc., who have joined the German Army to avoid starvation. They are simple, friendly people, who get on very well with the peasants and call the Contessa Boba (who is Russian) 'Mama' — but they don't think much of the dry soil of the Maremma, and long for their own rich, black soil.

April 21st

To-day the Jugoslav, Larig, has been 'liquidated' — to the great relief of us all. He had extracted further sums of money from several people at Abbadia (pretending that he was head of a band) and had taken an apartment at Montepulciano, to which he was about to take one of our farm-girls whom he had seduced, threatening to shoot her parents if they opposed him. There was nothing for it for his former companions but to take the law into their own hands. Early this morning five young men broke into his room, disarmed him, and took him away towards Monte Amiata — from where, presumably, he will not return. This morning our nurse met them on their way: Larig very pale between two armed men, and three others behind.

April 22nd

Bombs were dropped in the valley this morning, shaking the house — aimed at the bridge on the Orcia. Then the bomber formation (thirty-six) flew over our heads, and bombed Chiusi and the railway line. The explosions were loud even up here, and the children were frightened, especially those whose houses had been destroyed in Turin. Benedetta, never having seen any danger, was quite unmoved, and continues to refer to the airmen as *bon citti* (good boys). A lorry full of evacuees, all women and children, was hit at the Acquaviva crossing — twenty people wounded and eleven killed. Bracci, going down to help, had his car machine-gunned and only just escaped with his life.

The brother of Larig was also caught last night in Chiarantana, and taken off to Monte Amiata — where presumably he will share his brother's fate.

In the afternoon one of our peasants, living in a farm which has only narrowly escaped bombing, comes up to ask for advice, because *le mi' donne* (my womenfolk) are so frightened that they want to leave the farm. We can only say, while sympathizing, that there are no absolutely safe places, and that all any of us can do is to stay where we belong.

The Allies' intention is clearly to stop all German traffic, by air, road or rail. And in this, except at night, they are now being completely successful.

As we are weeding the garden, the gardener comes running up: 'The partisans are killing a Fascist! He has taken refuge in the clinic with his wife and baby.' We go down there and find a group of about fifteen partisans, in picturesque garments and very much over-armed, surrounding the clinic, from which they had turned out the patients and children. Antonio goes up to their leader, who chooses to call himself *Uragano* (Hurricane), and asks what it is all about. Apparently a Fascist (in uniform and belonging to the S.S.) who was on his way back from Rome, had got a lift with his brother, wife and small baby on a German lorry as far as the main road, and had then attempted to walk across our valley to Chianciano, wheeling the pram with their luggage. Just below the clinic, however, three partisans came out of the wood and demanded the Fascist's pistol. His brother threw himself upon the partisan, and, after a struggle, disarmed him: the three then ran off to call their comrades, who were resting in a farm near by, while the Fascists, with the woman and baby, took refuge indoors. Other partisans then appeared, surrounded the house, and were exchanging threats with the Fascists out of the window — until Uragano appeared and tried to calm them down. Antonio points out the idiocy of the whole performance, and tries to persuade them to release the man, after disarming him. This most of them are prepared to do, but two or three are sullen. 'It's all very fine,' they say, 'but they would show *us* no mercy if they had us in their hands.' Meanwhile I go indoors, and find the woman in hysterics, and the baby (only one month old) howling while its father was changing its diapers. Take them upstairs, and give them some coffee, while outside an interminable argument goes on. Some of the men want the Fascist's life, some only his badges, others want to take him as a hostage. One of the rebels says he wants the personal satisfaction of cutting off the badges, and goes indoors. Uragano goes up with him, I follow — and we find the ferocious Fascist rocking his baby in his arms. He docilely removes the badges with his nail-scissors, and the partisan explains that he has joined the patriots in order to avenge his brother, who had been killed by the Fascists. Then, quite amicably, he goes off with the badges, and outside the argument begins again. At last Uragano's men give way, and the whole party (in our pony-cart, and minus their shoes, which had been taken by the partisans) is allowed to set off for Chianciano.

April 24th

I walk down to the men's institute, and there meet B. — the real leader of Uragano's band. He only arrived last night, and was much annoyed about yesterday's silly performance. 'You are behaving exactly like Fascists yourselves,' he told his men, and to me he expresses his discouragement and the difficulty of persuading them to sensible behaviour. We then have a long and (under the circumstances) slightly comic conversation on the theme of the Liberal tradition of moderation, in the middle of which a messenger turns up with fresh news: a mopping-up of the bands is in progress just across the valley, at Vivo d'Orcia, Campiglia and Abbadia. Our young friends of yesterday, he told me, had now moved into one of our farms at the top of the hill, Palazzone — where no doubt those who escape across the valley will now join them. Four lorries of Fascists are also said to have arrived at Chianciano, on their way here.

On my way home I meet one of the lorries, at the turn of the road, by the nursery-school, bearing about twelve very anxious-looking Fascists, with their guns sticking out on either side. They slow down and I hastily tell the children to go indoors, thinking that we may have some fighting if the partisans turn up. But after a while the Fascists drive on towards Contignano. Ten minutes later another lorry, belonging to the Farmers' Association of the province, and laden with lambs, comes up the hill, and turns past the Castelluccio towards Montepulciano. But it never reaches its destination: at Pianoia it is attacked by the partisans, who order its driver to go up to the Palazzone. There they help themselves to as many lambs as they require, and then let the lorry and its driver proceed — having thus obligingly made their whereabouts quite clear to everyone. Antonio rather annoyed about this.

At lunch-time two peasant-women appear, carrying heavy sacks, which contain parcels for their sons, prisoners in Germany, and ask me to take their parcels to the Red Cross in Florence. The parcel-post here has ceased to function, but the poor women continue to get letters from their sons, begging for food. One of the women, not having received from her son the form without which no parcel can be sent off, has borrowed one from a friend — unaware, not being able to read, that the printed address is that of an entirely different camp. I have the greatest difficulty in persuading her that the parcel will never reach her son, and her misery when at last she realizes that it cannot be sent is pitiful.

At tea-time the fattore turns up to say that one of 'our' prisoners — Bert the cook — has turned up again with an urgent message. We walk up to our meeting-place in the woods, and he tells us that he and his mates have now joined one of the partisan bands operating on Monte Amiata. He has come to warn us about the mopping-up which has now begun in the district. It began early this morning at Vivo d'Orcia and Campiglia. About four hundred Germans with machine-guns surrounded the villages and arrested some of the civilian population — including the parish priest of Campiglia and about a hundred others. The partisans scattered into the woods, and, though there was some sporadic shooting, so far as he knows very few were caught. The Germans also went to some farms along the road, took some peasants away with them, and helped themselves to some pigs, flour, sheets, etc. Bert had also heard an optimistic rumour that the German line at Cassino has broken, and that this is the beginning of their retreat. We tell him that to-day's B.B.C. news in no way confirmed this story, but that the last report from Rome (brought by hand) is that the Allies are expected here before May 10th.

While we are talking another partisan turns up, bringing the news that the civilians have been released, and that the Germans are now coming in this direction. He is on horseback and is bound for our farm, Palazzone (where a large group of partisans are living) to give the alarm.

The same young man tells me that Larig was shot, after a trial by the partisans, on the evening after his capture. He was proved to have abstracted over two hundred thousand lire of partisan funds, and to have been in possession of information and lists of names (including ours) which he intended to hand over to the Germans. The poor girl whom he seduced is still expecting his return.

We spend the evening burying beneath the olive-mill such hams, sausages, oil and sugar as we still have above ground, in preparation for a German visit.

April 25th

The nurse comes to tell me that Giorgia, the young Venetian partisan who had pneumonia at the Sassaia, whom we had nursed back to health, and who had joined the local partisans, turned up here this morning with a violent haemorrhage. What are we to do? We dare not take him into the clinic, where he would immediately be captured, and he is not fit to walk. Finally, after the nurse has given him an injection to check the haemorrhage, we decide to send him up the hill to Palazzone in the pony-cart. There, among his friends, he will be safer, and yet not out of reach of nursing.

In the afternoon a German sergeant, looking for billets for a 'Pferde Lazaret', comes to inspect the Castelluccio; he thinks it will probably suit him, and says that his C.O. will come to-morrow to decide. The news spreads fast, and grows in the spreading, so that before he is well out of the house everyone on the place has already heard that the Germans are coming to mop up this district, too.

April 26th

A German officer comes up, and inspects the Castelluccio. Antonio points out (1) that it has already been reserved to store the goods of the hotel-keeper of Chianciano. (2) That there is insufficient water. (3) That there is no stabling. To which the German — a Prussian of the worst type — merely replies that he will require the whole of the castle for his three hundred men, stabling for eight hundred horses in the farms, and quarters for his eight officers in our house. As to the refugee children, we must find lodgings for them 'elsewhere'. He then goes off, saying that he will let us know his decision in three or four days.

Antonio drives down to Chianciano to get in touch with the Kommandantur there, and lodge a protest, but on arriving at the village he is stopped by a sentry who, pointing a pistol at him, orders him to report himself at once to the Albergo Centrale. Meanwhile the Maresciallo dei Carabinieri comes up and advises Antonio to go home. Someone has been killed — the Maresciallo does not know who or why — Germans and Fascists are searching all the houses, and several arrests have been made.

Antonio returns home, and together we hurry off to warn B., the leader of the partisans, to move his men farther away.

Meanwhile the fattore has had an account of what has happened on Monte Amiata. It appears that two German S.S. men, who pretended to be Austrian deserters, have for some time been wandering from farm to farm in the district of Vivo d'Orcia, Abbadia and Campiglia, saying that they had lost touch with the band to which they belonged, and asking for help. From one farm they were handed on to the next, until they had discovered the whole network of the farms in touch with the rebels. Finally they went to the old parish priest of Vivo d'Orcia — and, under false pretences, succeeded in extracting from him some more information including the whereabouts of the partisan command. Whereupon, last Monday, German troops appeared, surrounded the three villages and the outlying farms, and arrested all the men whom the two spies pointed out, including some women and the priest. About a hundred of them are still shut up in the school of Abbadia, with German sentries—and some of them are to be shot.

This is the second local instance of such spying by alleged partisans — so we warn everyone on the farm to be careful. Nothing is more likely than that a similar attempt will be made here, too.

In the afternoon we hear that the man who was killed at Chianciano this morning was one of our workmen, Mencatelli — a quiet, peaceable, hard-working fellow, totally unconcerned with politics, whose murder seems to us inexplicable. His wife rings me up, and implores me to go down to her. I drive down, and find two German sentries barring the road. They let me pass, and, as my car drives up the empty street, terrified faces appear at the windows. What new danger, they think, is coming now? In the dead man's little house, which, after thirty years of hard work and self-denial, he had at last succeeded in owning, the widow is hysterically moaning and sobbing beside the bed of her boy of eleven, who saw his father killed. The child is in a queer state of coma, from which he awakes at intervals to a fit of shivering and sobbing, then sinks back again. His mother and some other women continue moaning and crying, repeating the miserable story over and over again. It appears that, when the German and Fascist troops began to search the houses nearby, poor Mencatelli, terrified of being taken off to a labour camp, hid in his little attic. The boy, hearing that the attics in other houses were being searched, shouted to him to come down, but he was too panic-stricken to do so, and crouched there, in frozen terror, waiting. Finally the soldiers, a German and a Fascist, came tramping up the stairs and, throwing aside the weeping woman and child, climbed up the attic ladder. As soon as they saw the defenceless little man crouching there, the Fascist fired, hitting him in the head. He was killed instantaneously, before the eyes of his wife and child. When I saw him, already laid in his bed, his head swathed in white bandages, and a few faded stocks scattered on his pillow, his tired, drawn face still had a look of terror.

Of all the Fascist crimes that I myself have seen this is the ugliest, meanest and most purposeless. But we are *all* guilty. 'Any man's death diminishes me, because I am involved in mankind.'

I drive in to Chianciano, to try and make arrangements for the funeral – and find the streets entirely empty, and on the walls a notice stating that, while the German authorities deplore what had occurred, they consider it to be the fault of the local population, owing to their unco-operativeness and general hostility. In consequence, there will be a curfew at eight-thirty p.m., and the population is warned that any further attempt at sabotage will be followed by the arrest of ten hostages.

When I get home the nurse is waiting for me. She has been up to Palazzone to see Giorgia, and there has found him lying on some straw in the stable, in foul air, with eighteen other men. She and B. carried him upstairs to the only available room, where another boy was in bed with pneumonia, but the effort of moving caused another haemorrhage. When she got up to leave, slow tears poured down his face. He is only twenty-one, away from home, and probably dying.

We discuss what is best for him. What he needs is proper nursing at the clinic, but it is at the cross-roads, the first place Germans would search. In the end we decide to leave him where he is.

And so I go to bed, my heart full of the murdered workman, and of the young partisan who soon must die.

May 1st

Yesterday an uncomfortable little episode. Two German soldiers turned up in the farm, one in plain clothes and one in uniform. They immediately inquired whether there were any Fascists here, and then asked to see Antonio, told him that they were deserters, and asked for food, money and plain clothes for the one in uniform. Antonio, feeling something fishy about them, firmly refused, whereupon they professed great astonishment. 'But', they cried, 'haven't we come to the right place? Aren't you the gentleman who speaks German and English — and his wife too — and who have helped thirty-three British prisoners to escape? Didn't you give civilian clothes to two Austrian deserters? Why won't you help us, too?' Antonio firmly denied it all. And now they became threatening: 'You'll live to regret it — the Cassino line can't hold — and you'll see what will happen to you afterwards!' But in the end they went off, grumbling. Later on we discovered that they came here with the two so-called Austrian deserters, who have been wandering about the country for some time, and presumably got this information from them — that they lunched to-day at one of the farms, called and asked questions at the clinic and workmen's club (where they forced the men playing bowls to buy them some socks) and eventually asked the farmer, in whose house they had lunched, for arms, saying: 'Two hundred Germans are at the Castelluccio, and we must defend ourselves!' The farmer fortunately said he had none, and they went off. We still have no idea whether they were spies or genuine deserters.

To-day another incident of the same kind. While Antonio is out on the farm, I meet a young man in the courtyard who insists on speaking to me alone, tells me that he is a partisan, and says that he has got three wounded men hidden in the wood, for whom he needs bandages and medicines at once. Something about him makes me feel sceptical, and my doubts increase when he goes on to state that his men are three hundred in number, and are in hiding in a part of the woods which I know to be already inhabited by B.'s band. He then proceeds — in an increasingly truculent tone — to demand money and food for his men. I refuse point blank, but he insists in waiting for Antonio at the edge of the woods. I accordingly send out the fattore to him (first explaining my suspicions) — and the latter, unfortunately, has a bright idea. While they are standing talking, he sees one of 'our' partisans coming down the wood road (on his way to the farm to fetch some food), and signals to him: 'This man seems to be looking for you.' The partisan asks a few questions — takes in the situation — and, pulling out a pistol, points it at the young man. 'If you really need help and bandages, you'll find everything you need with us. Come along!' And, with his pistol in the small of the stranger's back, they disappear into the woods.

The fattore returns triumphantly to me — 'That's settled him!' — and is somewhat downcast when I point out that, on the contrary, if the young man succeeds in escaping from the partisans, and really is a Fascist spy, it is we who are up a tree: for the fattore has thus clearly shown that we are on the best of terms with the partisans. Nor are our anxieties diminished by the information proffered by one of our workmen (who happened to have been in the Army with my visitor) that he is the brother-in-law of the Segretario del Fascio of Chianciano.

After dusk the partisan leader, B., comes to tell us: the young man, he says, is still being questioned, and they cannot make up their minds whether he is a spy — in which case they know how to deal with him — or whether he was merely trying to get some money out of me on false pretences. He is now in tears, imploring the partisans to accept him as a recruit.

May 2nd

Drive to Montepulciano, where I am shown an unpleasant little article against me in the official Fascist paper of Siena, the *Republica Fascista*. It says: 'For four years of war it has been tolerated by everyone (first by the Fascist Party, then by the forty-five days' carnival, and now even by the Republican Fascist Party) that an Anglo-American woman, rolling in wealth (*straricca*) should comfortably live as she pleases in her own domain, under cover of large donations to public charities. But charity is one thing: the spirit behind it another.

'First the fifty British prisoners, who were sent to work on her land, and who, on September 8th, took refuge in the surrounding woods, called her their "loving sister"; then the refugees of Badoglio, on their way home, called her their "generous mother". Now her lonely property, alone out of the whole of this province, where rebel hands are committing deeds of violence of every kind, has not been included in the official reports of robbery and violence suffered by all the surrounding villages and farms. These are symptoms that cannot be neglected. All our enemies, male or female, rich or poor, must be isolated and put under guard, *all* of them!'

This virulent little note, clearly springing from some personal spite, would not in itself be worth our attention — were it not that the paper in which it appeared is under the direct control of the Prefect. Moreover, its appearance at the same time as that of our recent visitors — if indeed they were spies — may be something more than a coincidence. We accordingly decide that it is better to take the bull by the horns. Antonio will go to-morrow to Siena, and tackle the Prefect about it — and I will go on to Florence, take a report of our situation to the German Consul, and perhaps stay there for a few days until the storm has blown over.

At midnight, as we are sitting discussing these plans, there is a false alarm. We hear, in the silence of the night, a lorry driving slowly up the hill, and it stops at our door. Antonio says: 'Get your hat and coat while I go out to meet them — and go out by the garden door into the woods' — I get my things, and then stand in the hall waiting — until a few minutes later he comes back: 'They've gone on again.' We then laugh at ourselves. But it's a tiring way to live!

May 3rd
Leave at three-thirty a.m. for Florence to avoid machine-gunning on the road. Deep fog in the Val d'Arbia; we meet

long German horse convoys, which delay us. Otherwise the journey is without incident, and I arrive in Florence at seven a.m. My friends there are inclined to take the newspaper article and our situation very seriously — since it appears that there have been several recent arrests on much slighter foundation. At the German Consulate the vice-consul, Wildt, too, is not inclined to make light of it, and both he and the consul, Wolff, say that we have done well to go to them before there was serious trouble. They advise me to send them a written report of our situation, and say that Antonio should send in a similar report to the German C.O. at Siena. If we should be arrested later, they will show this document (or part of it) to the S.S., and it may help to get us out again. But they themselves confirm my anxiety not to show it to the S.S. *now*, for fear of arousing an inquiry into the affairs of this district. In the Casentino and Mugello, the punitive expeditions of the S.S., and especially those of the Hermann Goering division, have been indescribably brutal. At Stia (where German troops had been fired upon from a window) every member of the male population has been shot; in the Val di Chiana the village of San Pancrazio has been burned to the ground; at San Godenzo, women have been raped and a child killed. Everywhere farms have been plundered and burned. There is no reason to suppose that this district would be treated with any greater leniency. Finally the consul, with a certain humour, warmly implored us not to get arrested both together! He is spending his whole time, he said, in getting innocent Italian families out of prison — but it is so much more convenient when at least one member of the family is free to take some steps about it himself![1]

I accordingly reluctantly agree to stay on in Florence for a few days — and send a report of the circumstances to Antonio, who is waiting in Siena.

[1] Wolff and Wildt — both civilized and humane men — have probably done more than any Italian, in the last few months of the German occupation, to save innocent people from the Germans, and also to protect Italian houses and works of art. In doing this, with great courage, they incurred grave suspicion from their own countrymen.

May 4th

Here everyone is much shaken by the bombing of yesterday and the day before, which has been far more serious than any
preceding attack, and has caused much destruction in the Campo
di Marte area, and by the Porta al Prato, where there was a
repair-shop for engines — the only one in this part of Italy. On
the first day the bombs missed it — hitting instead the Teatro
Comunale (where a rehearsal of *Cosi fan tutte* was in progress)
and destroying many villini in the district.

May 5th

The murder of Gentile was followed by the arrest of four
university professors (anti-Fascist, but wholly unconnected with
the event) — but since then the matter has been dropped so completely by the authorities, that it is rumoured that it is the Fascist
extremists themselves who are responsible for the crime. Certainly it is true that Gentile had not concealed his opinion of the
weaknesses of the Republican Government, and it is said that he
had prepared a report for Mussolini — which he did not live to
deliver. Since then, a few days ago, there has been an attempt to
murder a colonel of the Fascist militia, and a reward has been
offered of half a million lire to anyone who will give any information on the subject. But it does not, alas, need so large a reward
for the Tuscan to turn traitor. Nothing has been uglier, in the
story of these tragic last months, than the avalanche of denuncia-
tions which have been showered upon both the Italian and the
German officials. Professional rivalry, personal jealousy, the
smallest ancient spite — all these now find vent in reports to the
Fascist police, and cause the suspected person to be handed over to
prison, to questioning by torture, or to a firing-squad. No one
feels safe — for who can be quite certain that no one has a grudge
against him?

In contrast with these, there are remarkable stories of individual
steadfastness and courage. Thus in Florence last week, O.C., a

boy of nineteen, sentenced to death for failing to report for
military service, spent the harrowing night before the execution
(during which the news of a reprieve, at midnight, was cancelled
three hours later) in prayer in his cell, supporting his two comrades — a peasant boy and a Neapolitan lieutenant — and enduring
with equal fortitude the terrible alternatives of hope and fear.
He then faced the firing squad, unbound, with unflinching
serenity, reciting 'Our Father'. On the following Sunday the
Prior of San Miniato, in his sermon, mentioned the death of these
three young men as a remarkable instance of Christian faith and
courage, and was promptly arrested himself. To the reproaches
of those who had arrested him (he is an old man of nearly eighty)
he firmly replied that he would take nothing back that he had
said — since it was his duty, as a priest, to point out examples of
a Christian death, wherever they may occur — and eventually was
released.

May 8th

There have been some more arrests of anti-Fascists,
following a German mopping-up at night in the poorer quarters
of the town. The papers are full of articles urging the 'rebels' to
report themselves before midnight on May 24th, when the
amnesty comes to an end. It is, the articles say, the 'rebels' ' last
chance to return to their families and become respectable members of society. After that date any of them who are captured
will be shot without mercy.

All Red Cross nurses are also now obliged to take a vow of
allegiance to the Republican Government — with the result that
practically all of them are resigning. Their places will be taken
by paid Republican nurses — very insufficiently trained — and the
whole character of the Red Cross work will (temporarily) be
altered. Fortunately the hospitals — except for German wounded
— are mostly empty.

May 9th

Hear from Pippo Cavazza, who has just returned from Arezzo, the story of his family's imprisonment there. It has already lasted twenty-nine days, on a score of trumped-up charges. The first (that of having listened to Radio Londra) was merely a pretext for the arrest, not only of his sister-in-law, Bianca Cavazza, and her husband, but of her two daughters, her son-in-law, a cousin who was staying in their house, and an unfortunate neighbour who had merely come to dinner. The latter was kept in prison for six days, and the rest of the family for twenty-nine days, until at last Pippo Cavazza succeeded in obtaining their release; but the Contessa herself and her husband are still under lock and key. For the first forty-eight hours after their arrest, none of the party were allowed any food or drink, not even a glass of water; and, during the whole time all of them (including the daughters and guests, against whom there was no charge whatever, and who were merely held as witnesses) slept upon lice-infested straw, were never allowed to change their linen, and ate nothing but prison fare. Moreover, during two severe air-raids which took place during this time, and in the course of which the house next to the prison was completely destroyed, they were left locked up in their cells, while the gaolers all ran away to a shelter. The questioning was conducted with rudeness and threats, especially the women's, but not with actual physical violence — but when the Contessa, after a heart-attack, asked to be allowed a camphor injection, she was brutally told that they were not interested in giving medical care to prisoners who would soon be shot. After a fortnight, her illness was so severe (she suffers from heart and kidney trouble) that she was moved to the infirmary, where she still lies, at the point of death. The charges against her are of 'favouring the rebels' and of having ordered arms for them from an arms factory in northern Italy.

May 10th

Antonio arrives from Siena, and tells me of his interview with the Prefect, which ended in his receiving from this official fervent protestations of esteem and trust. The Prefect went so far as to state that he had not seen the number of the paper containing the article against me, and to insinuate that the source of our troubles is the German Command in Chianciano — which we are inclined to doubt. In fact, the whole interview, while satisfactory on the surface, does not leave us wholly reassured — especially in view of the fact that Bianca Cavazza received equally eloquent protestations from the Prefect of *her* province — exactly forty-eight hours before she was arrested! Moreover, our local situation is still very unsettled. Two nights ago, the partisans marched into Montepulciano, disarmed and undressed three militia-men, and hung their shirts on the doors of the *Casa del Fascio* — fired off their guns under the windows of the Fascio secretary — and then returned to the shelter of La Foce woods! It is all childish and purposeless — and, in view of the penalties that may fall upon the civilian population in consequence, extremely foolish. Antonio persuades me to stay in Florence a little longer, until he has been able to see the head of the Fascist militia of Siena. All police measures are in his hands, and it is on his attitude that our future will depend.

May 15th

Met Heydenreich, the German archaeological expert, who is responsible for the preservation of Tuscan art treasures — a gentle, cultivated, human being. He said that when the Piero della Francesca 'Resurrection' was removed from San Sepolcro, the lorry which carried it stopped for half an hour at Arezzo; the town was bombed, and a bomb fell within twenty yards of the lorry — by a miracle, without exploding. Now he is engaged in moving back to Florence, from the tunnel near Incisa where originally they had been placed for safety, the great bronze doors of the Baptistry, a truly Herculean task. In the general destruction of Arezzo the Piero della Francesca frescoes in San Francesco have escaped and now (owing to Heydenreich's efforts) are being protected by an elaborate framework, at the expense of the German Government. It is his plan, too, which has made Siena into a 'hospital city', into which no traffic can now enter — and he is full of hope, he says, of reaching a 'gentleman's agreement' with the Allies about Florence, too. He speaks with respect and liking of his opposite members of the Allied Commission, Kenneth Clarke and Woolley, and with much nostalgia of the year he spent at Windsor, studying the Leonardo da Vinci drawings. A queer, comforting conversation, a reminder of eternal values, which may outlast the present madness.

May 16*th*

At last the car comes to fetch me, and I arrive home to find the children well, and the situation much quieter. The partisans have now scattered, and only one small group of fifteen or twenty remains in our woods. Moreover, Antonio has had a fairly satisfactory interview with the colonel of the Fascist militia of Siena. It started badly, the colonel producing a dossier of the accusations against us (including that of our having a deposit of arms and ammunition concealed in the Castelluccio), but there is no doubt that Antonio's policy of counter-attack is the most effective, and he does not think that any active measures will be taken against us, at any rate for the present. At the moment the Republican policy is one of leniency towards the partisans, and no effort is being spared to get them to report before the 25th.

May 18*th*

Meanwhile events, at last, are moving. The attack on the Cassino front has begun.

May 19*th*

Cassino has fallen.

May 20*th*

The Gustav line has broken, and the Allies are advancing towards the Adolf Hitler line — which is said, however, to be very strong.

The local situation is becoming more stormy again. Partisans have broken into the barracks of San Casciano, disarming the Carabinieri; they have also taken prisoner one of the monks (an ardent Fascist) in the Montefollonico Monastery. He was subsequently sent back to his monastery, completely naked. Other partisans have disarmed two German soldiers at Contignano; with the consequence that this morning two lorries of German soldiers went to the village and took nine men away with them as hostages. On their way back, at seven a.m., they stopped here, and sent up a message to Antonio to come down immediately.

Thinking it was some routine matter, Antonio dressed and shaved in a leisurely manner, until the officer, a captain, sent up an irate message to say that, if he didn't at once appear, he would come up himself and fetch him. When at last Antonio came downstairs the captain abused him for keeping him waiting, and then stated that he had come to search the house for rebels. His soldiers had already searched the surrounding houses and farms, but here they only entered the kitchen and servants' rooms, abstracting such small objects as caught their fancy. In the farm every room was examined, and everyone had to show their papers, and the captain then told Antonio to translate a little speech, in which he warned us all that any further help to the rebels would be given at the risk of our skins. He also asked Antonio to give him exact information as to the partisans' whereabouts, to which Antonio replied that they are to be found everywhere on the chain of hills running from Cetona to

185

Montichiello — about fifty miles — and are seldom more than twenty four hours in any one place! The Germans then went off again.

Leaflets have been dropped this morning by German planes in the Val d'Orcia, saying: 'Whoever knows the place where a band of rebels is in hiding, and does not immediately inform the German Army, will be shot. Whoever gives food or shelter to a band or to individual rebels, will be shot. Every house in which rebels are found, or in which a rebel has stayed, will be blown up. So will every house from which anyone has fired on the German forces. In all such cases, all stores of food, wheat, and straw will be burned, the cattle will be taken away, and the inhabitants will be shot.' The leaflet finishes with the reminder that 'the German Army will proceed with justice, but with inflexible hardness'.

Other leaflets scattered by Allied planes give precisely opposite instructions: 'At all costs refrain from reporting yourselves to the Army. Commit acts of sabotage on the communication lines. Enter into contact with the foreigners in the German Army. Go on organizing groups. The moment for decisive action is near at hand.'

The peasants read these leaflets with bewildered anxiety as to their own fate, and complete indifference (in most cases) to the main issue. *Che sarà di noi?* (What will become of us?) All that they want is peace — to get back to their land — and to save their sons.

All day a succession of young men come up, asking for advice, including the Sicilian and Calabrian soldiers who are working on the place. In the evening, too, we have a visit from some of the women from Contignano, whose husbands and brothers have been taken as hostages by the Germans. They have been to take food to them at Chianciano, where they are at present shut up.

Antonio promises to try to help, but we believe that probably these men are merely being detained as a warning.

May 22nd
      We were mistaken. This afternoon, the Bishop of Pienza arrived, and informed us that seven out of the nine hostages from Contignano are to be shot. He has succeeded in obtaining forty-eight hours' reprieve, but if, within that period, the arms which the rebels took away from the Germans are not returned, the execution will take place.

The Allied troops are advancing on Terracina.

Every day now, whenever I go out of the house, I find a little group of famished people sitting in the farm courtyard; haggard women, with babies in their arms and other children waiting for them at home; thin, ragged schoolboys or old men, carrying sacks or suitcases — all begging for food to take back to Rome. We give them all that we can, but Antonio begs me to remember that we must also go on providing food for our own population and for the two hundred partisans in the woods.

None of our young men are going to report for military service. They will all leave home and hide in the woods — and they are trusting to luck, and to the Allied advance, to save their families from reprisals. But Antonio has already, this evening, received a note from the Fascio of Pienza, warning him that in a few days German troops will arrive there, to remain 'until the mopping-up is finished'. Our personal crisis is just beginning.

May 25th
      Visit from the Maresciallo of Pienza. This is the last day of the amnesty, but it has been prolonged for a week, for this district at least, before the mopping-up is to begin. The little village of Castiglioncello, at the top of the hill, was surrounded this morning by German troops, who have found there the man

responsible for disarming the Germans at Contignano. The seven hostages from Contignano have consequently been released, but two men from Castiglioncello have been shot.

The only recruit to join the Fascist Army is a boy with pleurisy who consequently believes that he will be sent home at once.

The Fifth Army, after occupying Terracina, joins up with the Eighth on the Anzio beach-head.

May 26th

Anti-aircraft guns, stationed at Spedaletto, bring down five Allied planes out of an unusually large bomber formation, which is attacking German columns on the road. Some of the airmen save themselves by parachute. From our terrace we can hear the firing, and see the little silver balloons opening and drifting down from the sky. One plane, laden with bombs, explodes as it hits the ground. We see the great column of black smoke soaring up, and long to hurry to the scene to bring first aid; but the Germans will be there before us.

The Allied Armies, still advancing, have broken through the Hitler line.

May 28th

A young partisan comes to the clinic and asks the nurse to go up with him to a farm, where one of his comrades has been severely wounded — not as the result of an encounter with the Germans or Fascists, but shot in the stomach by one of his own friends! The nurse goes up the hill, and on her return reports that the wounded man is none other than the Fascist from Chianciano, whom the partisans had after all not executed as a spy. The bullet is still in his abdomen, and the nurse says that an immediate operation is necessary to save his life. Then follows a council of war. It is clearly dangerous to send the young man, whom we certainly have no reason to believe trustworthy, to the Montepulciano hospital, where the Fascist officials will question him. If he should talk (either under the anaesthetic or deliberately) he is in a position to betray not only us, but all his companions, many of whose families are still living at Chianciano or Montepulciano. Yet one can hardly let him die without help. The partisans accordingly decide, most humanely, to risk it, and at dusk the little procession, carrying a stretcher, winds down the hill. We put the wounded man in our car and, accompanied by the nurse, take him off to the hospital. There, a word in the surgeon's ear ensures that no one is present at the operation except one elderly and deaf nun, and our own nurse. And when the Segretario del Fascio turns up the next day, the young man declares that he was just about to report for military service, when he was shot by an unknown person, in La Foce woods! So far, so good. But the partisans, who do not trust him too far, propose to break into the hospital on the first day that he is fit to stand, and take him off with them again!

May 31st

Quite suddenly one of our refugee children, Nucci, aged eleven, completely loses her speech. She looks terrified, and cannot answer us, but writes down that when she was 'little' the same thing happened before, after a fright, and the doctor said 'it might perhaps be meningitis!' It seems necessary to take her to the hospital, but not convenient, owing to the machine-gunning of cars on the road. However, we decide to risk it at dusk, and take her to the doctor at Montepulciano, who clearly has not the faintest notion of what is the matter with her.

June 2nd

Nucci mercifully recovers her speech, as inexplicably as she had lost it.

June 3rd

The Allies take Valmontone, Velletri, Anagni. Violent fighting on the Alban hills. Now it can only be a matter of days.

Bombing and machine-gunning on the roads is now continuous. All day the planes fly over us, the big bombing formations of twenty-four or thirty-six planes for the large-scale attacks on trains or military objectives, and, far more dreaded by us, the small, swift-flying groups of six or seven fighters, swooping down in an instant, machine-gunning any vehicle on the road, and bombing lorries or bridges. They are at work from dawn until dusk, and, now that there is a moon, go on attacking all night.

June 4th

Wake to the sound of planes flying low, and look out of the window in time to see bombs falling — obviously aimed at the bridge on the Orcia in the valley. Drive down there and find that the bridge has been missed by a few yards, and so has the farm, a hundred yards away. Four large bombs have exploded within forty yards of the farm, but mercifully no lives have been lost. It seems likely, however, that the planes will have another shot, and that the family must move out. We accordingly spend the morning in loading their wheat and furniture on to carts, and transferring their smaller possessions to an underground cellar. Now and again we hear the familiar droning overhead: 'Here they are again!' and take cover under the trees until the formation has passed. Mariano, the farmer, shows a certain wry humour: 'Keep your stories for winter evenings *a veglia* (sitting up round the fire),' he says to the women, who are beginning to chatter about their experiences and feelings, 'and get on with the move.'

When we get home we turn on the radio: the Allied troops are within six miles of Rome.

We speculate as to the future. The fall of Rome is now a

matter of hours — but will the Allies be able to cut off the German retreat? If so, Tuscany will be saved: if not, our troubles are just about to begin.

Late in the evening we hear that fighting has begun in the suburbs of Rome. General Alexander issues a proclamation to the Roman people, urging them to help the Allied troops by every means in their power.

Shots from a fast-flying plane, at midnight, warn our partisans that, in the next few days, ammunition will be supplied to them from the air, within a given area. They will light fires to show the exact spot.

June 5th

The Allied armies have entered Rome! We hear the bare news at eight a.m. The Allies entered late last night by Porta Maggiore, and the fighting continued up to the Forum. A few hours later we hear that the Allied Armies, barely pausing in Rome, are pursuing the Germans in their retreat, on the road to Bracciano and Viterbo, which will bring them here. But the rest of the German forces, farther south, are still fighting violently in the Anagni-Fiuggi sector, the object of the Allies, presumably, being to cut off their retreat and force them eastwards, across the Apennines, towards Pescara. If so, Tuscany may largely be spared.

At ten a.m. three German officers turn up, part of the staff of a hospital at Monterotondo. They require the Castelluccio, the nursery school, and the schools, not for the wounded (who are to be quartered at Chianciano), but for the staff, provisions, etc. They will arrive this evening, and we have half a day in which to move all the children into the villa, and to clear out the furniture. Take up the carpets and curtains in the visitors' rooms, and put the children there, twenty-three in all, and turn the downstairs drawing-room into their dining-room and play-room with the nursery school furniture. The children, delighted, run up and down, 'helping'. At seven p.m. the officers turn up: the houses

are ready for them. They say that they have come from Monterotondo, and that the rest of the unit will probably arrive during
the night, but the roads are so blocked that they do not know
how or when they will get through. They also say that the
fighting has been violent and the casualties high.

Late at night, more news from Rome. There was fighting
inside the city between Germans and anti-Fascists, and there are
still thirty thousand Germans wounded in the city. The German
hospitals of Monte Mario, with their staff and wounded, have
been captured. The Allies state that they are attempting to cope
with the appalling situation of lack of food and water within the
city.

June 6th

All last night German lorries are travelling northwards,
and we hear planes bombing and machine-gunning the road by
moonlight. Some firing quite near here at midnight, and again
in the early morning.

In the morning I find the garage and the farm courtyard full
of German Red Cross lorries. Their drivers, utterly exhausted,
ask for coffee and food. Many of them have had no sleep for
three days – they look dazed and bewildered. One of them fell
asleep at the wheel, and took his lorry into a ditch; his face is cut
and bleeding. They all say that the state of the roads is appalling.
Planes continue to fly low over us, and I suggest that the Germans
should put their cars under cover, but their officer is still at
Chianciano, and they seem incapable of doing this without his
orders. Two bombs fell in the valley, near the bridge across the
Orcia. The children dance about the garden or play in the
sand-pile, no longer even glancing up at the planes.

Antonio has gone down to Chianciano. Last night the Commissario of the Commune rang him up, begging him to act as
an intermediary with the partisans. A few nights ago, one of the
Fascists of Chianciano was captured by the partisans – who now

say they will only give him up in exchange for several of their number, who are in Fascist hands. The partisans are now indisputably in control of the countryside, and take what they require: yesterday (with our connivance) all of our cheese on its way to the government stores; to-day, one of our horses from a farm. This morning the captain of the Carabinieri of Montepulciano telephoned to Antonio in great distress: he had woken up to find that all his Carabinieri had left! They too have joined the partisans.

Hear at eleven-thirty that the Allied troops have landed this morning on the coast of France. Proclamation of Eisenhower to the people of France.

Allied troops pursuing Germans north, north-east, and north-west of Rome on via Cassia, via Flaminia, and via Salaria. Fifth Army on via Tiburtina.

In the afternoon one of the Germans says that he has heard on his radio the news of an Allied landing at Genoa. All the evening we listen-in hopefully, but in vain.

June 7th

No confirmation of the landing at Genoa — but a rumour reaches us that Grosseto has been occupied by Allied paratroops and local partisans. General Alexander issues a broadcast to the Italian patriots, telling them that the hour of their rising has come at last. They are to cut the German Army communications wherever possible, by destroying roads, bridges, railways, telegraph-wires. They are to form ambushes and cut off retreating Germans — and to give shelter to *Volksdeutche* who have deserted from the German Army. Workmen are urged to sabotage, soldiers and police to desert, 'collaborators of Fascism' to 'take this last chance of showing their patriotism and helping the cause of their country's deliverance. United, we shall attain victory'.

Spent the morning in Montepulciano, driving there in the

pony-cart, and meeting a group of partisans guarding the cross-roads. Find the captain of the Carabinieri in despair over his men's desertion. What, he asks, is he to do now? How is he to keep order? It appears that his men have not only deserted, but have taken with them all their arms and ammunition, including the captain's own tommy-gun. The immediate cause of their desertion is the order to wear black shirts, like the Fascist militiamen, and still more the fear of being taken off to Germany — but the truth is that for a long time their sympathies have been with the partisans. With tears in his eyes the captain begs me to ask Antonio to persuade them to come back! They know perfectly well, he says, that he has made a secret exit for them, with an underground passage, by which they could at any time run away from the Germans! If they will only come back, they need not wear a black shirt, and no reference will be made to this episode. And then, as I am leaving, he adds: 'Let them come back even on the last day before the Allies arrive — and I shall be satisfied!'

At the Bracci's there is much rejoicing over the news, and the grown-up sons, fired by Alexander's message, propose to join the partisans at La Foce, but their father, who is the mayor of Montepulciano, thinks they can be of more use in the town itself. He and the *Commissario del Fascio* are meeting two leaders of the partisans this afternoon! Fascism is not so much being destroyed as crumbling before our eyes. By the time of the Allies' arrival here, nothing of the whole wretched structure will be left, and its supporters will have vanished into thin air.

Meanwhile Antonio has been spending the morning first in getting under cover the numerous large lorries that were standing round the house, an obvious target for planes — and then in talking to Beppe, the leader of our local partisans. They are prepared to give up the Fascist in their hands in exchange for ten of their friends who are held by the Fascists. This message has already been conveyed to the Prefect, and they are now awaiting his answer. As for the Carabinieri, they have no intention of going back until the Allies arrive, but are fully prepared to do so then! To-night the head of the local partisans will furnish us with the key to the special messages on the radio, so that we may hand them on, their own receiver being poor. If, later on, the retreating German troops begin to plunder and rob on their retreat, Beppe and his men will join up with Antonio and some of our own men to form a guard in defence of the farm.

In the course of the evening one of the p.o.w.s from our own camp, who is suffering from bronchitis, walks over from the other side of the valley to ask our nurse for some medicine — and is unpleasantly surprised to find himself in the midst of a German unit! 'Never mind,' says Antonio, 'just walk across the road with me, and no one will look at you.' And so indeed they do, and fetch the medicine.

The Germans have with them, as camp followers, two handsome girls from Monterotondo, who call themselves 'Red Cross helpers', a new name for one of the oldest of professions. German lorries continue to arrive in the morning, having travelled during the night, but many are still missing. The lieutenant in charge of the traffic is a rude little bully, and Antonio has a passage at arms with him. The young doctor who is with him, a tall, polite young man, apologizes later. The men are mostly 'correct', and express regret for turning out the children. All are tired and depressed, but all are convinced that the war will soon be over. The doctor once again repeats the story of the terrible 'secret weapon' that is to be used (very soon now) against England. He says it is not gas, but something terrible. Goebbels has wanted to use it before now, but Hitler has hesitated. Now, however, it *will* come into action, and will be decisive.

June 8th
The hospital at Montepulciano was hit early this morning, the bombs fortunately falling only on the outlying washing-

house, and no one was killed. But since the hospital is on the main road, on which German columns are passing, beside a bridge, it is to be evacuated at once, no easy matter, since the town is already full, and the hospital contains a maternity ward and an orphanage.

On the Pianoia road, between us and Montepulciano, the partisans have attacked a German armoured car, two men being killed on each side. This may bring German reprisals upon the whole district. Beppe tells us that last night some ammunition was dropped for the partisans in the valley, and that they believe that some paratroops have also come down. From our terrace, during the morning, we see the Allied light bombers sweep down on the roads, where the German convoys are going northwards, and watch the bombs dropping. We also hear, at midday, tommy-guns firing near by, in the direction of Pianoia, and wonder whether the German reprisals are beginning there.

The main road to the north is strewn with propaganda leaflets to tempt the retreating German soldiers to surrender. Each leaflet calls itself a 'safe-conduct' and states in four languages that 'The German soldier who carries this safe-conduct is using it as a sign of his genuine wish to give himself up. He is to be well looked-after, to receive food and medical attention as required, and is to be removed from the zone of combat as soon as possible'. On the other side of the leaflet, in German, is a somewhat highly-coloured description of the amenities of life in Allied prisoners' camps.

The Allies have now occupied Civitavecchia, Bracciano and Subiaco. The German radio forecasts a German line of defence on the hills immediately to the north of these places. It is now clear that the greater part of the German forces have *not* been cut off, but it remains to be seen whether any supplies will be able to reach those which are now slowly retreating. The slower the retreat, the worse for Tuscany.

In the evening, the true story of the Pianoia incident reaches us. It appears that, during the bombing of the Montepulciano road, four Germans got out of their car and took refuge in the farm called San Carlo, at the cross-roads. While they were sitting there a group of partisans came up, disarmed and captured them, and also took the car. Within a few hours, however, three of the Germans succeeded in escaping, promptly hurried to their unit, returned to the farm with an armoured car, burned the farm and arrested the farmers. The latter will be kept as hostages, and will be shot unless the captured German and his car are given up.

June 9th

A day of odd contrasts. It is Donata's first birthday. and while planes drone overhead and swoop down on the valley roads, we have a children's party in the garden. (The children have, by now, completely lost their original nervousness, and we want, if possible, to keep them like this, especially now that the danger is drawing nearer.) The planes are particularly assiduous overhead, however, during the sack and three-legged races, and it seems better to continue the party indoors.

The evening radio tells us that Viterbo, Vetralla and Tarzuinia are taken. The German hospital unit decides to leave to-morrow. The bombing on the road is increasing, and at Pienza the Germans have set fire to several farms, in reprisal for yesterday's incident. We begin to wonder whether the time has not come to move the children away.

June 10th

Send up ox-carts to the farm at the top of the hill, Pietra-porciana, laden with twenty small camp beds for the children, some pots and pans and some food, so that, when the time comes to move them, they will be able to get away quickly. We also pack our last valuables and personal papers and some more clothes in a tin trunk, and bury it at night in the garden.

At midnight a loud explosion tells us that the partisans have succeeded in blowing up a bridge on the Radicofani road, which should prevent a lot of traffic from coming this way.

At Pienza there is a German mopping-up, and eight partisans are captured. We are now completely cut off from Montepulciano, as no workmen will come by that road for fear of being caught.

June 12th

While I am still asleep, at five a.m., a message is sent up to me by Antonio to get up at once, as the Germans have arrived to 'mop-up' the district. They are in two large SITA buses, about eighty men. They tried to break into the granary at the Castelluccio, then came on here, but seeing the courtyard full of German Red Cross cars, scattered to the farms, which they searched for arms and ammunition. On our place they only steal some food, but we learn later on that just above us, at Castiglioncello, a farm has been burned and two men shot.

In the afternoon, while I am with the children in the garden rehearsing the 'Sleeping Beauty', I hear a lorry drive up, and some of these same German troops come tramping, fully armed, into the garden. They do not look attractive. I go up to them, not without some inner apprehension, and ask them what they want. But the answer is unexpected: 'Please — wouldn't the children sing for us?' The children sing *O Tannenbaum* and *Stille Nacht* (which they learned last Christmas) — and tears come into the men's eyes. '*Die Heimat* — it takes us back to *die Heimat*!' So they climb into their lorry and drive away.

Dr. W., a German doctor who had been here before, turns up, on his way north with this hospital, and tells us that yesterday he was obliged to shoot a German soldier, who, near Castiglion del

Lago, was raping a young girl. W. was passing by on his motor-bicycle, and the girl's father ran out, calling for help. He went in, and shot the man on the spot.

He also warns us to beware of the First and Fourth Division of German paratroops, if they should come this way. It is they who were formerly at Anzio, where they were attacked by the Italian Division which had been fraternizing with them until the previous day. They had many casualties, and their resentment extends to every Italian, soldier or civilian.

A message from the partisans summons us to the meeting-place in the woods, where their leader, Beppe, gives us the following warning. His brother has just come down after four weeks' imprisonment in Siena, during the course of which he was beaten and tortured with burning cigarette ends to make him talk. The information they wanted was about Antonio and myself, and we conclude that there is a spy on the place, since every one of our movements, and especially every meeting with the partisans, has been reported accurately, as well as much that is untrue, such as that we have given twelve million lire to the partisans, and have a deposit of ammunition at the Castelluccio. Both Beppe's brother and one of our British prisoners, who was also arrested, heroically refused to give away anything. It appears that for a long time we headed the list of suspects to be arrested, and that it was the German Colonel Bock (who formed part of the Court of Inquiry) who caused the arrest to be delayed. But now, Beppe warns us, though the Fascists are no longer to be feared, it is possible that the retreating Germans will receive orders to take us with them. So Beppe says we had better walk up the hill and join the partisans. They have cleared out a part of the farm they are occupying to make room for us, and have even gone so far as to clean the floors, in preparation for our arrival! We, however, think that if we were really going to be arrested it would have happened yesterday, and, in any case, we have no intention of leaving the children and the place, until the Germans actually come to fetch us.

We once again, however, keep a coat, shoes, etc., beside our beds at night, so as to be able to make for the woods at a moment's notice.

One can plainly hear cannon-fire beyond Radicofani, and we presume that the Allies must have reached Acquapendente. The B.B.C. bulletin says that Bolsena is taken.

In the afternoon I drive with Schwester Marie in the pony-cart to Montepulciano, as we need some medicine for Giovannino, the baby, and, since the Pianoia incident, none of our men wishes to take that road. We meet, however, no one, and only have to jump down into a ditch twice, as the fighter planes swoop down over our heads. At Montepulciano the population is very jumpy, as a German anti-aircraft battery has just been installed at the gates of the town, and a rumour has spread that the whole population is to be evacuated. This news appears to be based, however, on very slight foundation. A most lovely drive home in the sunset — the red clover in flower, the green cornfields waving in the breeze, the hedges full of briar-roses. Meet a few German cars, heavily camouflaged with branches, the troops sitting on the bonnet or the roof, so as to be able to observe the sky. Heavy bombing in the Val di Chiana.

In the evening, worrying news is brought by one of the keepers. It appears that some German officers have been up the hill at the top of our property, between Castiglioncello and Pietraporciana, to look for a suitable emplacement for guns. Five partisans fired upon them, and one of the Germans has been killed. So now, presumably, the whole of that district, and particularly the village of Castiglioncello, and the surrounding farms (of which Pietraporciana is the nearest) will be surrounded and searched. This settles the question of using that farm as a shelter for the children.

June 13th

Send up a cart to fetch away all our things from Pietra-porciana, in case the Germans choose this farm for their reprisals, and discover that all the partisans have left, presumably for the same reason.

The news is unsatisfactory. There seems to be some tough German resistance round the lake of Bolsena, and the Allies have now been stuck there for three days, while in the evening the B.B.C. tells us that three German divisions from the north have arrived there as reinforcements. Very scant activity, too, in the air, and we begin to wonder whether some of the planes on this front have been sent to France.

Another message summons us again to meet Beppe's brother and some other partisans, at dusk, in the woods. They tell us that, by order of the Central Committee of Liberation in Rome, they are forming a citizens' defence corps to take charge of each city, as soon as the Germans have left, and to enter into contact with the Allies on their arrival. The Chianciano Committee is already formed, and they wish Antonio to be the new Mayor of the Comune. He accepts, and they then show us the draft of the proclamation which they propose to issue on taking charge – an admirable document, urging the citizens to moderation, to return to law and order, and to refrain from all private vengeance for any injuries they may have received. 'Justice,' it says, 'will be performed – but this is no time for private grievances. We can afford to be generous.'

It is strange, after this conversation, to return down the hill, and find the courtyard still full of German troops.

June 14th

A company of German sappers arrives here during the night. The captain is billeted in the house, the men in the woods; they sleep in their cars, and wash in our laundry, greatly disturbing the women who want to get on with their washing, and find large naked young Germans occupying the tub.

Spend the day in widening and cleaning a deep natural trench in the woods, as a possible emergency bolt-hole for the children. Air activity again in the afternoon – bombs near the bridge on the Miglia, and machine-gunning on the Castelluccio road, hitting two German lorries.

In the evening, a messenger from Montepulciano brings the bad news that Bracci, together with nine other citizens of Montepulciano (the bank manager, head of the school, etc.) have been arrested by the Germans, apparently as hostages, following upon yesterday's attack of the partisans on Germans between Montepulciano and Pienza. An urgent message has accordingly been sent to Beppe that all partisan activity is to cease for the present in this district.

The news is slightly better, the Allies have passed Orbetello, and are proceeding towards Grosseto. American troops have taken Pitigliano, on the other side of Monte Amiata. At Bolsena, fierce fighting continues.

An important detail, from our personal point of view, is the news that the troops fighting in the Bolsena area are largely coloured Moroccan troops, and it is these that presumably will be the first to arrive here. After so many months and years of waiting for the Allies, this will be the Val d'Orcia's first impression of them! There is also, however, a South African division at Bagnoregio, so let us hope that these may turn up instead.

Some of the partisans come down to our cellar to fetch some wine, carrying up the demi-johns under the very noses of the Germans, who are sitting in the yard by their lorries, not twenty yards away. Among the partisans is a tall young South African, who comes into the house to talk to me and shares my anxiety that the Allies, when at last they do arrive, should not disappoint the high expectations of the population. 'I'm going to tell all my mates,' he says, 'about the kindness I've received here – and about the farmers who have risked their lives and homes to take me in. Now it is up to us to play the game.'

June 15th

Wake up to find that many more German cars have arrived during the night, and that the surrounding woods are full of them and their owners. While the men of the Red Cross units and the sappers quartered here have been 'correct', the stray units which are now straggling north — many of them on foot, their cars having been bombed — are very different. Yesterday at one of our farms three men stole a ham, some cheese, and a thousand lire; at another they took a woman's wristwatch; at yet another, some hens. The peasants, on their side, are incredibly slow-moving and stupid over hiding their possessions. This morning — while Antonio was away at Montepulciano — an alarmed messenger came running up from one of our farms to say that two German soldiers had ransacked the house, stolen three large hams, some sugar, bread, eggs, and flour, and had now gone on to another farm, presumably for the same purpose. I accordingly hurried off to the captain of the sappers to ask for help — but found him at lunch and much disinclined to be his brother's keeper. 'They certainly don't belong to *my* unit', was all he could say, but eventually I persuaded him to send a sergeant with me and we went down the hill to the farm-house, just in time to meet the German slinking away in the corn, carrying a large sack. The sergeant took out one ham and returned it to its owner, but where were the other two? The peasant then said that they had seen the second man hiding something lower down the field, and with some difficulty we found, hidden in the high corn, the other two hams, and so returned triumphantly home. In the afternoon, however, setting off on a similar mission to another farm, we were not so fortunate: a lorry carrying the stolen goods was already driving away.

Antonio, meanwhile, has been spending an exhausting day at Montepulciano and Chianciano. On arriving at Montepulciano, he discovered that the arrest of Bracci and nine other hostages was in consequence of the Castglioncello episode. When the German Command realized that it had not occurred in the Comune of Montepulciano, these hostages were released. Antonio accordingly saw Bracci freed, but as soon as he got back home, was called up by the greatly distressed secretary of the Comune of Chianciano, who informed him that ten citizens of Chianciano have now been arrested in their stead, and that all the other men in the town had run away, leaving him (who can speak no German) alone to cope with the situation. Antonio then set off for Chianciano, to find a deserted city, in which no one even knew who was responsible for the order of arrest. On hearing that the general of the Hermann Goering Division had arrived, he went straight to him, and found him coming out of the bathing establishment. 'Are you the Burgmeister?' — 'No.' — 'Then what are you doing here?' — 'Herr General, the Burgmeister has run away!' The general laughed, and said he would send a squad of 'Feldpolizei' to police the town to prevent its being looted, but that he could do nothing about the hostages, for this was the first he had heard of the matter.

Antonio brings back a basketful of cherries, the only thing for which poor Giorgio longs, and which have become practically unprocurable, since no farmer has the courage to take them (or anything else) to market. Giorgio is now a tragic sight, and his nights are made hideous by continual attacks of coughing and suffocation. He is as thin as a skeleton, and the other day, coming in suddenly when he was asleep, Antonio and I started back in horror, for we both thought that he was dead. But still, whenever we come in, his first eager question is about the news, his only complaint that all the fighting is being done without him, and he still, with the incurable hopefulness of consumptives, speaks of 'next month, when I am at home again'.

What to do with him, if we are are bombed or turned out of the house, is one of our greatest problems, but I suppose we shall carry him on a stretcher with us.

At midnight we walk round the farm-buildings to have a look round. It is a strange sight — the great bulks of cars, filled with sleeping men, concealed behind every arch and under every tree or thicket, camouflaged with young cypresses which they have ruthlessly cut down. Now and again a match shows the face of a man who is unpacking, or tinkering at a car; or the rumbling of an engine and the shouting of orders announces yet another car laboriously making its way up the dark wood-road. We wander about among it all, with a curious sense of detachment, feeling like ghosts of the past, who have no business here.

June 16th

Awakened at six-thirty by planes circling low above the house. We wonder if there is a column on the road, and if so, whether it, and we, will be bombed together. The speed with which the planes arrive shows the uselessness of any shelter in the wood; there would never be time to get the children to it. At the best we can only hope to take them down to the cellar. However, this time the planes only machine-gunned the road, about six hundred yards away, setting fire to a haystack beside one of our farms. All the morning *die Brüder* (as the Germans call them) were very active, and at about ten a.m. they again bombed the bridges on the Orcia and the Miglia. Cannon-fire is now to be heard, directed against the southern side of the Radicofani hill and Piancastagnaio. The front is very near.

The whole place is now full of troops. Several lorries drive up the hill-road towards Chianciano, and we hear later that they are after the partisans, who have stolen a lorry and killed two soldiers. At one of our farms, Fontalgozzo, a cow is stolen by the Germans; at another, Chiarentana, a donkey, a cart, and food. In both cases, a German Red Cross sergeant-major who is quartered here, intervenes, but in the second case, too late. A German colonel and two other officers turn up at midday from the front, and tell us that Viterbo has been badly bombed, and that the Allies have broken through at Orvieto, and are already half-way to Chiusi. The cannon-fire is louder now, and our first shell has fallen, beside one of our farms. The German colonel, a regular officer, is very bitter about Hitler's order to spare Rome and not to use any of the bridges. His men had to swim the Tiber in consequence, and there were many casualties. He advises us to keep the children here, and to take refuge, if necessary, in the cellar, but *not* in the woods, which, he says, are much more likely to be fired upon than the houses.

In the evening, the sapper captain who is quartered here comes to say good-bye. He says speculatively, 'I'd give a lot to be in your place, to be able to talk in a few days to some British officers, and find out what they really think about the war'. A great many other German officers have said something of the kind. As to the general morale, they are all quite frankly tired of the war and of five years away from their houses and families, appalled by the bombing of Germany, and depressed by the turn of events here and in France. But there is not one of them who does not still express his blind conviction that Germany *cannot* be beaten, and their equally blind belief in a terrible *Vergeltung* against England, which is close at hand. What form it will take, they say, they do not know, but the Führer has promised it to them, and he has never yet failed to keep his promises *to his own people*. Should this promise prove to have been only a bluff, then the whole nation's trust in the Führer would collapse, for they would feel that he had betrayed them. But, they hastily add, this will not, cannot happen.

June 17th

Cannon-fire all night. The electric light and telephone are both cut, so we get no news, which matters the less, in that the news is now happening *here*. The first wounded are beginning to come through on lorries and motor-bicycles, and a German medical officer who has stopped his ambulance at the cross-roads to ask the way, and of whom I ask: 'Are you going to the front?' laughs and replies: 'And where do you think *you* are?' This is a new idea to me, who, like most civilians, think that the front is somewhere where we are not. The fighting is now just beyond

Radicofani — and the Allied troops are said to be coloured. We can only hope that the German retreat, and their pursuit, will be equally rapid. Last night the Germans took with them, on leaving, our car, our mattresses, and towels from the captain's bedroom.

Carry Giorgio on a stretcher to a room in the office building, away from the constant traffic of the road. His colour is ashen; he is very much afraid.

At midday a German colonel, passing through, gives us the appalling news (which we have missed, as we have now no radio) of the beginning of the German *Vergeltung* in England. The details that he gives are so terrible that one can hardly either take them in or believe them. Rocket planes without a crew, carrying some terrible unknown explosive, have come down over London and the south coast. The explosion of these rockets, according to his story, brings utter destruction for a radius of over a kilometre. There are nearly two hundred thousand dead in London alone, and the Lord Mayor has stated that only five shelters are deep enough to be of any use. The town is being evacuated. Such is the German's tale, and all day — utterly unable to find out how much of it is a lie — I am haunted by it. What is happening here seems child's play in comparison.

Nevertheless, one must get on with what each hour brings. The gun-fire is now considerably nearer and one sees the shells falling on this side of Radicofani. A soldier tells us that the casualties there, among the civilian population, have been very high, as they all took refuge above the little town, in the old castle, which was precisely the area that was most heavily shelled. The people here are getting very jumpy. Fannina (the maid who helps to look after the refugees) has already gone off with her family (most prematurely) to camp out in a cave. The fattore's wife and family are preparing to do the same to-morrow morning. All are very nervous of the cellar. Meanwhile I try to keep the children happy and occupied, by rehearsing 'Snow-white' with them.

In the late afternoon, a billeting officer turns up: he requires quarters for the general of his division and a major, who both come into the house, and for several other officers, for whom he takes the school-buildings. This arrival suggests that events are not moving quite as quickly as we expected.

June 18th

Our 'guests' arrived at eleven p.m., and we at once discovered that they were precisely the paratroops against whom we have been warned. The colonel (acting general) is Trettner, and the chaplain turns out to be an acquaintance of Antonio's sister. The others are the most complete set of ruffians that I have ever set eyes upon. Tramping in (and looking even more sinister, by the uncertain light of a flickering acetylene lamp) they take possession of the house — set up a telephone in the dining-room, which is to be their office, and a bed for the colonel in Antonio's sitting-room, while the others sleep, smoke and eat all over the rest of the house. Before they have been here half an hour the chaplain — a tall, thin man in pince-nez, of a 'correct', not to say prim appearance, which is in comic contrast with that of his flock — comes up to Antonio, and solemnly warns him not to leave anything about that he may value. We accordingly remove waterproofs and coats from the downstairs cupboards, and anything else that occurs to us (unfortunately forgetting my sun-glasses and hair-net, which immediately disappear). We also lock the door of every room, both on entering and leaving — but hear the soldiers wandering about the house all night. Some break into the clinic during the night — and some others into the school — but Antonio is in time to save the teacher's mattresses. In the course of the day we get to distinguish them better. There are a few quiet fellows among them (one sergeant-major, like the chaplain, going out of his way to warn us about his comrades' long fingers) but most of them look even more ruffianly by day than the night before; more like figures out of a second-rate film of the Foreign Legion, than members of a regular army. They are all over the place, bathing stark naked in the laundry; preening themselves, in emerald green or scarlet bandannas or loin cloths; invading the kitchen, the fattoria, and every unlocked room in the house; sleeping behind every bush and under every tree. In the wood the keeper finds evidence of their recent activities in two large, empty safes, which they have picked, as well as numerous empty boxes and suitcases, presumably from the houses which they have just left. And all day a constant stream of terrified, anxious peasants flocks to us for help – which we are wholly unable to give – in the calamities that are overtaking them. All have had their food-stores stolen, most have lost at least a pig, or some geese or fowls, some have been turned out of their houses altogether, and three have had their daughters raped. One of these, a child of twelve, was saved at the last moment by her father, who brought her here, and she is now sleeping in the house.

The weather has chosen this inopportune moment to break, and all day it has been pouring. The firing becomes louder towards midday, and we realize that the German batteries have been moved down the road. Up to lunch-time the Germans tell us, 'You can keep the children here', but after lunch the colonel sends for Antonio and tells him that he advises him to move the children away, 'to any place that is not on a road, on a hill-top, or on the side of the valley facing Radicofani'. We then, together with the chaplain (whom we discover to be a Capuchin missionary, Father Leopoldo), discuss what we had better do. We reject moving the children to Chianciano or Montepulciano or any of the farms (which all face the valley or are on a hill-top), and finally reach the conclusion that the trench we had prepared in the woods, half a mile away, is probably the best place after all. It has, moreover, the great advantage of enabling us not to desert the place, for everyone agrees that, if we leave the house empty, we will return to find it destroyed. But it has begun to rain again, and the prospect of one or more nights in an open trench, with a three-months old baby and a dying man, as well as all the other children, is not wholly agreeable. However, there is a piece of waterproof sheeting, big enough to form a sort of shelter about ten yards long, for the children, and another smaller one for the ill man, and with that we must be content. Antonio and the men begin to place the supports for the roof, while I return to the house and prepare the food-supplies and children's clothes. We shall take the pram (which, under its hood, will be the one completely dry place), pack most of the children's clothes in it, and put the smallest babies to sleep in it in turn. The other children will have a blanket and a pillow apiece, a jersey and a change of socks. Straw to sleep on — plenty of bread and cheese — and a cow tethered in the woods for the babies. If only it would stop raining!

All the day, during these activities, there is the haunting undercurrent of the terrible news from England, and the longing for further details. Only the German troops have a radio, and it is being used almost exclusively for military orders. But in the late afternoon, as we are standing by the trench, a sergeant comes up and tells Antonio with glee that *die Vergeltung* is going on splendidly. The details, he says, come from the neutral radio, Swiss and Swedish. They say that it has been going on steadily since the 15th, and that the whole of London and the south coast is aflame. There is no possibility of the landing in France continuing, and the troops there will be encircled. 'What wouldn't I give to see it!' he cries. I feel sick and blind with misery, and go back to the house. Oh, England, England!

June 19th

This morning the paratroops have moved to Monticchiello, but have immediately been replaced by some gunners, under command of a stout Herr Major. His men are far less brigand-like in appearance and behaviour than the paratroops, but he has placed his batteries all round the house, and after lunch they begin firing in good earnest. The Allied fire is as yet directed on the main road and on Contignano, but presumably sooner or later they will respond to the fire from here. The Allied infantry, judging by the direction of the German fire, would seem to be at Contignano, just opposite. Meanwhile a persistent drizzle continues to fall, the trench (in which a small shelter has been erected) is deep in mud, and the prospect of a night or two there becomes less and less attractive. Moreover, the gunners are unanimous in reversing the advice of their predecessors, and in saying that, in their opinion, the children would be much safer in the cellar. Eventually the C.O. comes to see the cellar, and another smaller underground room beside it, where we propose to put the dying young partisan, and says that both will do. He will let us know, he says, when it is necessary to move the children there. We shall be about fifty people there, as, in addition to the twenty-three children, their two teachers and ourselves, there are all the men and boys of the fattoria (the fattore's wife and family have preferred a cave in the cliff), the members of our household, and several little peasant girls and women who have taken refuge with us from the Germans.

All the afternoon the gun-fire is very near and loud. At eight p.m. the major appears and says that they are leaving at once. 'And your batteries too?' I ask. 'Yes — but they will at once be replaced by others.' We learn with dismay that these will be paratroops again. The major can only tell us that they will arrive 'some time in the night', and adds, 'Get hold of an officer at once, if you can'. Antonio accordingly decides not to go to bed tonight. The news (according to German soldiers) is that *der Tommy* is already at Perugia, and that this district forms the last line of the local defence, so that we may hope to see the Allies soon. Another two days perhaps, the worst, will see us through.

For two days we have had no milk for the babies, as the cows have been let loose in the woods (to prevent their being stolen) and though one of the keepers succeeded in finding and milking them the milk was seized by the Germans, as it was being brought back to us. We only hope that they will not find the cows, too.

No more news of England.

June 20th

At five-thirty a.m. a deafening noise informs us that the paratroops have arrived. They are all round the house and in the farm, and are trying to break in the front-door, but Antonio is able to prevent this on the ground that it is a *Kinderheim*. They are camping in the front garden, together with two stolen donkeys laden with goods, and a sheep. They have also broken into the farm larder.

We take mattresses and benches down to the cellar, and get the children dressed and fed. The Germans look unspeakably worn out and dirty, and it is clear that all discipline has come to an end. Their O.C., however, is civil, examines the cellar and says it is pretty safe, and adds that he does not think anything much will happen until this afternoon. He gives orders to his men to keep out of the house, but whether they will respect this order up to the end, remains to be seen. They are placing machine-guns behind the parapet of the lower garden and of the vine-pergola, and have mined the roads.

All through the morning there is a lull, except for some Allied gunfire on Contignano, already largely destroyed. We sit about in a *desoeuvré* way, with our overcoats and waterproofs, like people waiting at a railway station, and try to keep the children occupied. In the course of the morning we hear that a neighbouring farmer has been shot by a German because he made a fuss over giving up his pig, and is now lying dead in a field. His daughters, in tears, come to take refuge with us. The Allied gunfire moves on from Contignano to Castelvecchio, which is also destroyed, and the German guns are now firing on Contignano, from which we conclude that the Allies have arrived there.

The day drags on interminably, but at about three o'clock the shells begin to fall on the Castelluccio hillside, and we move the children down to the cellar, blocking up the windows with sandbags. The children are rather amused by this novelty, and not, as yet, much frightened. We also carry Giorgio down to a little underground room beneath the oil-mill. His appearance is tragic. Already his face has the drawn, shrivelled look that precedes the end, and it seems brutal to cause him the suffering of being moved. But it would be still worse unnecessarily to expose the two women who are nursing him, or to leave him alone.

The day drags on and on, with sporadic shelling on both sides. Two dead Germans are carried down (killed by mines that they themselves had laid) and are buried late in the evening in our churchyard. Giorgio grows worse, and begs for morphia, which is given him. In the evening some German officers tell us that there is likely to be activity during the night, so we decide to settle all the children in the cellar, four small babies (of whom at least one is always wailing), twenty-three other children under ten, and about twenty adults, including some of the peasant women.

Three other German officers turn up and demand beds in the villa for the night, firmly stating that nothing will happen until after midnight. So Antonio and I decide to sleep upstairs, in our own beds (leaving everyone else below, for greater safety) — but at eleven p.m. we hastily spring to our feet, as some shells come whizzing past our windows, very near. I arrive in the cellar with only one shoe and rather shaky knees. Antonio, however, says that they are not very large shells. We then spend the night in the cellar, all the babies mercifully sleeping well. I am haunted all night by the thought of what these nights must be in the London shelters. If only, only, one could have news! The German soldiers all believe that the new weapon will bring the end of the war, but this may merely be propaganda to raise their morale. We have, however, no means of ascertaining the truth, and so one continues to wonder.

Giorgio dies at dawn, quite quietly, without suffering, under the influence of morphia. We still don't know whether the name and address he has given us are the real ones; only that his mother is waiting for him, somewhere in Bergamo.

The children are none the worse for the night, and in the morning there is a long lull, which enables us to pop up to the kitchen and get breakfast. Then, at about nine, the German firing begins again, and five Sherman tanks are to be seen at one of our farms in the valley, only five miles away. Surely they will soon arrive! But there are still German batteries all round us, and the roads are mined, including the one just outside the front door. A Moroccan prisoner, with a turban and large moustaches, is brought in to the German O.C., the first member of the Allied forces to reach La Foce.

The day drags on. In the lulls the children play under the vine-pergola outside the cellar door, and when the shelling gets worse, go underground again. They are very good on the whole, but their voices are nearly as deafening as the guns. A wounded German comes hobbling up, supported by two others, and receives little help from the Red Cross unit here, because he belongs to another detachment. Indeed, all through these days, we have been increasingly impressed by the curious inefficiency and apathy of the German Field Hospital Units. They hang about interminably with nothing to do, and never seem to be where they are really wanted, nor do any of the German troops show the slightest interest in, or helpfulness towards, members of other units than their own.

A great increase of activity at about two p.m., and in the evening we hear from a German sergeant that at that moment the Allied troops (we learn later on that they are a battalion of the Scots Guards) had broken through, about a mile away, but were then driven back again by increased German firing. Now they are circling round and trying to come down the hill-road track from Sarteano, but there are German batteries there, too. After supper the firing increases in a new direction, and when I go upstairs to my room to fetch some soap, some shells again come whizzing just past the window, one bursting in the garden just below, and one in the stables. I suddenly realise that I am quite alone in the upper part of the house, scurry down the stairs in the dark, and reach the cellar with my heart in my mouth, to find the children crying and the noise pretty loud even there. After a few minutes, however, it calms down, and we get the children to bed, and there are only two other bad bursts of shelling during the night. Benedetta, sharing a bed with her nurse, was very brave; not crying, but holding my hand or Schwester's very tight, and saying in a slightly quivering voice, 'But even if the bangs get louder still, they won't really hurt us, will they?' and then, as they get worse, 'Are the Germans really coming to eat us up?' A sack of bread, which had been placed between two vats, came tumbling down on the head of one poor woman, who believed it to be a bomb. All through the night, lying awake, and thinking of all those who are lying in shelters in England, under a greater menace, I went over and over the course of events, wondering if we could have taken the children to safety elsewhere, if we had been more foreseeing. In the morning Antonio told me that he had been doing the same. But the sequence of events has been such that I really do not see at what point we could have behaved differently. Ten days ago, when we meant to take the children up the hill, the farm was still full of partisans, and later on the German mopping-up was taking place. Earlier still, when we might have gone to Florence, the roads were practically impassable, owing to the bombing, even if we could have got hold of any transport. Last week all the Germans agreed in advising us not to take the children to Montepulciano or Chianciano, as most of the hill-towns near the main roads have been badly bombed — and indeed in these last days we have seen Radicofani and Contignano destroyed. Our trench in the woods was also condemned by the German gunners, and since then mines have been laid all round it, and bombs have burst near by. If we were alone, or only with our own babies, we would have taken to the woods, and tried to get through to the Allied lines, but with this pack of children, it is out of the question. There is nothing for it but to trust to the partial security of the cellar, and stick it out.

June 22nd

The day begins badly. During the first lull in the firing a tragic procession begins to struggle down to our cellar: those of our farmers who, until then, have preferred to take shelter in the woods. All night they have been under fire, and their drawn, terrified faces bear witness to what they have been through. They thankfully take refuge in the cellar and the vat-room — old men, women and children — about sixty more people to shelter and feed. An old grandmother from a neighbouring farm is among them; half paralysed, with a weak heart, she has been dragged along by her son and daughter, and now collapses, utterly exhausted. The babies whimper from cold and hunger. The older children go and whisper to ours, frightening them with the tales that I have tried to spare them until now. We go up to the kitchen (since fortunately the lull still continues) and produce hot barley-coffee and bread-and-milk, the keeper having succeeded in finding and milking the cows. The farmers' account of their nights in the woods is not such as to encourage us to try to get through to the Allied lines with the children, a plan which again, this morning, we had considered. Sporadic firing goes on all through the morning.

This glimpse of a tiny segment of the front increases my conviction of the wastefulness of this kind of warfare, the disproportion between the human suffering involved and the military results achieved. In the last five days I have seen Radicofani and Contignano destroyed, the countryside and farms studded with shell holes, girls raped, and human beings and cattle killed. Otherwise the events of the last week have had little enough effect upon either side: it is the civilians who have suffered.

Later

The above reflections were written during a lull in the shelling, in the kitchen, while boiling some milk for the children. But, in the midst of them, a louder burst of shell-fire than any we had experienced brought me down to the cellar, where we turned on the gramophone and started songs with the children, and waited. 'Now,' we felt, 'it really is beginning.' It had already been evident for some hours that shells of larger calibre were now being used, and both Antonio and I (though fortunately no one else) realized that the cellar was by no means proof against them. After a while, in another slight lull, the door opened, and a German sergeant came in: space would at once be required, he said, in the cellar (already filled to overflowing) for some German troops. A few minutes later an officer appeared: 'You must get out,' he said, 'and get the children away. You can't keep them here. And we need the cellar.' (That same morning we had again asked this officer what we should do with the children, and he had said emphatically, 'Stay on!') 'If you get out at once,' he added, 'you may be able to get out of range during this lull.' There followed a few minutes of considerable confusion. Antonio and I were besieged by a crowd of terrified people, asking when and where they should go, what they should take with them, what they should leave behind, and so on. We could only answer: 'At once. To Montepulciano or Chianciano, wherever you have friends. Take only what you can carry with you — the clothes on your back, and some food.' The babies were howling, and, with Donata in my arms, I couldn't help Schwester much, but we managed to pack a basket with the babies' food, and the pram with some of their clothes and nappies. I took a tiny case, which we had in the cellar, containing a change of underclothes for Antonio and me, a pair of shoes, some soap and eau de cologne and face powder, my clock and Giorgio's photographs; and that is all that we now possess. Each of the children carried his own coat and jersey. The grown-ups each carried a baby, or a sack of bread. And so, in a long, straggling line, with the children

217

clutching at our skirts, half walking, half running, we started off down the Chianciano road.

I did not think, then, that we should get all the children through safely. We had been warned to stick to the middle of the road, to avoid mines, and to keep spread out, so as not to attract the attention of Allied planes. German soldiers, working at mine-laying, looked up in astonishment as we passed. '*Du lieber Gott!* What are those children still doing here?' Some corpses lay, uncovered, by the roadside. A German Red Cross lorry came tearing up the hill, nearly running over us. And all the time the shells were falling, some nearer, some farther off, and the planes flew overhead. The children were very good, the older ones carrying whatever they could, the smaller ones stumbling along as fast as their small legs could carry them. Donata shouted with glee on Antonio's shoulder. No one cried except the tiny babies, but now and again there was a wail: 'I can't go so fast!' and someone would pick up that child for a few hundred yards. The sun was blazing overhead, the hill very steep, and none of us had had any food since early breakfast. But every stumbling, weary step was taking us farther away from the cellar, and from what was still to come.

When we got to the top of the hill before Chianciano we divided into two parties. Those who had friends in Chianciano went on there, the rest of us, sixty in all (of whom four were babies in arms, and twenty-eight others children) started across country towards Montepulciano. The road itself was, we knew, under continual shell-fire, but we hoped to be able to cut across to the Villa Bianca cross-roads. The first part went well, and when at last we had a ridge between us and La Foce, we called a first halt. The children fell exhausted and thankful on the ground, only to rise again hastily, having sat down on an ant-hill. They made, indeed, much more fuss about the ants than about the shells.

The shelling seemed farther off, the mined path was behind us, and a peasant brought us glasses of water. Until then, there had been no moment in which to stop and think, but now we began to realize, with dismay, all that we had left behind. The people in the vat-room — had they been warned? No one knew, and we looked at each other in horror. Then at last Assunta remembered: 'Yes, she had seen the fattore go in to warn them.' But what they could do next it was difficult to imagine, for the old grandmother who was with them was unable to walk, and there were also several children. Probably they would merely hide in terror in a ditch. One could only pray that none of them would be killed.

And then there was Giorgio's body. We had hoped to bury him the night before, so that at least we could show his grave to his family when we are able to trace them, but the firing on the road to the cemetery prevented us from getting there. So we had had to leave him in that little room, unburied.[1]

And then the dogs — they, too, had been forgotten. We fed them up to yesterday, but in the hurry of leaving we did not remember to go up to the kennels (five hundred yards away, and under shell fire) to fetch them. And poor Gambolino, the poodle, is terribly gun-shy. Even if he is not killed he will go almost mad with fear. It does not bear thinking of.

After a brief rest (too brief, but as long as we dared) we went on again — Antonio and the keeper, Porciani, taking the longer and more dangerous road, on which the pram could be pushed, and the rest of us scrambling along a rough track up and down steep gulleys. The children were getting very tired, but struggled manfully on, and we lifted them over the steepest places. Twice planes came hovering over us, and we all crouched down in a ditch. Then when we came out into the open cornland, beyond Pianoia, came the worst part of the journey. The shelling had begun again, and on the Montepulciano road, a few hundred yards below us, shells were bursting with a terrific din. The children were afraid to go on, but on we must. Some more

[1] When we got home we found the room empty, and under the cypresses, a few yards away, a fresh grave with a rough cross, on which was written *Unbekannter Italiäner* (Unknown Italian). It was many months before we were at last able to trace his family in Bergamo.

planes came over, and we lay down for cover in the tall corn. I remember thinking at that moment, with Benedetta lying beside me and two other children clutching at my skirts: 'This can't be real — this isn't really happening.'

At last we reached a farm on the road, occupied by a German Red Cross unit, and there again we got some water and a short rest. But the officer came out and, hearing that it was a *Kinderheim*, gave us disconcerting advice: take refuge at once in the Capuchin convent on the hill, he said, and don't push on to Montepulciano. 'What is happening at La Foce to-day, will happen there to-morrow.' For a minute we hesitated, but the convent, we knew, had no food and no sort of shelter, so we decided to risk it and push on. From this point onward, the Germans said, the road was safe, and so we took it, a long, straggling, foot-sore procession. Half an hour after we had passed, that very stretch of the road was shelled.

After four hours we got to San Biagio, at the foot of the Montepulciano hill, and there sat down in a ditch for a breather before the last pull. We were very tired now, and a dreadful thought came over us: 'What if the Braccis should have left?' 'What if we find no shelter here?' But as we sat there, a little group of Montepulciano citizens appeared, then yet another: they had seen us from the ramparts, and were coming down to meet us with open arms. Never was there a more touching welcome. Many of them were partisans; others were refugees themselves from the south whom we had helped; yet others old friends among the Montepulciano workmen. They shouldered the children and our packages, and in a triumphant procession, cheered by so much kindness, we climbed up the village street, Antonio at the head, with Donata on his shoulder. Bracci and his wife Margherita came out to meet us, the children were at once settled on cushions on the terrace, and the Montepulcianesi vied with each other in offering accommodation. Antonio and I acted as billeting officers. Three went to one house, four to another, and the Braccis nobly took in not only our whole family, but all the refugee children as well. The Braccis' mattresses and blankets, which had been walled up, were pulled out again and laid on the ground, the children (after a meal of bread and cheese) put to bed, and at last we were able to wash and rest. Only one child was the worse for the terrible experience: Rino, who had a touch of the sun and suddenly fainted. Benedetta (sharing a bed with me) woke up, when I came to bed, to say: 'We've left the bangs behind at last, haven't we?' and then fell into a twelve hours' sleep.

We have left behind everything that we possess, but never in my life have I felt so rich and so thankful as looking down on all the children as they lay asleep. Whatever may happen to-morrow, to-night they are safe and sound!

June 23rd

So we felt on our first arrival, and to-day the thankfulness endures, but the awareness of new problems also awakens. During the night the gun-fire seemed mercifully far away, compared with what it had been at La Foce, but it was quite near enough to remind us that we may soon be taking refuge in *this* cellar, too. Moreover, we find that yesterday's experience has left its trace; I was far more frightened last night than I was at the time, and lay in bed sweating. In the morning Schwester Marie said that the same thing had happened to her, too. Nor is the atmosphere of Montepulciano agreeable. The population is very jumpy, and when I went out in the morning to try to buy some necessities for the children and myself, I found every shop shut and barred. The Maresciallo of the Carabinieri is in hiding, and two sergeants are the only members left of the police force. There is no light and also no water, the piping having been blown up, and food is becoming scarce. The electric mill is also no longer working, so that there is a bread shortage; and the peasants are too frightened to venture into the town, so that there are no vegetables, milk or fruit. Two of our men ventured out to forage in the farms, and returned triumphantly with some milk and vegetables for the children — and the Comune has still got some rice — but if the situation goes on for long, the conditions will be those of a siege. The Comune reserves have been broken into by the Germans who have taken practically everything except the rice. However, for eight or ten days longer we can hold out, and surely it will not be longer than that? Little anxious groups gather in the streets exchanging views, and the wildest rumours spread. The Germans are going to defend Montepulciano; they are going to knock down the houses on both sides of the main street so as to be able to pass it with their tanks; the whole town is to be evacuated; and so on. At midday we gather clandestinely in the little back room of a mechanic who has succeeded in putting up a battery radio, and listen to the scanty news (Allied) from Rome. It is not good — Chiusi has been taken again by the Germans, and fierce fighting is going on in the district. And, as the day goes on, the cannon-fire in the Val d'Orcia increased imperceptibly, while more German batteries respond from this hill.

All day German officers call upon Bracci, the mayor, for whom Antonio acts as an interpreter, demanding cars, tyres, bicycles and so on, and when there is some opposition, one of them says: 'What's all this nonsense? Don't you realize that in two or three days' time your whole town will be flattened out?'

To protect this house from looting we have put up a notice *Kinderheim La Foce*, with a Red Cross above it, and the letter given us by the paratroops' captain at La Foce, stating that this *Kinderheim* is to be left alone.

In the afternoon there is horrible news: a young partisan, who is accused of having shot a German at Chiusi (and who was caught in a cypress tree up which he had climbed for shelter) has just been publicly hanged on a lamp-post in the main street. He is to be left hanging there for twenty-four hours, in sight of the whole population, as an example. Bracci believes the poor wretch is innocent, but a German soldier says that he has recognized him, and the alternative is the execution of ten innocent hostages from the town. The German captain who gives these orders is a most sinister brute, elegant, hard and cruel. The bishop is present at the hanging and, in spite of a protest from the Germans, courageously imparts his benediction to the dying man. The corpse's presence hangs like a blight over the whole town, and the people who live in the main street dare not open their shutters on the horrible sight. But at night a volunteer guard has to be formed to ensure that no one comes to cut him down, as, if this should happen, the German captain has announced that he will hold Bracci personally responsible.

In the evening the firing seems to be louder, and the news is still bad. We are all gloomy, foreseeing that Montepulciano, in its turn, will share the fate of La Foce. There are several good shelters, but not enough for the whole population, apart from the food and water shortage. And the thought of the corpse outside haunts us all.

June 24th

Antonio spends the morning with Bracci inspecting the air-raid shelters, and returns with the comforting news that they are excellent, and that the cellars beneath this house are sufficiently large to accommodate us all. Moreover, they give upon the garden, and, if necessary, we could carry down a small cooking stove to prepare the children's food. We are immensely relieved, for what was haunting us yesterday was the fear of having to drag the children on somewhere else, the whole weary trip once again. Now, whatever happens, we have decided to stay on here and see it out.

At six a.m. the corpse is at last taken down, but we are forbidden to bury it in the cemetery. The indignant Bracci sons say: 'We'll put up an inscription on the spot, telling what the Germans have done.' Their father says: 'No, we'll put up a *Madonna del Buon Consiglio* (Our Lady of Good Counsel). We've had enough exhortations to hatred for at least one generation.'

In the afternoon the news is better. Chiusi is again in Allied hands, and a report comes that a monk at the Capuchin monastery has seen Allied troops climbing up the ridge below Casalvento. If this is true, La Foce may already be freed.[1] Already our spirits have begun to rise, and we begin to speculate when we shall be able to go back. Even if our house is entirely destroyed, we could perhaps send the children up to Pietraporciana, where there is a spring of water, and ourselves camp near our own house, and see what, if anything, can be saved. It is a very odd feeling to be entirely possessionless, but it seems curiously natural. One feels that one is, at last, sharing the common lot. And the kindness of everyone is endless. One lady has lent us mattresses; another towels; yet another has given me some underclothes; another has provided Schwester and the nurse with some clothes, every shopkeeper has produced something for the children, and when Porciani and Gino visit the surrounding farmhouses in search of milk and vegetables, the peasants produce all that they have and flatly refuse to be paid.

In the evening some of the German batteries round Montepulciano cease firing, and we conclude, with renewed hope, that they have left. Moreover, some of the bridges on the roads between Montepulciano and Val di Chiana are being blown up by the Germans, from which we infer that they do not intend to use them for their retreat. Go to bed easier in mind, and sleep well for the first time.

June 25th

Poor Benedetta, who was all right the first day, is now showing the effect of what she has been through. Yesterday afternoon she was sick several times, slept uneasily all night, and this morning was tearful and headachy; slept again all the morning and complains on waking (although for the first time there is no heavy firing near by) that she hears 'the bangs' in her sleep. Two

[1] This story proved to be wholly without foundation.

of the other children were similarly affected, but at once, the first day.

Antonio sees one of the officers from the German H.Q. at Monticchiello, who says that heavy fighting is still going on in that region. This means that our peasants are still under fire. We watch Allied planes bombing German batteries at Acquaviva and near Chiusi, and there is a good deal of sporadic firing all through the day in the Chiusi-Trasimeno district. The midday radio announces the capture by the Allies of Sarteano, but still they seem to be getting on no farther either in the Foce or the Chiusi area. Perhaps the medieval prophecy, that the decisive battle of the war will be fought on the shores of Lake Trasimene, is about to come true!

In the afternoon a man who had gone out into the country foraging, reports that our two assistant factors, Michele and Piero (who had set forth for Montepulciano behind us, and had never turned up) have been captured by the Germans, and shut up in a pig-sty in the very farm on the road where we had met the Red Cross unit. Antonio accordingly sets off to the German lines, and discovers that the two men captured are Michele and a friend of his, a Carabiniere. They are both suspected of being rebels and spies, and, according to the German officer's account, they seem to have lost their heads altogether, and to have told a lot of obvious lies. The officer said that he had already sent them off to H.Q. for examination, but on Antonio's way back he met a car containing both the unfortunate young men, their hands tied behind them. Antonio succeeded in stopping the car and identifying Michele to the escort, and we trust that this may save him, and that some of the Germans at Monticchiello, who were billeted at La Foce, may also recognize him. But Bracci is pessimistic: he says that Pianoia, where all the trouble with the partisans was, is a bad place to be caught in, and that their hands being tied is a bad sign. Poor Michele! He is no hero, and it is his blind panic on the first day, when he did not come with us, that is responsible for this. But it is horrible to feel so powerless to help him, or any of our people: the fattore and his family in that cave in the cliff, where the firing has been unceasing — our wretched peasants, crouching in their shelters or in the caves, homeless and foodless — and even our poor dogs. What tragedies shall we find, when at last we do get back?

And meanwhile, with every day that passes, harvest-time is drawing nearer. If only we are liberated by the end of the month, the corn can yet be saved. As soon as we get back, before digging for our possessions, before anything else, every able-bodied man must set to reaping. But shall we get back in time?

June 26th

A good deal of firing during the night and morning. Later on we learn that it was directed against Chianciano, and in the afternoon some bombs are dropped there, and some wounded are brought to the hospital here. In Chiusi the street-fighting still continues between the German and Allied forces. The wretched population has had a terrible time, for when first the Allies occupied the town, five days ago, the anti-Fascist leaders immediately and prematurely showed their rejoicing, and pasted up manifestoes proclaiming the beginning of a new era. The next day the Germans occupied the city again, plundered every house and hanged, according to the account that has reached us here, no less than nineteen citizens in reprisal.[1] Since then the fighting has been continuous, each side occupying the city in turn, and little enough can be left of it.

At Cetona, too, the greater part of the destruction is due to a similar cause. On the Allies' arrival the town bells were prematurely rung in rejoicing, whereupon the retreating Tiger tanks turned their fire again upon the city.

The news from abroad (heard secretly in the same little room) is good: Cherbourg occupied and Vitebsk taken. The local news not quite so good: Piombino is occupied, but severe fighting

---

[1] This was not true.

continues on the shores of Lake Trasimene. We do not, however, need the radio to tell us about the fighting in this district, which we observe by merely looking down on the plain from the balcony of this house. In the evening we hear that Castiglione and Rocca d'Orcia are occupied by the Allies, and that they have reached the stream Astrone, between Chiusi and Chianciano.

Our hopes for Montepulciano begin to rise again; very possibly the retreat may take place towards the Val di Chiana, and we shall be spared. However, as the shelling grows nearer, we prepare the cellar in case it seems better to move the children there. Many people in the town are already sleeping in shelters, as yet quite unnecessarily. Late at night German soldiers enter the shelters and announce to the inhabitants that the whole population of Montepulciano will be evacuated at five o'clock next morning. The story is entirely without foundation (as is proved by the soldiers' refusal to repeat the order to Bracci), its object being merely to sow panic and to empty the houses for German looting. Bracci tells everyone not to budge.

June 27th

Michele has turned up! Antonio's statement to the German escort identifying him has saved him, and he and his companion were both freed early this morning. And he brings, at last, news of La Foce. It is better than we dared to hope. The house is still standing. One shell has fortunately burst just behind the farm kitchen, in such a manner that the rubble is covering the entrance to the ditch beneath the house in which all our suitcases are hidden, thus, perhaps, saving them from being stolen. Two other shells have fallen in the little patch of garden just outside the cellar, where the children came out to play, and many others in various parts of the garden, stables, etc. But on Saturday night, when Michele left, the villa itself was still untouched.

Several of the farm-houses, on the other hand, have been hit, particularly Casalvento, where a German battery was placed. The line of fire has been all along the hillside. An old peasant from one of those farms turned up here last night in search of his family, but they have not appeared, and are presumably hiding in some cave. (Two three-months-old twins among them, whose mother is short of milk.) The fattore and his family, according to Michele, are still in the cave in the cliff.

The local news to-day is better. The Allies have at last retaken Chiusi and are pushing on towards Chianciano, and on the lake towards Castiglion del Lago. We watch their progress by the artillery fire which we can see from our balcony. German sappers are already mining the bridge immediately beneath this house: we watch the dynamite being prepared, open all the windows, and wonder when the explosion will be.

In some ways, these days have been more trying to the nerves than the more dangerous ones at La Foce. Then, there was a constant need for activity and decision. Now we are just sitting about, in someone else's house, and waiting. The children are tired and whine, Benedetta has a digestive upset, I have the worst attack of hay-fever that I have had for ten years, we all feel bound to be careful of every scrap of food and drop of water, and everyone's nerves are on edge. Beneath our windows the Allied and German forces appear to be dancing the Lancers — back and forth, forward and back. Now the gunfire seems nearer, and our spirits rise — now it is farther again, and they fall. 'Listen to the firing over Chianciano! They are German guns, hurrah — that means that the English are there already!' Half an hour later: 'No, it was the British guns, as before.' (And the wounded begin to arrive at the hospitals.) And every day the pall of fear — reasonable and unreasonable — hangs heavily over the little town. More and more Germans arrive, ordering that the shops be kept open to supply their demands. They demand a car, bicycles, a gramophone, a watch, and all these demands are enforced at the point of a pistol. This house, so far, seems to have been protected by the *Kinderheim* notice.

June 28th

Go to the hospital to visit the Chianciano wounded. The shelling appears to have been in answer to a German battery situated just behind the town. Hear to our great relief that none of our people from La Foce have been killed,[1] and that the whole party in the vat-room, even the old grandmother, reached Chianciano in safety. A boy of fourteen, who had called out some insult against the Germans, immediately received a pistol-shot in the head and was killed.

No military news of any kind. The Allies still appear to be between Chiusi and Chianciano. But in the night some German tanks have gone northwards, and we see little clouds of smoke and hear explosions all over the valley, where ammunition is being blown up. Undoubtedly the Germans are on the move at last.

In the afternoon the Germans blow up some houses inside the town, to obstruct the inner road, and also, alas, destroy the magnificent Medicean gateway at the foot of the town. Antonio tries in vain to save it, but does succeed in saving the fine fourteenth century arcades of the old hospital. The Germans say that we must expect some shelling here to-morrow, but that that should be the last day.

'You want der Tommy: well, by Friday you'll have him!'

The Montepulcianesi, however, as the end draws near, are more and more jumpy. When I went out this evening, they were standing about in little knots, looking at the ruins of their gateway, and finding some comfort in the fact that the image of the Madonna, which stood in the upper part of the arch, is miraculously intact. Little family parties with prams and bundles were making their way to the shelters for the night.

The evening news brings little change. The guns go on rumbling, and we go to bed expecting the bridge to be blown up during the night.

[1] This unfortunately was not true.

June 29th, Eight a.m.

Our expectations were realized. At eleven p.m., Allied batteries in the direction of Monticchiello opened fire on the German batteries just beyond Montepulciano, and the firing continued, with short intervals, until four-thirty a.m. The shells whizzed just over our heads and fell mostly on the road by Sant' Agnes, about eighty yards from here. The noise was considerable. Benedetta and I left our bedroom on the front of the house, and slept, half dressed, in a back bedroom with Schwester and the other two babies, and the other children were also dressed, ready to go down to the cellar if necessary. Then, at four-thirty, there was a sudden, terrific din. The whole house shook, the walls trembled, there was a crash of falling glass, tiles and mortar. The bridge had been blown up at last! For a few seconds it felt as if the house was falling down — then everything steadied itself, and I hurried to the older children's room to reassure them and the maids. The children were huddled together, silent but very frightened. There was a little more sporadic firing, but no one paid any attention to it. Most of the Montepulcianesi hurried out into the dawn to look at their bridge — the rest of us settled down to two hours of unbroken, blessed sleep. The Germans have gone at last!

Eleven a.m.

Not only have they gone, but the Allies are here! The first good news came to Antonio, who (while standing beside one of the Germans who are still left in the town) was hurriedly summoned by a partisan: some English soldiers, he said, were looking for him. He accordingly hurried down into a wheat-field, and there found a small patrol, headed by a subaltern in the Scots Guards, who had actually come from La Foce. He wanted information as to the number of Germans who are still in the town, the lie of the land, the bridges that had been blown up, and so on, all of which Antonio gave him, and in return, he gave us fairly good news of La Foce. The house has only been hit in two or three places, and though the damage inside is considerable, it is not irremediable. All this conversation took place hurriedly, hidden in the wheat, with sentries posted, and just as it was over, a pretty peasant-girl came up with a basket on her head, on her way to town. What next? She said she would hold her tongue, but it seemed safer for the soldiers to take her off with them for a few hours, to which indeed she agreed very willingly. The plan is for the regiment to occupy the town this afternoon. Meanwhile, we are having some German shelling for a change, and Palazzo Ricci and some other buildings have been hit. La Foce has had the honour of being mentioned in the midday bulletin as 'liberated' — together with Pienza and Montalcino. But we can hardly listen to the news now: we want to see with our own eyes. Every minute, now, the Allies may arrive!

Ten p.m.

Well, they have come — at last! All day the partisans have been watching the roads, and at four p.m. the first news reached us: 'They are coming!' The news coincided with a burst of German shelling, but meet them we must, so we hurried along the narrow streets, climbing over the rubble and dodging into doorways until we reached the Bersaglio, the Braccis' stretch of hillside garden overlooking the road to Villa Bianca. And at last, scrambling up the steep grassy hillside, we saw the first British helmet! Beneath it was the round, flushed face of a very young subaltern, who (as we afterwards were told) had no business to be there at all, but had set out on a little reconnoitring party of his own. He was followed by an officer in the R.E. (who wanted to find out about the bridge) and by four or five men. We came forward and greeted them with tears in our eyes — we all shook hands — the peasants brought out glasses of wine. A young partisan sprang up from nowhere and demanded a gun, to fight by their side. Remembering, however, that twenty Germans were still just above our heads, and the fate of Chiusi, I went straight to the point: 'How many of you are there?' But the young officer, in addition to breathlessness, had a severe stutter: 'B-b-b-b-barely t-t-two d-d-d-dozen!' he brought out with maddening slowness, and I found myself replying crossly, 'It isn't nearly enough!' The young man's actions, however, were less hesitant than his speech, and as soon as the partisan was able to tell him in what part of the town the Germans were, he and his men set off there at once. We then hurried back, and under the arch of the old gateway of the town we met the other platoon. Very strange it seemed, to see them marching up the Montepulciano street — and oh, what a welcome sight! In every doorway there were beaming faces to greet them. Remembering the fate of Cetona, the population abstained from too loud rejoicings, but I heard one old man saying, as tears streamed down his cheeks, 'I don't mind dying, now that I've seen them arrive!'

Meanwhile, a German shell had dropped just outside this house, and we herded all the children down to the cellar, as it seemed probable that there would be more German shelling during the night. When I came upstairs again an English officer was at the door: 'Are you Marchesa Origo? The whole Eighth Army has been looking for you!' It was Major Petre, who, he explained, had spent last night at La Foce (in the nursery, among the Kate Greenaway pictures — 'very odd', he said, 'in the middle of a battle') and who brought me the exciting news that my cousin, Ulick Verney, is at G.H.Q., only a few miles away. La Foce, he says, is still standing, 'but I'm afraid you'll have rather a shock when you see the rooms'. Now, an hour ago, he has come back again with his delightful colonel, Derek Cardiff. I wish very much that I had a clean frock to put on in their honour, but, of course, have only the same clothes which I have been wearing ever since I slept in them in the cellar at La Foce. They are very reassuring about the flying bombs in England, saying that their damage, although extensive, is too erratic to be considered a serious military menace. We sit talking by the uncertain light of the only lamp – now and again a shell falls outside – the Braccis produce glasses of wine, Colonel Cardiff has some biscuits – we discover mutual friends at home. It is like a party in a dream. The colonel offers to take us back to La Foce with him, but the shelling seems to be increasing, and one of us must stay with the children in the cellar. So Antonio, who can at once start work at home, goes off with the officers, and I descend to the Braccis' cellar, where we all spend an extremely stuffy, crowded and unpleasant night. At one a.m. the house is hit, but with damage only to a top-story room. And my thoughts are too agreeable to be disturbed: our long nightmare is over at last.

June 30th

A very English day. The Scots Guards leave the town, but the Coldstreams, who are attached to a South African division, take their place, and attack a position below the town held by the Germans, from which they had been firing on us.

The steep, narrow streets of Montepulciano are filled with British soldiers, and all the population is out to greet them. A doorway suddenly bears the sign, *Comitato di Liberazione*. Partisans with tricolour armlets and guns slung across their shoulders stand at every street crossing – children crowd round the tanks – pretty girls in their best frocks walk up and down arm in arm, with a glance at the soldiers over their shoulders. Old Italian uniforms, too (hidden by their owners for many months) are suddenly to be seen again. The shops are all flung open, so are the house-doors, so are our cellars and our hearts. It has been so long, so long! The soldiers walk about the town, grinning a little sheepishly when someone tries to embrace them, accepting the glasses of red wine, giving some sweets to the children, friendly, detached, a little bored. They have done it all before. But to us it is new – and still almost incredible. I find myself talking to the first soldier I meet for the sheer delight of hearing English spoken. Then I go into the Comune and act

233

as interpreter for Bracci with the A.M.G. officer, explaining to him Bracci's odd position as an ardent anti-Fascist yet mayor under Fascist rule. An occasional German shell has still been falling in the morning, but no one pays any attention to them, and by midday they cease. A young captain in the Coldstreams comes back to lunch, and we talk of mutual acquaintances in England — of the flying bombs — of Gloucestershire. My sense of unreality increases and is brought to a climax when, turning round, I see my cousin, Ulick, standing in the doorway.

July 1st

And now we have come home. This morning Ulick sent a staff car to fetch us, and Schwester Marie and I, with the two babies and Benedetta, triumphantly drive back over the road which we had taken — so much less agreeably — ten days ago in the opposite direction. (The other children are to follow in a few days.) Plenty of shell and bomb-holes on the road and in the fields, and as we got nearer home we looked out anxiously for damages. At the Castelluccio there are some large shell-holes; the clinic, too, has been badly hit. Then, as we drive up to La Foce, chaos meets our eyes. The house is still standing, with only one shell-hole in the garden façade, another on the fattoria, and several in the roof. The latter have been caused by the explosion of a mine, the Germans' parting gift, bursting on the road to Chianciano, not thirty yards from the house. An enormous crater marks the spot, but has not blocked the road, since the Allies merely made a diversion into the field beside it.

In the garden, which has also got several shell-holes and trenches for machine-guns, they have stripped the pots off the lemons and azaleas, leaving the plants to die. The ground is strewn with my private letters and photographs, mattresses and furniture-stuffing. The inside of the house, however, is far worse. The Germans have stolen everything that took their fancy, blankets, clothes, shoes and toys, as well, of course, as anything

234

valuable or eatable, and have deliberately destroyed much of sentimental or personal value. Every drawer of my writing-desk has been ransacked, and stained or torn-up photographs, torn out of their frames, strew the floors. In the dining-room the table is still laid, and there are traces of a drunken repast; empty wine-bottles and smashed glasses lie beside a number of my summer hats (which presumably have been tried on), together with boot-trees, toys, overturned furniture and W.C. paper. In the library, where the leather has been ripped off the arm-chairs and some books have been stolen, more empty bottles lie in the fireplace. The lavatory is filled to the brim with filth, and decaying meat, lying on every table, adds to the foul smell. There are innumerable flies. In our bedroom, too, it is the same, and only the nurseries, which the maids have been cleaning ever since they arrived (five hours before us) are habitable. Some of the toys have been stolen or deliberately broken, but curiously enough, the English Kate Greenaway alphabet is still upon the wall, and the children's beds are untouched. So we put the children to bed for their afternoon nap, and then go on investigating the damage. There is no water in the house, and also, of course, no light.

Antonio is away, having had to go down to Chianciano to take up his work as mayor, and cope with the spearhead A.M.G. officials, but in the farm courtyard, in a wilderness of refuse, gravel and waste paper, a few men are standing about gloomily. They come forward to greet me — and later the fattore, too, appears, and with tears in his eyes takes both my hands in his. He and his family are all safe, but have had a very bad time. And he gives us tragic news. Gigi — our beloved gardener, with his crooked mouth and limp, with his passion for flowers, and his short temper and wry smile — Gigi has been killed by a shell in the ditch in which he had taken shelter. It was not even possible, owing to the mines that are strewn in the woods, to bring his body back to the graveyard for burial, and his son has buried him in the woods where he fell. One of the peasants of our home-farm, Giocondo, has also been killed by shells, and two children from another farm, and the Capoccia of Chiarentana, Doro; all these, too, are buried in the fields where they fell.[1] And all the survivors are profoundly downhearted. At least ten of the farmhouses they say (later on we learn that it is fifteen) have been destroyed, and those that have not been shelled, have been looted. A third of the cattle and sheep and pigs have gone (either stolen, or killed by shells); all the chickens and turkeys, and many of the farm instruments.

I go back into the farm, and there, crouching under a sofa, I see a black shadow. I whistle, and, half incredulously, he crawls out, then leaps upon me in wild delight, and from that minute never leaves my side. It is Gambolino, the poodle, miraculously safe, but pitifully thin, and so nervy that the slightest noise sends him trembling under the nearest bed. But our other dog, Alba, the pointer, was not so lucky. The fattore tells us that he found her inside the fountain with a wound in her side — dead.

In the lower part of the property, where the French coloured troops of the Fifth Army have passed, the Goums have completed what the Germans have begun. They regard loot and rape as the just reward for battle, and have indulged freely in both. Not only girls and young women, but even an old woman of eighty has been raped. Such has been the Val d'Orcia's first introduction to Allied rule — so long, and so eagerly awaited!

July 5th

But now, at once, we must begin again. On the first day Antonio set the men to reaping. There has been an accident in one field already: a mine has blown up an ox-cart, killing the oxen and smashing the driver's legs; there will no doubt be others. But the harvest will be saved.

We cannot hope that the Allies, who have already enough to

[1] Later on, they were all moved to our little cemetery, and lie there beside Giorgio, the young partisan.

do in clearing the main roads for the troops, will be able to help us with mine-detectors. But the resourceful postmaster of Chianciano, who says he has some knowledge of explosives, has volunteered to attempt the job, so we will try to clear at least those mines and bombs that are lying on the surface. The Germans have been very lavish: in the mine just outside the garden door, alone, they laid three quintals of dynamite.

We have now been round the most-damaged farms. Of those on the Castelluccio ridge, two — San Bernardino and Poggio-meriggi — are totally destroyed; in the others, one or two rooms still have a roof, no more. In all of them the looting has been thorough: either the Germans or the Goums have taken all that was not destroyed by shells or fire. In one farm thirteen people are sleeping in two beds, and the neighbour's family, nine persons more, are camping downstairs in the stable. At Lucciolabella eleven people are sleeping on the floor. All the farms have lost their cooking utensils, their linen, most of their blankets, and their dearly-prized furniture (*la camera in nocino degli sposi*),[1] bought one piece at a time, year by year, and all their clothes, except those on their backs. The houses at Chiarentana — a medieval group of houses around a stone courtyard, which have seen other wars, other invasions — are almost equally bad. Here, in addition to the destruction caused by shells, the inhabitants have suffered the looting of the room in which they had walled up their most valuable possessions; the Germans discovered, by tapping, that the wall was hollow. One young woman, who is expecting a baby, has seen its whole layette deliberately burned before her eyes. Since they have no furniture left, and the roof lies open to the sky, their few remaining possessions are being devoured by mice. In all these farms there is no doubt as to what must be done first: we must get a roof on to at least two or three rooms before the winter. The furnaces which make the tiles and bricks are not working now for lack of lignite, and transport is an almost insuperable problem. But I expect that we shall

[1] 'The bride's walnut suite.'

237

manage somehow.[1] Glass for windows, however, will be practically impossible.

Almost the most immediate necessity is to get cooking-pots and pans, and these I have been lucky enough to find in Montepulciano. (The shops had buried them during the German occupation.) No less than fifty farms have to be provided for! Next, before the winter, will come clothes, especially for the small children. We will do what we can with the wool of the sheep that have not been taken, and perhaps later on there may be help from the Red Cross. After that, the imagination boggles: where, at a time like this, shall we find linen, blankets, or shoes?

There is cause for anxiety, too, about the general health. The place is still strewn with unburied corpses, both of men and of cattle. At San Bernardino there is still an unburied man in the stable, and six or seven other German corpses on the hill were only burned yesterday. And the flies swarm everywhere, bringing infection with them. In every farm there are severe cases of gastro-enteritis and we fear something worse — paratyphoid or what here is called *colerina*. When I drove into Montepulciano yesterday I heard that there is an epidemic there, too, and that eleven out of the twenty children in the Foundling Hospital have died. So we have brought our little refugees home as quickly as possible — singing all the way — in a great lorry provided by the British Army. For the sick I have bought some milk ferments, the only remedy available. At the hospital there is a lack of all medicines and medical supplies; they have even come to an end of their anaesthetics.

In Chianciano, too, where Antonio is working all day, the problems are numerous: lack of Diesel oil for the threshing, of light, of water, of sugar and salt and soap, of all medicines or hospital supplies, of any transport. The refugees from southern Italy clamour unceasingly to be sent home, but the A.M.G. refuses permits, as we are still in the battle area, and the roads

[1] We did. Thanks to help from A.M.G. in transporting a few lorries full of building materials, and to the industry and tenacity of the local labourers, a few rooms in every farm were habitable before the winter.

must be kept clear. I have formed a women's committee, have issued an appeal for old clothes of any sort, and hope to set up a little workroom to prepare babies' layettes, etc. But at the moment, with very little stuff or thread, there is not much that we can do.

Nevertheless, for the future I am hopeful. The whirlwind has passed, and now, whatever destruction it may have left, we can begin to build again. And it is here that the deepest qualities of the Italian people will have a chance to show themselves. To speak of the patience and endurance, the industry and resourcefulness of the Italian workman has become almost a commonplace. But, like other commonplaces, it is true, and, sometimes, in times of crisis, these qualities reach a degree that is almost heroic. Time and suffering have engraved them in the lines of the peasant-women's faces — a sorrow too deep for complaint, a patience that has something sculptural, eternal. Resigned and laborious, they and their men-folk turn back from the fresh graves and the wreckage of their homes to their accustomed daily toil. It is they who will bring the land to life again.

The Fascist and German menaces are receding. The day will come when at last the boys will return to their ploughs, and the dusty clay-hills of the Val d'Orcia will again 'blossom like the rose'. Destruction and death have visited us, but now — there is hope in the air.